Praise for Leonard Sax's
The Collapse of Parenting

"One of the premier experts on parenting, Dr. Leonard Sax brilliantly articulates the problems parents experience with their children, then gives solutions. *The Collapse of Parenting* is academic but practical, simple but deep. If you have time to read only one book this year, *read this one.*"

—MEG MEEKER, MD, BESTSELLING AUTHOR OF *STRONG FATHERS, STRONG DAUGHTERS* AND *STRONG MOTHERS, STRONG SONS*

"The family unit is in unprecedented decline and under assault from a wide variety of cultural forces. With years of experience and research working directly with parents and children, Dr. Leonard Sax provides an important glimpse into parenting in modern times, where it's gone wrong, and how to fix it. Being a parent has never been more important and Dr. Sax explains how to avoid parenting pitfalls and raise your children well."

—DR. BILL BENNETT, FORMER UNITED STATES SECRETARY OF EDUCATION

"If you're going to read one book on parenting this year, make it *The Collapse of Parenting* by Leonard Sax. What makes a good nonfiction instructional book is an author who has extensive real world experience in the subject matter and who has the ability to write clearly. Leonard Sax has both.... This is quite simply a good book that is easily read and will provide sound advice for giving our children the best chance to succeed in life."

—*NEW YORK JOURNAL OF BOOKS*

"Based on years of extensive clinical practice and interviews with students and parents internationally, Sax presents a sobering and alarming picture of the collapse of parenting in this country. But he does not leave the reader without hope; he offers simple, if not easy solutions, giving parents an accessible guide to help them regain their rightful roles."

—DR. NANCY KEHOE, ASSISTANT CLINICAL PROFESSOR OF PSYCHOLOGY AT HARVARD MEDICAL SCHOOL, AND AUTHOR OF *WRESTLING WITH OUR INNER ANGELS: FAITH, MENTAL ILLNESS, AND THE JOURNEY TO WHOLENESS*

"It is time for us to get real as a society. Dr. Leonard Sax has issued both a warning and an encouragement for parents to take up their proper roles in leading their children to a truly mature adulthood. His book is a highly readable and well-informed challenge for us."

—DR. TIMOTHY WRIGHT, HEADMASTER, SHORE SCHOOL, SYDNEY, AUSTRALIA

"There are many 'holy' trinities, but in educational terms, one of them is definitely the relationship between parents, children, and schools. I certainly will be recommending this book to the parents of my school. It does not preach; it cajoles, encourages, guides, and helps. It allows one to stand back and step back on one of the most important aspects of life—looking after our youngsters."

—ANDREW HUNTER, HEADMASTER, MERCHISTON CASTLE SCHOOL, SCOTLAND

"A comprehensive breakdown of where parents have gone awry and how they can get back on track to teach virtue and character to their children.... Sax provides a series of easy-to-follow solutions that help bring parents and children back to the same page, working toward a healthier, more respectful, and conscientious attitude.... With the author's solid advice, parents have a good shot at achieving these goals."

—*Kirkus*

"The Collapse of Parenting is one of the best books I've ever read on the subject of raising children. It's not written from a religious perspective, but it's chock-full of information every parent should have."

—*National Catholic Register*

"[Sax's] guidelines are clear and well-supported."

—*Booklist*

"The Collapse of Parenting may sound like a lone voice in the world of American parenting these days, but it's a desperately needed one.... If you're going to read a single parenting book this year, please make it this one."

—*Treehugger.com*

"Dear Dr. Sax, thank you so much for your brilliant book. Two days ago I was on the phone with a friend. She was distraught because that morning she and her husband asked their ten-year-old son to shovel [the snow off] the walk. From the couch not ten feet away, he texted to her, 'I think it is rude that you ask me to shovel the walk when all you do is slouch around.' I asked her where her son could have learned to say such a thing. She was at a loss. Later that day I heard an interview with you on NPR and I immediately downloaded an audio version of your book. Listening to it was like having all my parenting instincts affirmed. I kept saying, 'Yes! Yes!

Yes!' I know your book is a tough sell in this town that is rife with permissive parenting, but I am recommending it to everyone I know. I will use your book as a shield when people ask me why we don't have a PS4 or a Gameboy, why our kids (nine and ten) don't have a Facebook account, etcetera. I hope your book marks a sea change in parenting. It's high time."

—VIVIENNE PALMER, BOULDER, COLORADO

"Dear Dr. Sax, I want to thank you so much for validating with experience and research what has always seemed like common-sense parenting to me and my husband. I know we are not perfect parents, but we are those parents about whom people whisper one minute and then tell us the next, 'You don't understand how lucky you are that you have such good kids.' They never connect the dots between our authoritative parenting, of which they disapprove, and the resultant respectfulness of our children, of which they are envious. Incidentally, we have six children, three biological and three adopted, so their respectfulness can't be pinned on biology. We aren't perfect parents. Our kids aren't perfect kids. But they are good kids, and we have been parenting, to the best of our abilities in the manner you prescribe for eighteen years now. Thank you for helping me to feel a little less alone as I navigate parenthood in this culture of disrespect. May *The Collapse of Parenting* reach a vast audience and help effect true cultural change."

—ELAINE BOURRET, SUBURBAN DETROIT, MICHIGAN

"I just wanted you to know that this is one of the best books about TEACHING that I have ever read. I LOVED IT! Perhaps it is confirmation bias on my part, but you expressed everything I have learned about good teaching over the past twenty-six years. I have recommended your book to all of my colleagues and during my recent parent interviews I had your book sitting at the table and recommended it to all the parents with whom I met. I am not a parent, but you can bet that your book has made me a better teacher."

—ANDREA VAN SLYKE, TORONTO, ONTARIO

"Dear Dr. Sax, It is unusual for me to read a book in one sitting, especially a book on parenting, but I could not put down *The Collapse of Parenting*. Please know this book will be talked about, studied, recommended (maybe as a requirement of attendance!), and referenced in newsletters for many years to come. Brilliant! Thank you for writing it."

—LLEANNA MCREYNOLDS, HEAD OF SCHOOL,
RAINTREE MONTESSORI SCHOOL, LAWRENCE, KANSAS

"In *The Collapse of Parenting*, Leonard Sax identifies and addresses children's social, educational, and behavioral issues and connects these factors back to the home. The emphasis of this book is not putting blame on parents. The focus is on explaining how this situation developed, and suggesting what can be done about it. This book is the first book I have come across that makes sense of what caused the shift in education, why current efforts aren't achieving desired outcomes, and what the family unit has to do with all of it."

—SUSAN DEIERLEIN, PHD, LAPEER COUNTY, MICHIGAN

"Whenever parents ask me for the 'secret' to raising my three hardworking, thoughtful, polite boys, I tell them, 'No secret!' and then I hand them a copy of *The Collapse of Parenting*. I am the manager of a homeschooling co-op that serves over 35 families, and I can tell you that this eye-opening book has singlehandedly changed the way most of our parents are raising their children. We've seen only positive changes as a result!"

—HINA KHAN-MUKHTAR, SAN RAMON, CALIFORNIA

"As a school principal, I have observed firsthand the 'culture of disrespect' which Dr. Sax describes so accurately in his book. While designed primarily as a guide for parents, the book provides concrete examples that school leaders and teachers can use to encourage character building in children. Clear, insightful research and practical solutions make it an excellent resource for any school or classroom."

—SARAH BLAIR, PRINCIPAL,
PINE CREEK COLONY SCHOOL, AUSTIN, MANITOBA

The Collapse of Parenting

Also by Leonard Sax

Girls on the Edge

Boys Adrift

Why Gender Matters

The
Collapse
of Parenting

How We Hurt Our Kids When
We Treat Them Like Grown-Ups

Leonard Sax, MD, PhD

BASIC BOOKS

New York

Basic Books
Hachette Book Group
1290 Avenue of the Americas, New York, NY 10104
www.basicbooks.com

Printed in the United States of America

Second Trade Paperback Edition: October 2024

Published by Basic Books, an imprint of Hachette Book Group, Inc. The Basic Books name and logo is a registered trademark of the Hachette Book Group.

The Hachette Speakers Bureau provides a wide range of authors for speaking events. To find out more, go to hachettespeakersbureau.com or email HachetteSpeakers@hbgusa.com.

Basic books may be purchased in bulk for business, educational, or promotional use. For more information, please contact your local bookseller or the Hachette Book Group Special Markets Department at special.markets@hbgusa.com.

The publisher is not responsible for websites (or their content) that are not owned by the publisher.

The Library of Congress has catalogued the hardcover edition as follows:
Sax, Leonard.
The collapse of parenting : how we hurt our kids when we treat
them like grown-ups / Leonard Sax.
Description: New York: Basic Books, 2015
Includes bibliographical references and index.
Identifiers: LCCN 2015036659 |
ISBN 978-0-465-04897-7 (hardcover : alk. paper) |
ISBN 978-0-465-07384-9 (e-book)
Subjects: Parenting. | Parent and child. | Children and adults.
LCC HQ755.8.S298 2015 | DDC 306.874—dc23
LC record available at http://lccn.loc.gov/2015036659

ISBNs: 9781541604537 (paperback), 9781541604544 (ebook)

LSC-C

Printing 3, 2025

Dedicated to my wife, Katie,
and our daughter, Sarah

Contents

PART ONE
Problems

Introduction:
Parents Adrift

It takes a lot to make my jaw drop. That day, my jaw dropped.

Mary McMaster* brought in her daughter, Margo. Margo was 6 years old, and she was sick: fever of 102, flushed, irritable. Mom said Margo had a bad sore throat.

"OK, it's time to take a look," I said, after mom had told me the story. "Margo, would you please open your mouth wide and say Aah?" I leaned over to look in her throat. Margo shook her head No and clenched her mouth shut tight. I said, "Mom, it looks like I'm going to need your help here. Could you please ask your daughter to open her mouth and say Aah?" Mom arched her eyebrows and said, "Her body, her choice."

Wow. "My body, my choice" is a longtime slogan of abortion-rights activists, later adopted by activists opposed to COVID-19 vaccines. Mom was invoking that slogan to defend her 6-year-old

---

*All names have been changed, except where noted.

3

daughter's refusal to let me, the doctor, look at her throat when she was sick with a fever.

Something's not right here. And I'm not just talking about extreme cases, like this mom who expects me to make a diagnosis without looking at her child's throat. The great paradox of American parenting today is that we are investing more time and more money in our kids than parents have ever invested before, but the outcomes are worse, across a wide range. American kids today are more likely to have anxiety, depression, and Attention Deficit Hyperactivity Disorder (ADHD) than kids in the past, by a wide margin. American kids are heavier and less fit today than they have ever been. By many measures, American kids are more fragile than they were a generation ago. And these changes affect kids from every demographic, regardless of race, ethnicity, and household income. On some parameters, as we will see, more affluent kids are actually at greater risk than kids from low-income households.

I'm going to argue that two big factors are driving these changes. One factor is the change in the culture. American culture has become a culture of disrespect, a culture that undermines the authority of parents and prioritizes the relationships that kids have with other kids their own age over the relationship between the parent and the child. That's a big problem. The other factor, which is related to the first, is that many American parents are no longer confident of their authority. They are uncomfortable enforcing rules. They think good parenting means letting kids decide in almost all circumstances, including those where parents would unequivocally have made the call not so long ago. Mary and Margo are an extreme case. More common is the parent who knows she should be setting and enforcing boundaries, but she isn't, and she isn't sure what to do about it.

Another child, another patient, this time a 4-year-old boy with a rash. Well, there are lots of rashes. There's poison ivy, there's eczema, there's scabies, and then there's meningococcus, which begins as a rash but can be fatal within hours. In order to make the right diagnosis, I have to see the rash.

"Where's the rash?" I asked mom.

"It's worst on his tummy," mom answered. "And on his chest. And some on his back."

"Let's take a look," I said.

Again, this kid did not want to cooperate. This mom—unlike the other mom—was actually trying to get the job done, to get the kid's shirt off so that we could see the rash. Mom had turned on a *SpongeBob SquarePants* video on her phone, cranked up the volume, and handed the phone to her kid, who promptly threw the phone on the floor. The kid was fighting back, kicking, screaming. "You are being such a GOOD BOY!" mom was saying as she struggled with his shirt. He thrashed harder as she tried to get his shirt up. The SpongeBob video was still blaring. "You are doing such a GREAT JOB!" she said, as though *saying* that he was doing a great job would somehow, magically, make it so. He tried to smack her in the face, but she pulled her head back just in time and he missed. "Good job!" mom said. I wasn't sure whether she was praising herself for evading the blow, or him. She did finally get his shirt off.

That was weird. When her son took a swing at her, it would have made more sense if mom had said "missed me!" or "please don't hit." It would have made even better sense for mom to say, "You are going to lose all privileges for a month if you try to hit me again." Kids are not born knowing the meaning of words. They have to be taught. When a child fights his mom when she is trying to get his shirt off, and he is praised for doing a great job, what lesson is he learning? The boy could reasonably conclude that he is being praised for fighting his mom. How are kids supposed to learn courtesy and respect when they are praised for being irrational and stubborn?

Jim and Tammy Bardus have one child, Kimberly, 8 years old. After carefully researching the local public schools, Jim and Tammy were concerned about what they considered an over-emphasis on basic skills such as reading and writing, and the elimination of what the public schools now call "enrichment" programs, art and music in particular. Those programs had been cut because of shortfalls in the district budget. So Jim and Tammy decided to enroll Kimberly in a private school, even though it wouldn't be easy for them financially.

Tammy took Kimberly to visit four different private schools. Tammy and Jim both liked school X: the atmosphere was warm and nurturing, the teachers were enthusiastic and engaged, and the long-term outcomes of the students were well-documented. But Kimberly liked school Y. On her visit to school Y, Kimberly had clicked with the student escort, a 9-year-old named Madison. Madison and Kimberly discovered that they both liked the *Beezus and Ramona* books by Beverly Cleary, and they both liked American Girl dolls. But the parents were concerned about the dilapidated condition of the school, the boredom evident among both the teachers and the administrators, and the school's refusal to disclose where graduates of the school (a K–8 school) went to high school. Tammy and Jim advised their daughter to attend school

X. But Kimberly insisted on school Y. And that's the school where she is now enrolled: school Y.

When I asked Tammy why she and her husband allowed their 8-year-old daughter to have the final say, Tammy answered, "I think good parenting means letting kids decide. That's how kids learn, right? If I make all the decisions for her, how will she ever learn to decide on her own? And if I force her to go to a school that wasn't her first choice, what can I say if she complains about the school?"

Forty years ago, most parents who sent their kids to private schools didn't ask the child which school the child preferred. Forty years ago, the parents made that decision, often overruling their children's preference. Forty years ago, when I was in medical school, it would have been unusual for parents to let their 8-year-old have the final say in the choice of school. Today it is common.

I'm not suggesting that 40 years ago were the good old days, or that we should prefer the 1980s or the 1990s to our own era. Every era has its shortcomings. But I don't think we are facing up to ours.

My friend Janet Phillips and her late husband, Bill Phillips, (their true names) have four sons. When the boys were in high school, Janet and Bill became concerned about stories they heard about kids drinking. Then they saw it for themselves: high school kids who had been drinking and who appeared to be drunk, but who were nevertheless getting behind the wheel of a car. What to do?

Bill bought a Breathalyzer. The next time there was a party at their house, Bill saw a boy who appeared to be drunk. Bill told the boy, "Come with me." He handed the boy the Breathalyzer and told him to blow into the device. Sure enough, the boy was drunk. Janet called the boy's parents and asked them to take their intoxicated son home. To the surprise of both Bill and Janet, the boy's parents were offended by the phone call. The boy's mother did take her son home, without a word of thanks to either Janet or Bill.

Janet and Bill's Breathalyzer strategy was not received enthusiastically by other parents as well. One parent, Ms. Stoltz, gave Janet a piece of her mind. "Kids these days are going to drink, whether you like it or not," Ms. Stoltz said. "I think our job is to teach them to drink responsibly."

"At 15 years of age?" Janet asked.

"At whatever age. I'd rather have them drink in my own home than hide their drinking from me."

Several days later, Janet happened to be standing just a few feet away when Ms. Stoltz picked up her youngest son, about 12 years old, from school. The boy climbed into the back seat of the car. Ms. Stoltz turned around and asked him, "How was school today?"

Her son said to her, "Turn around. Shut up. Drive."

Ms. Stoltz glanced at Janet and drove away, without saying a word.

As near as Janet can recall, she and her husband only actually used the Breathalyzer twice. But they always kept it in full view, where every kid could see it, whenever any of their teenage sons had a party. Their home became known as the home where "those crazy parents will use a Breathalyzer on you." And that had consequences.

Some of the consequences were predictable, and some were not. The four boys were popular, so their house was a favorite hangout—*early* in the evening. Then around 9:30 p.m., a certain contingent would leave to go to other parties where alcohol would be freely available. But other kids would stay.

And sometimes, still other kids would arrive. That's what was unexpected. Not all teenage kids like to get drunk. Some don't. But in contemporary American culture, it's hard for a teen to "just say no" without looking uncool. An excuse is helpful. A girl or boy could say, when offered a drink, "Hey, I'd love to, but I'm on my way to the Phillips' house and you know their crazy dad—he's the one with the Breathalyzer." And that provides a respectable excuse not to drink.

As I mentioned: We parents are spending more and more time and money on parenting, but when you look at the results, things are getting worse, not better. American kids are now much more likely to be diagnosed with ADHD and/or bipolar disorder and/or other psychiatric disorders than they were 30 years ago (I will present the evidence in Chapter 3), and they are heavier and less fit than they were 30 years ago (Chapter 4). Long-term outcome studies suggest that American kids are now less resilient and more fragile than they used to be. In Chapter 7 I will explain what I mean by "more fragile," and I will present the evidence supporting that claim.

What's going on?

The first half of this book poses the problems. The second half provides the solutions. I think I understand where we have gone wrong, and I think I know how to make it better. My prescription is based primarily on what I have seen in my medical office over the past 30+ years, but it also draws on what I have learned from my conversations with parents, teachers, researchers, and kids both across the United States and around the world.

You may be wondering, *Who is this Leonard Sax guy, and what makes him the expert?* It's a fair question. I am a family physician, board-certified in family medicine, currently in practice in the suburbs of Philadelphia. I also have a PhD in psychology. I grew up in the suburbs of Cleveland, Ohio, where I attended public schools K through 12. I earned my undergraduate degree in biology from MIT in Cambridge, Massachusetts. I earned both my PhD in psychology and my MD at the University of Pennsylvania. After doing a three-year residency in family medicine, I practiced for 19 years in the Maryland suburbs of Washington, DC. I then relocated to Pennsylvania, where I continue to see patients on a part-time basis. My primary sources for this book are the more than 120,000 office visits I have conducted in my role as a family physician between 1989 and today. I have seen children, teenagers, and their parents, from a wide variety of backgrounds and circumstances. I have seen, from the intimate yet objective perspective of the family physician, the profound changes in American life since 1989. I have witnessed firsthand the collapse of American parenting.

In 2001, I began visiting schools and communities—first just across the United States, and then in Australia, Canada, England, Germany, Italy, Mexico, New Zealand, Scotland, Spain, and Switzerland—meeting with teachers and parents, talking with students, learning from professors and other researchers. From July 2008 through June 2013, I took an extended leave from medical practice in order to devote myself full-time to these visits, and I have continued visiting schools in the years since. I have now visited more than 500 schools across North America and around the world, meeting with students, teachers, and/or parents face-to-face.[1]

In this book, I will share with you what I have learned. Like any competent physician, I will first review the evidence. Then I will make a diagnosis and I will prescribe a treatment. The treatment will be strategies that you can put in place today, in your home, without spending any money, that will improve the odds of a good outcome for your child.

And I will share success stories. We will hear more about Janet and Bill Phillips and their four sons, and other families like theirs: families who have resisted the tide and have achieved good outcomes, despite the odds. These stories, supplemented by recent scholarly research, will provide the basis for what you must do if you're going to raise a healthy child in the modern world. It's still possible to raise a healthy child. It is not easy, but it can be done.

Some aspects of the collapse of parenting are just as problematic in Scotland and New Zealand as they are here. In every country I have visited, I have found parents who are unsure about their role. They ask, "Should I be my child's best friend? But if I am my son's best friend, how can I tell him that he is not allowed to stay up past midnight playing video games?" When Dr. Timothy Wright was headmaster of Shore, a private school in Sydney, Australia, he told me how a parent called him one day. Mom asked, "Dr. Wright, would you please give my son some advice about which video games are OK to play, and which aren't OK? And would you tell him how much time spent playing video games is too much time?"

"Umm...No. Actually, I will not do that," Dr. Wright answered. He explained that it is *not* his job, as head of school, to provide answers to those questions. The job of guiding and governing a boy's use of video games is the job of the parent, not the job of a school administrator.

So some aspects of this problem are found worldwide. But other aspects of the collapse of parenting are peculiar to North America and especially to the United States. Chief among those is the culture of disrespect.

I

The Culture of Disrespect

A long time ago—September 2009, to be precise—in a culture now far, far away, President Barack Obama gave a prime-time speech to a joint session of Congress, outlining his healthcare proposal. Joe Wilson, a congressman from South Carolina, heckled the president from the floor of the Congress, shouting, "You lie!" The next day, Mr. Wilson issued a formal apology to the president in writing and by phone call. President Obama promptly accepted Wilson's apology, saying, "We all make mistakes. He apologized quickly and without equivocation and I'm appreciative of that." Wilson's outburst was condemned by fellow Republicans. Joe Barton, a Republican congressman from Texas, said, "We ought to be able to get our message across to the president without resorting to playground tactics." Bob Inglis, a Republican congressman from South Carolina, said, "The president deserves respect, especially when speaking to a joint session of the Congress. Our opposing views should be presented decently and in order, not as interruptions."[1] Five days later, the House of Representatives passed a bipartisan measure of rebuke, stating that Wilson's outburst was "a breach of decorum and degraded the proceedings of the joint session, to the discredit of the House."[2]

Fast-forward to February 2023. President Joe Biden was giving his State of the Union address when Marjorie Taylor Greene, Republican of Georgia, repeatedly shouted out "Liar!" Other Republicans also heckled the president during the same address, one calling out "Bullsh*t!"[3] This time there were no apologies. Greene went on Fox News the next day to reiterate that "Joe Biden is a liar" and that she was proud to have interrupted him.[4] Republican leaders, including then Speaker of the House Kevin McCarthy, defended Greene's interruptions.[5]

A few months later, Speaker McCarthy was rushing to get members of the House to vote on a spending bill to keep the government open. Democrats were stalling for time. Jamaal Bowman, Democrat of New York, pulled a fire alarm, prompting a mandatory evacuation of the Cannon House Office Building and postponing the vote for almost two hours. Bowman, who was previously the principal of a middle school, surely knew that pulling a fire alarm when there's no fire is against the law. (Some newspapers ran a cartoon showing Bowman standing at a school blackboard writing *Don't Pull Fire Alarm Falsely* in chalk, over and over.)[6] Bowman subsequently pled guilty to one charge of making a false alarm and paid a $1,000 fine.[7] Two months later, the House of Representatives passed a resolution to censure Bowman by a vote of 214 to 191, largely along party lines.[8]

This is not a book about American politics, thank goodness. But I do think that the change in how a member of Congress heckling a president is viewed by colleagues—over a span of less than 15 years—is a symptom of a transformation in American culture.

Likewise: 20 years ago, it would have been inconceivable for a member of Congress to pull a fire alarm when there's no fire. Now it seems unsurprising, even amusing. American culture has become a culture of disrespect, by which I mean a culture in which it is now considered not only permissible, but also entertaining and fun, to be disrespectful, to use bad language, to break the rules.

What is acceptable within a culture, and what is not acceptable? Or to dig even deeper: What constitutes a good life? Each culture answers those questions differently. A century ago, American kids were immersed in the *McGuffey Readers* and other books of that ilk, which portrayed the good life as a life which was morally grounded and biblically sound.[9] In that era, education pioneer John Dewey insisted that schools should teach morality "every moment of the day, five days a week"; in 1951 the National Education Association affirmed that "an unremitting concern for moral and spiritual values continues to be a top priority for education."[10] American kids today are reading much less,[11] and spending more time on YouTube, TikTok, and video games. They still listen to songs, but the songs have changed. A generation ago, the most popular songs were about love. Kenny Loggins scored a huge hit in 1971 with "Danny's Song": *Even though we ain't got money / I'm so in love with you honey / Everything will bring a chain of love.* A decade earlier, Sam Cooke had a #1 hit song in which he admitted he didn't "know much about history," but vowed that he would work hard to become an A student because he believed that becoming an A student, "I could win your love for me." Now the most popular songs are about sex, often transactional sex in which the act is offered in exchange for money.[12] In their #1 hit song titled "WAP"—an acronym for Wet Ass Pussy—Cardi B and

Megan Thee Stallion advised women to "ask for a car" while having sex with a man, adding that a man "paid my tuition" in return for sex.[13] Bruno Mars earned six Grammys for his song "That's What I Like," in which he offers a woman jewelry and a shopping spree in Paris if she will just "turn around and drop it for a player" because "that's what I like."[14] Drake recently had a #1 song on the Billboard Hot 100 titled "Jimmy Cooks." A sample of the lyrics: *F*** a pigeonhole / That s*** good to go / You don't like the way I talk? / Spin the same hood where I get my d*** sucked.* The *New York Times* reviewer praised Drake for his "lyrical vividness."[15] The lyrics of "Jimmy Cooks" are typical of Drake's songs, which are replete with the n-word, the a-word, and the f-word.[16] Incidentally, Drake is by many measures the most successful entertainer in American history. At this writing, he has had 78 songs reach the Top Ten on the Billboard Hot 100. Taylor Swift is second on the list of most songs to reach the Top Ten, with 59. The Beatles had 34. Michael Jackson had 30.[17]

A similar transformation has occurred on television. The most popular TV shows of the 1960s through the 1980s consistently depicted the parent as the reliable and trusted guide of the child. That was true of *The Andy Griffith Show* and *My Three Sons* in the 1960s; it was true of *Family Ties* and *The Cosby Show* in the 1980s. But it's not true today. Looking through the list of the 100 most popular TV shows on American television right now, I found only a handful which even occasionally depict a parent as reliable and trusted.[18] It's now more typical to encounter a dad like the character of Phil Dunphy on *Modern Family*, the straight dad whose idiotic antics are the butt of the joke on almost every episode in which he appears. His three kids are usually wiser and more insightful than their pathetic father. There was simply no top-ten show from the 1960s or even the 1990s which portrayed a father as a pitiful, clueless loser. Today it's common.

You will find this transformation even on television intended for children. The Disney Channel actively promotes the culture of disrespect and undermines the importance of parents. Consider some of the shows on the Disney Channel, such as *Jessie*, a sitcom in which the parents are almost always absent (and irrelevant), while the three kids are more competent than the bungling butler or the ditsy nanny. Or *Liv and Maddie*, in which the out-of-touch mom—who happens to be a school psychologist—is regularly put to shame both by her girly-girl daughter and by her tomboy daughter (who are both played by the same actress). Or *Dog with a Blog*, in which the father is a child psychologist—another psychologist!—who knows nothing about what kids want or what kids need, a peculiarity which leads to much well-deserved mocking of the father by his children. The father's cluelessness is a recurrent laugh line in the show. The talking dog is always more insightful than the dumb dad. Or *Bunk'd*, a spin-off of *Jessie* in which the director of the summer camp is psychotic, jealous, and irrational, while the kids patiently work to fix the messes made by the grown-ups.

One mother of an 8-year-old said to me, "Our son has recently started to be just amazingly disrespectful, talking back, smirking at us when we ask him to do stuff. I have no idea where this is coming from. His father and I never behave like that."

"Does he watch the Disney Channel?" I asked. "Nickelodeon? Nick Jr.?"

"Well sure," mom said.

"Lock it down," I suggested. "No more Disney Channel. No more Nickelodeon or Nick Jr. I'm not saying all television is bad. Home and Garden TV is fine. The History Channel is fine, mostly. But not Disney or Nickelodeon."

Three weeks later, mom called me. "It's amazing," she said. "The talking back, the smirking—it's all stopped. He's our sweet boy again. He was learning that stuff from the Disney Channel!"

The singer known as SZA (pronounced "sizza") scored a big hit with her song "I Hate You," which includes the memorable lyric "I be so bored with myself, can you come and f*** me?" The reviewer for *The Atlantic* magazine called SZA's album a "poisonous fog...of [expletive] talking," and the reviewer meant that as a *compliment*, lauding the album as "the final great pop album of the year."[19]

Lil Nas X won two Grammy awards for his hit song and video "Old Town Road." His song reached #1 in the United States for 13 consecutive weeks, and also reached the #1 spot in Canada, the United Kingdom, Ireland, Australia, New Zealand, and South Africa.[20] In that song, Lil Nas X—speaking to the world in general, apropos of nothing—says *You can't tell me nothin' / can't nobody tell me nothin'.*

That is the culture of disrespect in a nutshell. *You can't tell me nothin'.* If you can't tell me nothin', then why bother with school? Who cares about Shakespeare or the War of 1812 or the Pythagorean Theorem? Why listen to parents? Why go to church? *You can't tell me nothin'.*

Comedian Bill Maher recently noted "the most fundamental trade-off in life: you're beautiful when you're young, wise when you're old."[21] It follows that any successful culture will teach kids to learn from their elders and to respect their parents, because with age comes wisdom, or so one hopes. Older people are more likely to have learned valuable life lessons which they can share with the kids. The culture of disrespect breaks those bonds across generations. *You can't tell me nothin'.*

The culture of disrespect isn't limited to the United States Congress or to hit songs and videos and TV shows. It is *everywhere.* It's on T-shirts. Here are some of the slogans which I have seen kids wearing on T-shirts:

"DO I LOOK LIKE I CARE?"

"IS THAT ALL YOU GOT?"

"BUY ME ANOTHER DRINK, 'CAUSE YOU'RE STILL UGLY."

"I DON'T NEED YOU, I HAVE WIFI."

"YOU LOOKED BETTER ON INSTAGRAM."

"DUCT TAPE: IT CAN'T FIX STUPID, BUT IT CAN MUFFLE THE SOUND."

"BOOBS: PROOF THAT MEN CAN FOCUS ON TWO THINGS AT ONCE."

"I'M NOT ALWAYS RUDE AND SARCASTIC. SOMETIMES I'M ASLEEP."

"I'M NOT SHY. I JUST DON'T LIKE YOU."

"I DIDN'T MEAN TO PUSH YOUR BUTTONS. I WAS JUST LOOKING FOR MUTE."

These T-shirts are not intended primarily to display to adults. These are meant to be seen by other kids. The slogans on these T-shirts communicate young people's disrespect *for one another.*

What is childhood for? When I put that question to parents, they think I'm being silly. Childhood is for growing up, for biological maturation, right? Isn't that obvious? Actually, no, that's not right, and the answer isn't obvious. A horse is a mature adult at four years of age. The Kentucky Derby is raced with three-year-olds. But a four-year-old child has barely begun. So childhood and adolescence can't just be about biological development, because a horse is a bigger animal than a human, and a horse is fully mature at 4 years of age. Humans are children or adolescents for more years than most animals live. How come? What's the point? Why are we humans so different from other animals?

The answer is *culture*. It takes many years for parents and other grown-ups to teach the culture to the child. There's no shortcut.

The variation from one human culture to the next has no analogue in any other species.[22] Imagine a child raised in Kyoto, Japan, and contrast that child with one raised in Appenzell, Switzerland. The two children speak different languages. They observe different rules of behavior, both with other kids their own age and with their parents. They eat different foods, and they eat them differently (chopsticks versus fork/knife/spoon). The Swiss child may learn a great deal about the making of the local Appenzeller cheese, and by 12 years of age may be able to perform some of the tasks of the cheesemaker. The Japanese child raised in Kyoto knows nothing of cheesemaking but may know something about the protocol of a tea ceremony.

These differences are not genetically programmed. They are specific to the culture. Suppose the Japanese child and the Swiss child are switched at birth: the Swiss child is raised in Kyoto, and the Japanese child is raised in Appenzell. The experience of adoptive parents teaches us that the Japanese child will speak Swiss

German as well as any other child raised in Appenzell and will master that culture with the same ease as a native-born child; and the Swiss child raised in Kyoto likewise will speak Japanese as well, and will be as culturally proficient, as any child born and raised in Kyoto.

Scholars generally agree that the purpose of the extraordinarily long childhood and adolescence in our species is **enculturation:**[23] acquiring all the skills and all the knowledge, all the customs and behaviors which you must know in order to be competent in the culture in which you live. It takes years to master the details of Japanese language and culture and behavior, and the same is true of Swiss language and culture and behavior. If you or I were to move to Kyoto or to Appenzell as adults, we might struggle for the rest of our lives to master the intricacies of the language, the local arts, the local *culture*. It's likely we would always feel as though we were still outsiders, even if we did manage to master at least the language after 20 years or so.

But we are adults. The adult brain is harder to change in any fundamental way, compared with the brain of the child or the adolescent. There has been much buzz in recent years about "neuroplasticity," the ability of the adult human brain to change.[24] It's true that the adult human brain is not fixed in concrete. But it's also true that the adult human brain is much harder to change than the brain of the child or the adolescent. Once the process of puberty is complete, it becomes harder to fully master a new language, a new culture, a new life.[25]

What does it mean to learn a culture? It's more than learning a particular trade or profession, or a language, or a cuisine. It means learning how people get along with one another in that culture, what that culture considers right and wrong.

Four decades ago, a pastor named Robert Fulghum wrote a short essay titled *All I Really Need to Know I Learned in Kindergarten*. His essay, published in book format, sold more than 15 million copies. Here's an excerpt:

> Share everything.
> Play fair.
> Don't hit people.
> Put things back where you found them.
> Clean up your own mess.
> Don't take things that aren't yours.
> Say you're sorry when you hurt somebody.
> Wash your hands before you eat.
> Flush.
> Live a balanced life—learn some and think some and draw and paint and sing and dance and play and work every day some.
> When you go out into the world, watch out for traffic, hold hands, and stick together.[26]

You might think that these rules are universal and/or innate, but they are neither. The son of a samurai, raised in Japan circa 1700, would not have been taught "Don't hit anyone," nor would he have been taught to "say you're sorry when you hurt somebody." Let's contrast Fulghum's book with some lines from *Hagakure: The Book of the Samurai*, written by Yamamoto Tsunetomo in the early 1700s:

> The arts bring ruin to the body. In all cases, the person who practices an art is an artist, not a samurai, and one should have the intention of being called a samurai.

Common sense will not accomplish great things.

All of man's work is a bloody business.

The way of avoiding shame . . . is simply in death.

When there is a choice of either dying or not dying, it is better to
die. . . . The Way of the Samurai is found in death.

A real man does not think of victory or defeat. He plunges reck-
lessly towards an irrational death.

If you are slain in battle, you should be resolved to have your
corpse facing the enemy.

[The best way] of bringing up the child of a samurai: from the time
of infancy one should encourage bravery.[27]

Each culture constructs its rules of right behavior differently.
I'm not saying our way is right and that of the Japanese samurai
was wrong. I am saying that *no child is born knowing what the
rules are.* Every child must be taught.

You don't have to go to Japan three centuries back to confront
rules fundamentally at odds with Fulghum's kindergarten. In the
Western tradition, Nietzsche's preference for "master morality"
over "slave morality," Ayn Rand's "virtue of selfishness," and the
racist eugenics promoted by Margaret Sanger, founder of Planned
Parenthood, all illustrate values which are fundamentally at odds
with the unselfishness of Fulghum's Rules.

You can't take values for granted. We used to take more seriously the job of teaching kids to be kind, to think of others first.
Forty years ago, kindergarten and first grade in American schools
were all about teaching "socialization," as it was then called:
teaching Fulghum's Rules, and more. In 1951, as noted above,
the National Education Association affirmed that "an unremitting concern for moral and spiritual values continues to be a top

priority for education." But beginning in the 1990s, many American schools and school districts decided that the focus of early elementary education should not be on socialization or enculturation but should instead be on literacy and numeracy. There was great concern at that time because Japanese students had pulled ahead of American students on some measures of academic achievement.[28] The unspoken assumption seems to have been that kids would learn the basic rules of good behavior—the most important part of enculturation—in some other way: either at home, or from the larger culture.[29] At the time, and throughout the 1990s—and in many districts, continuing today—school administrators prided themselves on introducing "rigor" into early elementary education. I was living in Montgomery County, Maryland, when our county superintendent garnered national attention for making kindergarten "academically rigorous," cutting down on "fluff" such as duck-duck-goose and field trips and singing in rounds, requiring that kindergarten teachers spend more time teaching phonics instead.[30] And in my school visits nationwide, I have observed the same shift—a shift away from teaching socialization and how to get along with other people, to an emphasis on academic skills that can be assessed on standardized tests. As New York Times columnist David Brooks recently observed, "We [now] inhabit a society in which people are no longer trained in how to treat others with kindness and consideration. Our society has become one in which people feel licensed to give their selfishness free rein."[31]

The shift in the early elementary curriculum and the consequent neglect of teaching socialization place a greater burden than ever before on the American parent. But just when kids need parents more than ever to teach them the whole package of what it means to be a good person in this particular culture, the authority of parents to do that job has been undermined. We now live in a culture where kids value the opinion of other kids their own age more than they value the opinion of their parents, and where the authority of parents has declined, not only in the eyes of children but in the eyes of parents themselves.

Many parents today suffer from *role confusion.* "Role confusion" is a plausible translation of *Statusunsicherheit,* a term used by German sociologist Norbert Elias to describe this change.[32] Elias observed that in the second half of the 20th century, Western Europeans became less comfortable with any sort of power differential in social relations. Before World War I, Elias notes, there were sharply defined power differentials in multiple domains: between aristocrats and the lower classes; between men and women; between managers and employees; between parents and children. Throughout the 20th century, and especially in the decades after 1945, people in Western Europe—and in North America too, I might add—became uneasy with all such power differentials. With regard to the power differential between men and women: as a matter of social justice, women acquired equal rights, though at a varied tempo across the developed world (women in Appenzell, Switzerland, did not gain the right to vote on local issues until 1990). Regarding the power differential between managers and employees: in recent decades, many companies have abandoned the old-fashioned hierarchical management system in favor of "giving employees a voice." With regard to the former deference of the lower classes to the upper classes: the aristocracy has nearly vanished, and the children of the wealthy now pay extra money for jeans that have been deliberately torn at the factory, to simulate the look of a lower-income kid. And with regard to parents and children: the authority of parents, and even more significantly the *importance* of parents in the lives of their children, has declined substantially.[33]

What do I mean when I say that the importance of parents in the lives of children has declined? More than 60 years ago, Johns Hopkins University sociologist James Coleman asked American teenagers this question: *If all your friends belonged to a particular club, and all your friends wanted you to join that club, but one of your parents did not approve, would you still join the club?* In that era, the majority of American teenagers responded No. They would not join the club if one of their parents did not approve.[34] In that era, the opinion of one parent mattered more than the combined opinion of all the teenage peers.

Not today. I have posed an updated version of Professor Coleman's question to hundreds of children and teenagers at dozens of venues across the United States in the past 15 years, before and after the pandemic. I have asked them, "If all your friends were on a particular social media app, and they all wanted you to join, would you consult your parents first?" The most common response to the question isn't Yes, it isn't No, it's laughter. The notion that kids would bother to consult their parents about joining a social media site is so implausible that it's funny. *My parents don't even know what ASKfm is. They would probably think it was some kind of radio station! So why would I ask them?* If all my friends are joining that site, then *of course* I am going to join. These kids sometimes say that they love their parents, and maybe they do. But they care what their peers think more than they care what their parents think.

In American culture today, same-age peers matter more than parents. Parents matter less. I'm not saying parents *should* matter less. I'm saying that in contemporary American culture, parents *do* matter less, by which I mean that parents no longer have the authority or the standing that they had a generation ago. And parents are reluctant to change the rules, to insist that time spent with parents and family is more important than time spent with same-age peers, because parents are suffering from the "role confusion" described by Elias. They are unsure of what authority they have and how to exercise it. As a result, it's much harder for American parents to teach Fulghum's Rules, or any rules, to their kids. And the older the child, the more true that is. In one study, the most common attitude of American teenagers toward their parents was described as "ingratitude seasoned with contempt."[35]

Why did this change occur? I think Norbert Elias, mentioned above, understood why. Elias noted that throughout the 20th century, the idea of power and authority became suspect throughout Western Europe and North America. Politically, the story of the past seventy years might be summarized as the empowerment of the previously disenfranchised. People of color were empowered. Women were empowered. Employees were empowered (at least in theory and in lip service). And children were empowered. As writer Alana Newhouse noted in her viral essay "Everything Is Broken," our contemporary culture is now characterized by "an allergy to hierarchy, so much so that the weighting or preferring of some voices or products over others is seen as illegitimate."[36] I would add that nobody stopped to say, "Yes, it is right that adults should have equal rights in their relations with one another. It is right that women, people of color, etc. should have equal rights relative to White males. But what is true for adults in their relations with other adults may not be true for parents in their relations with children." Abolish every hierarchy! Empower everybody! Including kids! Why not?

My answer: Because the first job of the parent is to teach their culture to their children. And authoritative teaching requires hierarchy within the family, requires respect for the authority of parents. But in our current moment, the concept of respecting authority has come to seem absurd. The financial crisis of 2008/2009, the bungling of American interventions overseas, the sex abuse scandal in the Catholic Church, Elon Musk, and innumerable other recent examples of people in positions of authority screwing up big time have undermined the whole concept of respecting authority.[37] The notion of trusting people in positions of power to do the right thing now seems quaintly ridiculous. In 1964, 77 percent of Americans said that you can trust the government to do the right thing all the time or just about all the time. In 2023, only 16 percent of Americans said that you can trust the government to do the right thing all the time (1 percent) or just about all the time (15 percent).[38]

I am not asking you to trust the government the way people in 1964 trusted the government. I am just asking you to recognize how harmful it might be when our contemporary disdain for authority seeps into family life. The parent who is understandably and reasonably skeptical regarding the competence of government officials or of corporate CEOs is uncomfortable saying to her child, "Because I'm your mother, that's why." But a major claim I will make in this book is that children need to respect their parents and their parents' authority—in the best interest of the child.

American youth today are immersed in a culture of disrespect. Young people overestimate the importance of their own culture and disrespect the culture of their elders. How is a child, or a teenager, or an adult supposed to decide what is art and what is trash?

I have discussed this question with middle school and high school students on many of my school visits over the past 23 years. Most students reject my suggestion that I, or anybody, can distinguish authoritatively between art and trash. They insist that there is no objective standard of value by which to judge, no fundamental criteria that would allow anyone to say that one work of art is any better than another.

"So you can't say that Shakespeare's *Hamlet* is a greater work of art than, say, the movie *Superbad*?" I asked one group of high school students. "Right!" one boy answered. "Personally, I think *Hamlet* sucks. We had to read it last year. What. A. Bore! And *Superbad* is a great movie. One of the all-time best ever. But if you like *Hamlet*, that's fine. What you like is none of my business. Whatever floats your boat."

Children are not born knowing what makes Shakespeare or Beethoven great. They must be taught. If we don't teach them, they look to their peers and to the popular culture. And what do they find there? Cardi B and Megan Thee Stallion. Drake. SZA. Profanity as lyric. Vulgarity as normative. The culture of disrespect.[39]

There is somewhat greater cultural ballast in Western Europe and the UK than in the United States. When I have met with Scottish students and their families in Edinburgh and Perthshire and Stirling, I have found many boys, and some girls, who are proud to wear the traditional clothes that were worn by their parents and grandparents. Kilts are passed down from one generation to the next, not as museum pieces but as clothing to be worn whenever the occasion arises. And the occasions for a boy to wear a kilt do arise, typically several times a year. Boys in Scotland have been happy to give me an impromptu lecture on the characteristics of a proper Scottish kilt and how to distinguish the genuine article from the cheap imported frauds sold to tourists at Edinburgh Castle.

It would be unusual to find an American girl or boy who is proud to wear her or his grandparent's clothes.

But as far as our job as parents is concerned, it doesn't really matter why parents lost their authority, or why this trend may be more pronounced in the United States than elsewhere. We need to understand *what to do about it*, which will be one of our objectives in this book.

As Canadian psychologist Dr. Gordon Neufeld has observed, in most cultures in most times and at most places, the job of enculturing the child is not primarily the job of the mother and father. The entire culture takes part: schools, the community, and even popular stories all are in sync in teaching the basic rules, the fabric of the culture.[40] In our time, many schools have retreated from normative instruction about right and wrong, in part to emphasize academics, and in part because normative instruction about right and wrong now can be politically risky. It's now easier to focus on teaching phonics than to teach Fulghum's Rules or any other absolute notions of good behavior. It's easier for teachers or school administrators to suggest that a child has "Oppositional-Defiant Disorder," and suggest a visit to the doctor, than to exhort parents to work harder at the task of teaching basic social skills to their child. The end result is that parents today must shoulder a greater burden than parents in previous generations, while having fewer resources to enable them to do their job.

Before we go any further in our discussion of the loss of parental authority, I want to make sure you and I are on the same page with regard to what I mean by "parental authority." I have learned that when I speak to parents, many confuse "parental authority" with "parental discipline." They think that parental authority is all about enforcing discipline. In fact, parental authority is mostly about *what is valued*. Strong parental authority means that parents matter, and the parents' culture matters, more than same-age peers and the culture of same-age peers. In contemporary American culture, peers matter more than parents and peer culture reigns supreme.

For most of the history of our species, children have learned culture from the adults. That's why childhood and adolescence have to be so long in our species. But in the USA today, kids no longer learn culture from the grown-ups. American children and teens today have their own culture, a culture of disrespect, which they learn from their peers and from social media and from popular songs, movies, and TV shows, and which they in turn teach to their peers.

It's tough to be a parent in a culture which constantly undermines parental authority, a culture in which parents are most often portrayed as clueless idiots, whether on the Disney Channel or on social media. Two generations ago, American parents had much greater authority, and the culture supported the authority of parents. In that era, American parents were more likely to teach right and wrong in no uncertain terms. *Do unto others as you would have them do unto you. Love your neighbor as yourself.* Those were commands, not suggestions.

Today, most American parents no longer act with such authority. They do not command. Instead they **ask**, "How would you feel if someone did that to you?" The command has morphed into a question. And parents don't know what to say when their son replies, "If someone did that to me, I'd kick him in the nuts, then I'd sit on his face." Even when kids produce the canned answer which they know the grown-ups want to hear, the answer is mere regurgitation. Nothing has been digested. No real communication across the generations—the most important feature of enculturation—has occurred.

What does it mean to assert your authority as a parent? It doesn't mean being a tough disciplinarian. Among other things, it means that **the parent-child relationship takes priority** over the relationships between the child and his or her same-age peers. Not just for toddlers, but for teenagers as well. It means that parents are doing their job—fulfilling their biological niche, if you like—of teaching the child how to behave both within and outside the family unit, of teaching the child what matters, of teaching the child what's acceptable and what is unacceptable. Recall that the purpose of a prolonged childhood in our species seems to be, first and foremost, for the child to learn the grown-up culture, from the grown-ups. When parents lose their authority—when same-age peers matter more than parents—then kids are no longer interested in learning the culture of the parents. They want to learn the culture of their same-age peers, the culture they see on social media and on popular TV shows. Throughout this book we will see just how harmful that is.

The benefits of parental authority are substantial. When parents matter more than peers, then parents can teach right and wrong in a meaningful way. They can prioritize attachments within the family above attachments between kids and their same-age peers. They can nurture and grow better relationships between their children and other adults. They can help their child to develop a more robust and more authentic sense of self, grounded not in how many "likes" a selfie gets on social media but in the child's truest nature. When the parent-child relationship is the foundation of the child's world, then the child can rest secure because the parents will never stop loving the child. (Of course that isn't true of abusive or neglectful parents, but abusive or neglectful parents don't read parenting books. You are a loving parent, or you wouldn't be reading this book.) When the relationship a child has with a same-age peer is the foundation of the child's world, on the other hand, the child's world is precarious because the regard of your peers can change in one day. In five minutes. And every kid knows that.

The issue for parents isn't always that they are unwilling to assert their authority. Sometimes they believe that they are helping their children by letting kids make decisions which are really not age-appropriate. Here's an example of what NOT to do—in other words, an example of how many parents now behave. Megan and Jim are both 40-something parents. Their daughter, Courtney, was 12 years old when Megan and Jim planned a ski vacation between Christmas and New Year's. Four days, three nights.

Their daughter politely declined. "You know I'm not crazy about skiing," she said. "I'll just stay at Arden's house for those four days. Her parents said it's OK."

So her parents went on the ski vacation by themselves, and Courtney spent four days as the guest of her best friend. "I didn't mind. In fact, I was pleased that Courtney could be so independent," Megan told me.

But Megan is mistaken. Courtney isn't independent. No 12-year-old truly is. Instead, Courtney has transferred her natural dependence from her parents—where it should be—to her same-age peers, where it shouldn't be. Courtney's top priorities now lie in pleasing her friends, being liked by her friends, being accepted by her same-age peers. Her parents have become an afterthought, a means to other ends.[41]

You love your child. It's natural to want to please someone you love. If your daughter doesn't want to join you and your spouse on a ski vacation, it feels harsh to say, "Nevertheless, despite your protests, you are coming with us." But that's what you must say. Why? Because having fun together is one foundation, maybe the best foundation, for authoritative parenting in the modern world (we'll come back to this thought in Chapter 11, "Joy"). Because if most of the good times come when your kid is having fun with other kids, and not with you, then it's no wonder that your kid doesn't want to hang with you over the holiday. Because if you can't find a way to have fun with your kid on a vacation, fun that both of you really enjoy, then you've got big problems. Because your kids won't value time with you above time with their same-age peers if they rarely spend any time with you doing fun stuff. That's part of what it means to exercise parental authority.

I mentioned Dr. Neufeld, the Canadian psychologist who recently retired from active practice after 40 years of working with children and adolescents. Over the past four decades, he has observed firsthand a fundamental change in the ways in which kids across North America form and prioritize attachments. Forty years ago, kids' primary attachment was to their parents. Today, for most kids in the United States and Canada, kids' primary attachment is to other kids. "For the first time in history," Neufeld observes, "young people are turning for instruction, modeling, and guidance not to mothers, fathers, teachers, and other responsible adults but to people whom nature never intended to place in a parenting role—their own peers.... Children are being brought up by immature persons who cannot possibly guide them to maturity. They are being brought up by each other."[42] Today, most North American kids find their primary attachment in their relations with same-age peers. They care more about what other kids think of them than about what their parents think of them.

Neufeld describes a girl, Cynthia, who "had become rude, secretive, and sometimes hostile" toward her parents, while remaining "happy and charming" when around her friends. "She was obsessive about her privacy and insistent that her life was none of her parents' business. Her mother and father found it difficult to speak with her without being made to feel intrusive. Their previously loving daughter appeared to be less and less comfortable in their company.... It was impossible to sustain any conversation with her."

I personally have found this scenario to be common, from late elementary school through high school, not only in my medical practice, but in my meetings with parents all across the United States and Canada. How best to understand it?

Neufeld asks,

Imagine that your spouse or lover suddenly begins to act strangely: won't look you in the eye, rejects physical contact, speaks to you irritably in monosyllables, shuns your approaches, and avoids your company. Then imagine that you go to your friends for advice. Would they say to you, "Have you tried a time-out? Have you imposed limits and made clear what your expectations are?" It would be obvious to everyone that, in the context of adult interaction, you're dealing not with a *behavior* problem but a *relationship* problem. And probably the first suspicion to arise would be that your partner was having an affair.[43]

Neufeld observes that the primary problem in Cynthia's relationship with her parents is that she had come to place a higher value on her attachment to her peers than on her attachment with her parents. Once that happens, any attempt by parents to set limits on their child's interactions with their peers—for example, no texting or phone calls after 9:30 p.m.—can prompt sulking, or a tantrum. Parents need to recognize such tantrums or sulking as symptoms of a shift in the child's primary attachment from parents to peers.

Too often, parents today allow their parenting to be governed by their desire to please their child. If your relationship with your child is governed by your own desire to be loved by them, the odds are good that you will not achieve even that objective.

There is something hardwired going on here. The child expects to look up to the parent, to be instructed by the parent, even to be commanded by the parent when appropriate. If the parent instead is serving the child, that relationship falls out of its natural balance. You may not earn your child's love at all—and the more you try, the more pathetically unsuccessful you will be. I have seen precisely this dynamic play out at least a hundred times in my own medical practice since 1989. The parent who puts the child's wishes first may earn only their child's contempt, not their love.

But if you are not primarily concerned about your child's love and affection, and you instead focus on your duties as a parent—to teach your child right from wrong, to communicate to them what it means to be a responsible man or woman, within the constraints of the culture you are trying to teach and to share—then you may find that your child loves you and respects you. When you're not looking for it.

When I was a young doctor, back in the 1990s, I saw no connection between politics and parenting. Left-of-center parents were no different in their parenting style, on average, compared with right-of-center parents. Some left-of-center parents were Too Hard, some were Too Soft, and some were Just Right—and the same was true of right-of-center parents.

But over roughly the past ten years, I've noticed something new. For the first time, I am seeing a political dimension to parenting. Specifically, left-of-center parents have become more permissive, compared with right-of-center parents. I'm seeing a growing number of parents who truly believe that it's virtuous to let the kid be in charge. Recall that mom who wouldn't help me when her daughter refused to open her mouth, the mom who said, "Her body, her choice."[44]

Almost every day that I am in the office, I now encounter parents who believe in "gentle parenting" or its close relatives, mindful parenting or intentional parenting.[45] The gentle parent always lets the child decide. The gentle parent never uses punishments of any kind, not even time-outs. The gentle parent does not toilet train the child, but instead "models" toileting for the toddler, which will (it is hoped) inspire the toddler to want to use the toilet instead of the diaper.[46] One mother was playing with her son, then gently let him know that she needed to take a break from playing with him in order to do some housework. Her son exploded in anger, hitting and kicking his mom. That mom reached out to Robin Einzig, a leading guru of gentle parenting, to ask what she should do in that situation. Einzig responded without hesitation, "He's telling you very clearly that right now he needs your presence."[47] Forget the housecleaning. You have to play with the boy until *he* decides to stop. Jessica Winter, writing for *The New Yorker*, observes that gentle parenting requires the parent to transform himself/herself into "a self-renouncing, perpetually present humanoid who has nothing but time and who is programmed for nothing but calm."[48] Winter predicts that the next generation can "anticipate blaming their high rates of depression and anxiety on the overvalidation and undercorrection native to gentle parenting."

As a family doctor, I simply did not encounter this kind of parenting 10 years ago. Now I see it almost every day that I'm in the office. And the parents who practice gentle parenting are almost always politically left-of-center.

This change may help to explain some new findings. Let's talk about depression in teenagers. Researchers have known for decades that teenage girls are more likely than teenage boys to be depressed. But some recent studies have called attention to the interaction between politics and depression among adolescents: namely, the finding that left-of-center adolescents are increasingly more likely to be depressed compared with adolescents who are politically right-of-center. This finding is so pronounced that left-of-center *boys* are now significantly more likely to be depressed than are right-of-center *girls*.[49]

Catherine Gimbrone and her colleagues at Columbia University tried to explain this finding in political terms, asserting that the country veered steadily rightward beginning in 2012, causing left-of-center kids to be more depressed. Michelle Goldberg, a left-of-center columnist writing for the *New York Times*, dismissed that assertion by Gimbrone and colleagues as simply not accurate.[50] Goldberg observed that President Barack Obama was reelected in 2012; she noted that the United States Supreme Court legalized same-sex marriage nationwide in 2015. Those events should have encouraged left-of-center kids, but depressive symptoms rose steadily nevertheless. Goldberg suggested instead that left-of-center kids are more likely to be on social media than right-of-center kids. She drew on a growing body of research showing that teens who spend more time on social media are more likely to be depressed compared with teens who spend less time on social media (we will take a close look at this research in Chapter 5, "Screens"). Left-of-center teens are now more likely to be depressed than conservative teens because left-of-center teens spend more time on social media—so says Goldberg.

NYU professor Jonathan Haidt rejects both Gimbrone's conjecture of a steady rightward shift and Goldberg's attribution of blame to social media in explaining the political dimension of this rise in depression.[51] Haidt argues that the real reason left-of-center kids are more likely to be depressed compared with right-of-center kids is that left-of-center kids have been taught to catastrophize events, to assume the worst, while right-of-center kids are taught to be more optimistic.

I think both Goldberg and Haidt make good points, and their arguments are not mutually exclusive. Goldberg's argument about social media being the mediating factor driving the growth in depression is certainly valid, and we will return to that factor in Chapter 5. But Goldberg and Haidt are both missing another explanation which, from my perspective as a family doctor, is definitely an additional contributing factor. As I mentioned, I am now encountering more and more parents like the mom who said, "Her body, her choice": parents who might be described as aggressively permissive. They think it's actually virtuous to let kids decide *everything*. And those "gentle parents" are not randomly distributed along the political spectrum: they are overwhelmingly more likely to be left-of-center. Conservative parents still insist that their kids open their mouths and say Ah when they bring their kids to the doctor with a fever and a sore throat.

This is a big change. As recently as 10 years ago, it wasn't unusual to find left-of-center parents who were authoritative, even strict. That is less common today. Permissive parenting is now more common among left-of-center parents than right-of-center parents. That's important, because researchers have found that permissive parenting leads to young adults with "less sense of meaning and purpose in life, less autonomy and mastery of the world around them."[52] Other researchers have found that permissive parenting leads to lower emotional intelligence and lower personal growth.[53] Still other researchers report that permissive parenting is associated with an increased risk of drug and alcohol abuse and lower academic achievement, while authoritative parenting is associated with lower risk of drug and alcohol abuse and higher academic achievement.[54] The children of permissive parents are more likely to become anxious and depressed.[55] Two decades ago, University of Virginia sociologist Brad Wilcox presented evidence that conservative religious parents were the parents most likely to be authoritative, Just Right parents.[56] And from my perspective, that's even more true today: conservative religious parents are now the most likely to be the Just Right parent, not Too Hard and not Too Soft (there are still a few conservative religious parents who are Too Hard, but they are a dwindling minority). Left-of-center parents are now the parents most likely to be permissive, Too Soft in their parenting style. Both left-of-center parents and right-of-center parents have become more permissive over the past decade—that's a major theme of this book, for which I will present more evidence as we go along—but left-of-center parents are now more likely to be permissive compared with right-of-center parents. That, I believe, is part of the reason why left-of-center kids are now more likely to be depressed compared with right-of-center kids.

Today, when I counsel permissive Too Soft parents on the importance of being more authoritative—setting rules and enforcing those rules while still communicating love for the child—left-of-center parents are now more likely to push back. They tell me that they don't want to be "controlling." They don't want to be "coercive." Ten years ago, I could persuade such parents that kids need structure. Kids need rules. Kids need consistency. Today, I don't have much luck with permissive left-of-center parents. "Her body, her choice."

I am a family doctor, not a politician. I am not suggesting that left-of-center parents should adopt right-of-center politics. (And, because you asked: I am a registered Independent.) I just ask that you keep your politics out of your parenting. Your child, your teenager, needs you to provide structure, to set boundaries, to lay down guardrails that are enforced. This has nothing to do with blue states versus red states or Democrat versus Republican. This is about what your kid needs. Kids are not born courteous or respectful. Courtesy and respect are not genetically programmed. Those virtues have to be taught. You must teach them.

I visited multiple schools across Scotland, meeting with students, talking with parents, and leading workshops for teachers at each school. To get to Scotland, I flew from Philadelphia to London-Heathrow, and then connected on a smaller plane from London-Heathrow to Edinburgh.

I arrived well ahead of time for the first flight, the long haul across the Atlantic on a big Airbus A330. Waiting at the gate in

Terminal A at the Philadelphia airport, I watched an American family: a mother, a father, a teenage daughter, and two younger sons.

"Where are my doughnuts?" one of the boys said. He looked to be about 8 years old.

"Sweetie, I thought we should save those for the plane," his mom said.

"I want them right now!" he said more loudly.

"Honey, you just had dessert. Let's wait till—"

"I WANT THEM RIGHT NOW!!" he shouted at the top of his lungs. His mom looked guiltily around, as though the TSA might arrest her. Without another word, she fished in her bag and handed over the entire box of doughnuts to him.

The voice of the gate attendant came over the public address system. "In a few minutes, we will begin boarding American Airlines Flight 728 to London's Heathrow airport. We board by zone number. You will find your zone number on your boarding ticket. Please have your passport open to the photo page..."

The teenage daughter was texting on her cell phone. "Trish, it's time to put the cell phone away. We need to get ready to board," mom said. Her daughter ignored her. "Trish?"

"Mom, would you please SHUT UP. Can't you see that I am BUSY."

"Trish? We need to get ready to board? The plane?" The mom's words sounded like questions. Her daughter continued to ignore her. Mom glanced at me. I felt uneasy and walked away.

I could sense mom's discomfort. I was uncomfortable too. But the kids are in their element. They are living in a different culture. Mom has not *encultured* her kids into her own culture. Instead, mom is trying to adapt to the children's culture, the culture of disrespect, which they have learned from their peers. No enduring society does this. No enduring society expects the grown-ups to conform to the culture of the children. And while these kids might be enjoying themselves now—after a fashion, eating the doughnuts—their parents' failure to enculture and instruct their children rightly means that these kids will be ill-equipped to withstand the challenges of later adolescence and adulthood.

Sometimes you have to wait before you eat the doughnuts. Sometimes you don't get to eat the doughnuts at all. That's life.

2

Food

American kids are heavier today than they used to be. The trend started in the 1970s and continued steadily through 2000. Since the mid-2000s, the trend has tapered. But the shape of childhood has changed.

In the early 1970s, only 4 percent of American children 5 to 11 years of age were obese. According to the latest data, 20.7 percent of American children 5 to 11 years of age are now obese. The proportion of obese kids more than quintupled—from 4 percent to 20.7 percent—over five decades. There was a similar rise in the rate of obesity among American adolescents 12 to 19 years of age, from 4.6 percent in 1970 to 22.2 percent in the latest survey.[1] And we're talking *obese*, not merely overweight.[2]

Fitness is not the same thing as slenderness, and lack of fitness is not the same thing as obesity. Yes, fat kids tend to be less physically fit than slender kids. But there are plenty of slender kids in the United States who are out of shape: they can't run a quarter mile without huffing and puffing. The most recent studies available show that the average fitness of both girls and boys has declined significantly regardless of weight. To put it another way: a slender girl or boy today is less physically fit compared with an equally slender girl or boy from 1999, even if their height and weight are identical.[3]

American kids are becoming less fit. "This is not good news," said Janet Fulton, a lead investigator at the Centers for Disease Control and Prevention (CDC). Her comments were echoed by Dr. Gordon Blackburn, a cardiologist at the Cleveland Clinic. "Thirty years ago, we would not have expected to see 12-year-olds with symptoms of cardiac disease," Dr. Blackburn said. "Now we've had to start a pediatric preventive cardiology clinic."[4]

A mom and dad brought their 11-year-old son into the office. The boy had been running around on the playground with his friends when he felt chest tightness and shortness of breath. We did a thorough evaluation including EKG and chest X-ray. (The boy put aside his video game on his iPad so that I could listen to his chest.) Everything was normal. I concluded that the cause of his chest tightness and shortness of breath was "deconditioning," which is a fancy word for out of shape.[5] The parents wanted me to say that he had "exercise-induced asthma." But this boy didn't have exercise-induced asthma or any other kind of asthma. His lungs were clear. He was just an overweight boy who easily became short of breath because he spent more time playing video games than anything else.

I see this a lot.

What happened over the past five decades? In 1974, it was rare to find a child or teenager who was obese, or who couldn't run a quarter mile without gasping for breath. Today it's common. How come?

Researchers now generally agree on three factors which have driven the rise in obesity and overweight and the decline in fitness among children:

1. What—and how—kids *eat*
2. What kids *do*
3. How much kids *sleep*

Other factors—such as endocrine disruptors, intestinal bacteria, consumption of genetically modified wheat, and antibiotics—may play a role, but there is less consensus regarding those other factors.[6] Let's talk about factors 1, 2, and 3, so you can see the pivotal role played by parental authority—or more precisely, by the abdication of parental authority and by parents' role confusion—in each of these factors.

What—and how—kids *eat*. I was speaking to parents at Horace Greeley High School in Chappaqua, New York. After my talk, a mother and father told me how they had made a healthy and nutritious supper for their son and daughter. Their kids came home and said, "Yuck, we don't want to eat that. Can we just order pizza?" So dad sat down at his laptop and placed an order for pizza to be delivered, one personal pizza for his son and a different pizza with different toppings for his daughter.

I said to dad, "Why did you do that? Why didn't you just tell them, *this is what's for supper. If you don't like it, you can go to bed hungry.*"

Dad blanched. "We don't believe in using starvation as a means of discipline," he said.

"They're not going to starve," I said. "Look. Fifty years ago, if mom made a healthy and nutritious supper for her kids, and the kids didn't like it, she didn't run out and buy them a pizza. She would say, *this is what's for supper. If you don't like it, you can go to bed hungry.*"

When parents are unequivocally in charge, then the parents decide what is for supper, and their kids either eat what is offered or they go hungry. That was the norm in American families as recently as the 1970s, but today it is the exception. In the 1970s, it was common for parents to say, "No dessert until you eat your broccoli. No snacking between meals." Today it's less common to find parents who tell kids what's for supper. Instead, it's more common to hear of parents who *ask* their kids what the *kids* want for supper. When you ask a 12-year-old what they would like for supper, there are some kids who will choose broccoli, Brussels sprouts, cabbage, cauliflower, spinach, asparagus, and kale. Good for them! But many other kids will choose pizza, French fries, potato chips, and ice cream. Most 12-year-olds, and many 15-year-olds for that matter, are not competent to choose what's for supper. That's why they have parents. But when parents abdicate their responsibility and let kids decide what's for supper, one result is more fat kids.

Parents—especially affluent parents—now commonly carry bags of snacks in the car on the way to and from school. Heaven forbid that the children should experience even a moment of hunger. "I don't want them to get hypoglycemic," is the answer one parent gave me when I saw her toting a cooler of refrigerated snacks into the car for the 30-minute trip to her children's private school. I didn't criticize. Better that the kids should eat carrot sticks from home, than that they should stop at Burger King for a cheeseburger and fries.

New evidence suggests that allowing kids to have on-demand access to food may be one factor promoting obesity, independent of the total number of calories consumed. *Ad lib* feeding throughout the day appears to disrupt circadian rhythms, interfering with normal metabolism and disturbing the balance of hormones which regulate appetite. Studies with laboratory animals have found that animals with access to food whenever they want it become fatter than animals that have only scheduled access to food, even when the total calories consumed is kept the same in the two groups. Restricting the amount of time when food is available to 9 or 12 hours out of 24—without restricting calories—improves health and brings weight back to normal. "Time-restricted eating didn't just prevent but also reversed obesity," said Dr. Satchidananda Panda, author of one of the studies on laboratory animals.[7]

Anyhow, since when did a few minutes of hunger become unacceptable? When kids have the final say, then the parents must make every effort to ensure that the kids are not uncomfortable. Not even for five minutes. Hunger—even just for a few minutes on the car ride home from school—is now intolerable. Kids who have never been hungry grow up to be heavier, yet psychologically they are more fragile. They haven't learned to be master of their own needs.

When parents begin to cede control to their kids, food choices often are the first thing to slide. *"No dessert until you eat your broccoli"* morphs into *"How about if you eat three bites of broccoli, and then you can have dessert?"* The command has melted into a request, capped with a bribe. I was at a restaurant where I watched a well-dressed father pleading with his daughter (who looked to be about 5 years old). "Honey, could you please do me a favor? Could you please just *try* a bite of your green peas?" Kids take such pleadings literally. If this girl does condescend to eat a bite of her green peas, she is likely to believe that she has done her father a favor, and that he now owes her a favor in return.

Eat dinner with your kids. Every meal counts. In a survey of 26,078 adolescents from a wide range of backgrounds—urban and rural, affluent and low-income—researchers asked each kid, *In the last seven days, how many days have you had a meal with a parent?* Kids who had more meals with a parent were less likely to have "internalizing problems" such as feeling sad, anxious, or lonely. They were less likely to have "externalizing problems" such as fighting, skipping school, or stealing. They were more likely to help others and more likely to report being satisfied with their own life.

The difference wasn't just between the kids who had seven evening meals a week at home with a parent compared with kids who had none. At almost every step, from zero evening meals a week up to seven evening meals a week, each extra dinner a child had with at least one parent decreased the risk of internalizing problems, decreased the risk of externalizing problems, increased prosocial behavior, and increased the child's general satisfaction with life.[8] The change was statistically significant at almost every step. For example, when you compare kids who had six dinners per week with a parent with kids who had five dinners per week with a parent, you find that kids who had six dinners a week enjoyed significantly better well-being, demonstrated significantly more prosocial behavior, had significantly fewer internalizing

problems—anxiety, depression—and significantly fewer externalizing problems—acting out, fighting—compared with kids who
had five dinners a week with a parent. That one extra meal with a
parent—the difference between five evening meals a week together
and six evening meals together—makes a difference. In a separate study, researchers found that kids who regularly eat meals
with their parents are at lower risk for becoming obese.[9] Multiple
studies have shown that kids are more likely to eat healthier foods
when they are eating with their parents.[10]

American families today are significantly less likely than
families in most other developed countries to have a meal together.[11] "We have a lot of adolescents who've devolved to having
all of their meals in their bedroom," says Dr. Ellen Rome, head
of the Center for Adolescent Medicine at Cleveland Clinic Children's Hospital in Ohio. "It's a significant step away from family
connection."[12]

Not everybody is convinced of the benefits of family meals.
Researchers at Boston University "controlled" for other variables such as parents' involvement with their kids, the amount
of time kids spent watching television, the parents' level of education, etc. When they factored in all those other variables, they
found that family meals no longer predicted outcomes in their
sample.[13] I think the Boston University research suggests that parents who eat meals with their kids are more likely to be involved
with their kids, less likely to allow their kids to spend 30 hours a
week watching TV, etc. In other words, the family meal may be a
marker for a constellation of behaviors which collectively predict
good outcomes: behaviors such as limiting the amount of time
watching TV or on the Internet, parents being involved and engaged with their kids, etc.

The bottom line on family meals:

- A family in which kids often have meals with parents is likely to be a family in which parents still have authority, a family in which parents, and family interaction, still *matter*.
- But just insisting that everybody eat together, while the TV is blaring and the kids are texting at the dinner table, probably won't accomplish much by itself.[14] We actually have good evidence that when the TV is on during suppertime, many of the benefits of a family meal evaporate.[15]

Across North America today, both in the United States and in Canada, I find many parents who seem to believe that their kids' participation in sports, or dance, or some other extracurricular activity is more important than an evening meal with the family, sitting around the dinner table. Maybe those parents won't come right out and say it, but those parents *act as if* those activities are more important than a family meal together. They are scheduling their kids for computer coding class across town at a time that makes a sit-down family meal at home almost impossible. I think those parents are making a mistake. The family should be a higher priority than the after-school class or the sport. Healthy eating begins with the family eating together, as a family, around a table. Scarfing down food in the car on the way from one activity to another doesn't count as a family meal. Maybe once a week if necessary because of unusual demands might be OK. But when you make a habit of having your kid eat a meal in the car on the way from computer coding class to travel team soccer, day after day, week after week, you are sending the unintended message that all these extracurricular activities are more important than enjoying a relaxed meal at home with family. Don't send that message.

What kids *do*. American kids are substantially less active compared with American kids 50 or 60 years ago. The most common leisure activity of American kids in 1965 was outdoor play. American kids today are more likely to be sitting in front of a TV or computer screen. In 1965, the average American spent just 10 hours a week watching TV. Even more importantly, in 1965 most American households had just one TV, which meant that the parents and children were watching TV together.[16] There were only three television channels in 1965: ABC, CBS, and NBC. Cable television didn't exist. In the late 1960s and early 1970s, daytime television meant soap operas such as *As the World Turns*, *Love Is a Many-Splendored Thing*, and *General Hospital*. Not the sort of thing that kids wanted to watch. According to the latest nationwide survey, the average American 8- to 12-year-old now spends more than 38 hours per week being entertained by an electronic screen, whether a TV or a laptop or an iPad or a cell phone. The average American teenager now spends more than 60 hours per week being entertained by looking at a screen.[17]

When I was growing up in Ohio in the 1960s and 1970s, most of the kids on my block—and definitely all the boys—spent their free time outdoors. We came inside for meals, but that was pretty much it. Our backyard was so worn down from our games of baseball that three years after the last of us had moved away, you could still see where the pitcher's mound and the bases had been.

Not long ago, a mother I know said to her 11-year-old son, "It's such a beautiful day. Why don't you play outside?" He answered, in all seriousness, "But where would I plug in my Xbox?"

American children have less free time for play than they used to, and the play is more likely to be supervised and organized by the grown-ups. But the biggest change is simply that many American kids today would prefer to "play" with an electronic device rather than going outside to play hopscotch or jump rope or dodgeball. Many school districts have even banned some traditional American games, such as dodgeball, because of liability considerations, because of the belief that such games promote bullying, and because of the concern that such games might lower a child's self-esteem.[18]

Turn off the screens and get your kids outdoors. Go outside and play with them if you can. If your children are within walking distance of the school and you live in a safe neighborhood, why not ask them to walk to school? In 1969, 41 percent of American kids either walked or rode their bike to school. By 2001, that proportion had dropped to 13 percent, and there is evidence of further decline since 2001.[19] If there is a grocery store within a mile of your home, then take a daily or every-other-day walk to the grocery store with your child and carry a few bags home.

Encourage your kids to do more and sit less. But you can't just talk the talk; you have to walk the walk. Practice what you preach. If the store is three blocks away, as I just said, walk, don't drive, and encourage your kid to walk with you.

How much kids *sleep*. In recent years, researchers have recognized that getting less sleep at night appears to lead to overweight and obesity. This effect appears to be more pronounced for children and teenagers than it is for adults.[20]

When I first started reading the research on the relationship between sleep deprivation and obesity, it didn't make sense to me. How could sleeping *less* cause you to *gain* weight? If you are sleeping less, then presumably you are more active because you aren't sleeping. Almost any activity burns more calories than sleeping does. But it turns out that if kids or grown-ups are sleep-deprived, the hormones that regulate appetite get messed up, which confuses our brains in all kinds of bad ways. Your brain starts to say, *I'm so tired, I **deserve** some potato chips / ice cream / candy / cookies / cake and I need them right **NOW**.*

It's bad.[21]

American kids are not getting the sleep they need. Here's the expert consensus on the amount of sleep children should have:[22]

- 3 to 5 years of age: 10 to 13 hours per 24 hours (naps count toward this total)
- 6 to 12 years of age: 9 to 12 hours per 24 hours
- 13 to 18 years: 8 to 10 hours per 24 hours

But most kids aren't getting that much sleep. In every age group from 6 to 18 years, the average American kid is sleep-deprived relative to these guidelines; and the older the kid, the more sleep-deprived she or he is likely to be. Among high school seniors, fully 84 percent are getting less than eight hours of sleep a night.[23] And American kids today are getting significantly less sleep compared with American kids 20 or 30 years ago.[24]

How come? Many researchers now agree that the presence of devices in the bedroom is one factor contributing to sleep deprivation among American kids.[25] If a child or teenager has a TV in their bedroom, or a smartphone, or a video-game console, or a laptop, or an iPad, there's a temptation to use those devices rather than go to sleep. There is now good evidence that screens in the bedroom—whether a smartphone or a TV—interfere with sleep, even if the device is turned off.[26] Researchers don't fully understand how the mere presence of a smartphone in the room can interfere with sleep if the device is turned off. Perhaps some part of the brain knows that the phone is there, and that the phone could be turned on, and that possibility keeps the mind from relaxing fully. But it's a significant effect.

Time spent on social media, or playing video games, or watching YouTube videos, has a more toxic effect on sleep—reduced sleep time and reduced sleep quality—compared to just watching TV, which appears to be less toxic.[27] Other researchers have found that time spent on social media, and time spent surfing the Web, has especially disruptive effects on kids' sleep, making it harder to get to sleep, resulting in less total time sleeping and more awakenings after falling asleep.[28]

The benefits of a good night's sleep go beyond a lower risk of obesity. Kids who get more sleep are more likely to be physically active the next day.[29] Kids who get sufficient sleep are sharper in class the next day.[30] Teens who get sufficient sleep are more resilient and less likely to feel down the morning after a stressful day.[31] Adolescents who are sleep-deprived are much more likely subsequently to become depressed; and that depression is likely to result in impaired sleep, making it even harder for the depressed teen to get a good night's sleep, in a malignant feedback loop.[32] Curiously and counterintuitively, with anxiety the arrow of causality points in only one direction: sleep deprivation among teenagers increases the risk of anxiety, but anxiety does not increase the risk of subsequent sleep deprivation.[33]

I started leading workshops for children and teenagers back in 2001. My workshops for students are neither sermons nor didactic presentations, but conversations. I ask the kids questions, and I call on those who have their hands raised. Then I ask other kids to respond: "What do you guys think about what Tyrone just said?" One question I have asked regularly since 2001 is, *What's your favorite thing to do in your spare time, when you are by yourself with no one watching?* One objective of the workshop is to help kids realize that the choice of how you spend your free time is important. It influences the kind of man or woman you will become. From 2001 through about 2012, I heard lots of different answers. But in the years since 2012, one answer has become predominant among American kids, especially middle-income and affluent kids: sleep. American kids are now so busy trying to do so much that the majority of them now appear to be sleep-deprived. They are so chronically sleep-deprived that their favorite leisure-time activity is not music or art or sports or reading, but sleep.

That's sad.

I have already suggested several ways in which the culture of disrespect results in more fat kids. There is some intriguing evidence that appears to support a direct link: the child who is most disrespectful is also the child who is most likely to become fat.

Many studies have now reported just that finding: namely, that children and teenagers who are defiant, disrespectful, and just plain bratty are more likely to *become* overweight or obese, compared with kids who are better-behaved.[34] It turns out to be a big effect. In one study, kids who were chronically defiant and disrespectful were about three times more likely to become obese, compared to kids who were better-behaved. The study found that the odds ratio for all kids who misbehaved becoming obese was 2.95. An odds ratio of 3.0 would mean that the kids who misbehaved were exactly three times as likely to become obese. When the researchers restricted their analysis to kids who were of normal weight at baseline, the odds ratio increased to 5.23. In other words, normal-weight kids who misbehaved were more than five times as likely to become obese, compared to normal-weight kids who did not misbehave.[35]

It makes sense. If kids are being defiant or disrespectful, and refuse to eat their vegetables, some American parents will let those kids have pizza and French fries for supper. Because those parents are allowing their kids to get away with disrespectful behavior, those parents are unlikely to say, *No dessert until you eat your vegetables.* Those parents may find it easier to give the child pizza and ice cream rather than take a stand if the child is prone to misbehave. And the effect will be larger if the child is of normal weight at the beginning of the study, because if the child is already overweight when the study begins, then there's not as much room to see a big effect. If a child is normal-weight and then becomes obese, that's a big effect.

Now here's a surprise. This relationship between bad behavior now and obesity later, which has been confirmed in many studies conducted in the United States, may not hold in New Zealand. Only one prospective study on this topic has been conducted in New Zealand, but in that one study, girls who misbehaved were somewhat *less* likely to become obese compared with better-behaved girls (boys were not studied). The researchers speculated that the badly behaved girls in New Zealand may weigh less than "good girls" because the "bad girls" are more likely to smoke cigarettes.[36] I am not persuaded by that conjecture. Bad girls are more likely than good girls to smoke cigarettes in the United States, just as in New Zealand. I propose a different hypothesis, based on my conversations with parents and teens across New Zealand in Auckland, Hastings, Hawke's Bay, and Christchurch. I haven't found many parents in New Zealand who would permit their daughter or son to decide what's for supper. I suspect that if parents in New Zealand prepare a healthy supper, and they happen to have a defiant and disrespectful daughter who refuses to eat what the parents have prepared, then that girl is going to go to bed hungry. Which, over a period of months or years, might cause her to lose some weight.

It's not the end of the world. She won't die.

In the second half of the book, we will focus on concrete strategies to build your authority in the context of the contemporary culture of disrespect. But those strategies will be effective only if you begin with confidence about what you are trying to teach your child. Here's what you need to teach, regarding diet and exercise:

Eat right: Broccoli and Brussels sprouts come before pizza and ice cream. Prioritize the family; make time for suppers at home with at least one parent.

Eat less: Don't supersize. Prepare small servings and insist that kids finish everything on the plate, including vegetables, before they get second helpings.

Exercise more: Turn off the devices. Go outside. Play.

You can do this.

3

School

It was a big disappointment for me when I discovered the truth: Australia isn't that different from the United States.

Like many Americans, my notions of Australia prior to my first visit were a confused mix of kangaroos, koala bears, half-remembered scenes from *Crocodile Dundee,* and the late Steve Irwin saying "Crikey!" on Animal Planet. I have now visited more than 40 schools across Australia on six different tours, in all six states as well as in the capital city, Canberra. I remember my disappointment when I arrived at the airport in Sydney for my first visit and saw magazine covers featuring Brad Pitt and Angelina Jolie in the bookstore. No different from the airports back home. I'm not sure what I expected to find: maybe magazines for hunters tracking crocodiles in the outback? But the magazine racks in Sydney—and in Melbourne and Perth and Hobart and Brisbane and Adelaide and Canberra—look pretty much the same as what you would find in an American city, except that the Australian bookstores do tend to have more magazines devoted to the British royals.

I have met with students in Australia on many occasions. I often ask them to name their favorite TV shows. Invariably they answer with the same shows that American students name. Rarely does any program produced in Australia crack the top five.

Mainstream Australian culture is not that different from mainstream American culture. That's one reason I felt comfortable accepting invitations to lead workshops for teachers in Australia. Because the cultures are so similar, I assumed that the issues which mattered to American teachers would be similar to the issues which matter to Australian teachers.

Big mistake.

I was leading a workshop for teachers at Shore, a private school in the North Bay suburb of Sydney. From the school library, which is magnificent, there's a stunning view of the water and of the Sydney Harbour Bridge.

I began the workshop at Shore by promising the teachers that I would share what I have learned from my visits to hundreds of schools—mostly in the United States and Canada—about how to create a culture of respect in the classroom. "Even if the majority of your kids are respectful," I said, "there are always some who will try to undermine your authority and bring you down. That's true even at the most elite schools serving the most affluent neighborhoods."

After a few minutes of this, one of the teachers, Cameron Paterson, could take it no longer. He raised his hand. I called on him. "I'm sorry, Dr. Sax," Mr. Paterson said. "But I have no idea what you are talking about. And I don't think what you are saying makes any sense to my colleagues, either. We don't have students who are trying to undermine our authority and 'bring us down.' We simply do not have this problem."

I asked for a quick poll of the other teachers who were present. Did they agree with Mr. Paterson? Or did they at least occasionally find themselves struggling with disrespectful students?

All the teachers agreed with Mr. Paterson. A culture of respect prevails at this school. For example, students at Shore routinely thank their teachers at the conclusion of every class. One by one, as students walk out of the class, each student says, "Thank you, sir" or "Thank you, ma'am," as the case may be. It's not unusual for a student to say, "Great lesson, sir!" That would be weird today even at the most elite schools in the United States.* If an American student today were to compliment a teacher at the conclusion of a lesson, other American students might make fun, or they might suspect that student of apple-polishing. Not in Australia.

I felt silly. But I also learned something. *Don't assume that what's true in the United States is true in Australia or Scotland or the Netherlands.*

The popular culture as reflected in the magazine racks may not differ dramatically between the United States and Australia. But the culture of disrespect which is pervasive among children and teenagers throughout the United States is less prevalent in Australia. In the United States, you will find kids in almost every classroom who disrespect the teacher or who are actively trying to undermine the teacher's authority. That's true, as I told the teachers in the workshop, even at the most elite schools serving

*When I share this story, some Americans will describe a similar experience— a respectful student thanking a teacher for a great lesson—from their own school, in 1975 or 1985 or even 1995. But not today.

the most affluent neighborhoods. Girls texting during class. Boys making belching noises.

You will find this behavior outside of North America most often in schools serving low-income neighborhoods. That was the situation in our country as well, 50 or 60 years ago. American public schools serving low-income neighborhoods have often had to contend with a culture of disrespect, at least since the end of World War II. Movies such as *Blackboard Jungle* (1955) and *To Sir, with Love* (1967) depicted the culture of disrespect in schools serving low-income neighborhoods in the United States and in England. One reason these movies were so popular may have been because the disrespectful culture they depicted seemed exotic to middle-class moviegoers.

Today, movies such as *To Sir, with Love* seem quaint. The pranks those students played on their teachers seem playful in comparison with the mayhem which American students now inflict on their teachers. A student at Northeast High School in Oakland Park, Florida, attacked his teacher, pummeling her in the face until she was "dazed and crying," according to the police report. She was transported to the hospital via ambulance. The student received a three-day suspension but was not arrested or charged, and was back in school three days later.[1]

In 2014, a team of researchers from seven American universities surveyed 2,998 teachers at elementary schools, middle schools, and high schools in 48 states across the United States. Among teachers surveyed, 73 percent reported being harassed at school, and 44 percent of the teachers reported having been physically assaulted at school, a figure which the researchers noted was "substantially higher than previously reported."[2] An updated survey by the same team published in 2022 found roughly the same rates of harassment and physical assault.[3]

One of my own patients experienced this violence firsthand. Her student, a 12-year-old boy, was on the playground for recess. She let him know that there were ten minutes left, then five minutes left, then one minute left, then the timer went off and it was time to go back inside. "Time's up! Time to go back in!" she announced. Without warning, he attacked her, grabbing her left forearm and biting her. It was a deep, tearing bite, leaving a gaping wound. I know, because I cleansed and sewed up the wound. No disciplinary action of any kind was taken against the boy, neither after this episode nor after any of the other similar previous episodes. "He can't help it, he's on the [autism] spectrum," the parents say, and the school does nothing. In a later email, the teacher told me, "His parents are unwilling/unable to implement any of the behavioral strategies I outlined."[4] This teacher is not even persuaded that this boy is truly on the autism spectrum. She thinks he is just a violent and aggressive boy who enjoys inflicting pain on others. (There is, and always has been, a small minority of boys and men who enjoy inflicting pain on others.[5] One function of a civilized society is to correct and reform such boys.) She notes that the diagnosis of autism spectrum was made at a brief office visit with the child's primary care provider, without any confirmation by anyone trained in pediatric psychological assessment and based primarily on the parents' reports of the boy's violent behavior. The teacher had to return to the school, still instructing the same boy, who received no reprimand of any kind for attacking a teacher.

I visited an American school serving an affluent neighborhood. The teacher was trying to create a more courteous and orderly atmosphere in the classroom. She explained that she would no longer tolerate students interrupting one another, or interrupting her (the teacher). As she was talking, one of the boys in the back of the class belched loudly, and then said, "Oh just SHUT UP."

"You see, that's exactly what I'm talking about," said the teacher. "That was an uncalled-for interruption. That is rude."

"Oh, I'm sorry," the boy said. "*Please* shut up." Other students, both girls and boys, giggled.

Do not confuse insubordination with originality. There is nothing original or creative about an American child or teenager saying "shut up" to an adult. On the contrary, such behavior today merely signifies conformity to the prevailing American culture of disrespect. Nikki Hertzler, a teacher in Nevada with 18 years of classroom experience, emailed me to say, "In the media you hear that teachers are quitting because of the low pay. I see that as a falsehood. Teachers are quitting because of poorly behaved, disrespectful children. In the past, those children were the exception and we could deal with one or two. Now, at least half the class is disrespectful and they also see no purpose to being in school."

The most widely accepted measure for comparing students' achievement in different countries around the world is the PISA, the Program for International Student Assessment. First administered worldwide in 2000, the PISA test is offered every three years. Students take the PISA at 15 years of age.[6] Within each participating country, schools are randomly chosen. The program has received wide praise for its thoroughness and its ability to test real understanding and creativity, not just rote mastery of facts. The PISA also has maintained a constancy of methods since its first administration in 2000, so it provides a constant yardstick over time.

As recently as 2000, when the PISA was first administered, the United States still maintained a respectable mid-position in the world list in math. Here's where we stood on the math test in 2000 (the actual PISA raw score on the math scale is shown as well):[7]

Rankings in 2000

1.	South Korea	547
2.	New Zealand	537
3.	Finland	536
4.	Australia	533
5.	Switzerland	529
6.	United Kingdom	529
7.	Belgium	520
8.	France	517
9.	Austria	515
10.	Denmark	514
11.	Sweden	510
12.	Norway	499
13.	**United States**	493
14.	Germany	490
15.	Hungary	488
16.	Spain	476
17.	Poland	470
18.	Latvia	463
19.	Italy	457
20.	Portugal	454

By 2012, we had dropped to the bottom among the same group of nations listed above, falling from #13 to #20:[8]

1.	South Korea	526
2.	Poland	516
3.	Switzerland	515
4.	Denmark	509
5.	Belgium	508
6.	Finland	507
7.	Sweden	502
8.	United Kingdom	502
9.	Norway	501
10.	Germany	500
11.	Austria	499
12.	France	495
13.	New Zealand	494
14.	Portugal	492
15.	Australia	491
16.	Latvia	491
17.	Italy	487
18.	Spain	484
19.	Hungary	481
20.	**United States**	**478**

And here are the most recent figures, released in 2023, after the pandemic. We are still at the bottom, but our absolute score on the math exam has dropped even further:[9]

1.	South Korea	527
2.	Switzerland	508

3. Poland	489
4. Denmark	489
5. Belgium	489
6. United Kingdom	489
7. Austria	487
8. Australia	487
9. Finland	484
10. Latvia	483
11. Sweden	482
12. New Zealand	479
13. Germany	475
14. France	474
15. Spain	473
16. Hungary	473
17. Portugal	472
18. Italy	471
19. Norway	468
20. United States	**465**

There was considerable churn in the rankings after the pandemic. Australia climbed from #15 in this list to #8; Finland dropped from #6 to #9. The disruptions in education due to the lockdowns of 2020/2021 had negative impacts on students, which varied significantly from country to country. But on this measure, the United States continued to trail all the other countries listed, although the United States did much better on the reading assessment than on the math assessment.[10]

Did you notice that Poland, which trailed far behind the USA in 2000, has now soared far ahead of us—despite the fact that our per capita spending on education is more than twice what it is in

Poland?[11] Many theories have been advanced to explain the drop in academic achievement of American students relative to students elsewhere. In her book *The Smartest Kids in the World: And How They Got That Way*, American journalist Amanda Ripley made a careful comparison of the United States with Poland, Finland, and South Korea, three countries which widely outperform the United States on the math portion of the PISA exam. Ripley identifies three major factors where she thinks the United States has gone wrong:

- **Overinvestment in technology:** Ripley notes that while Poland was investing in teacher training, American schools—especially schools serving affluent neighborhoods—invested in tablet computers, high-tech smartboards, and other wireless gadgets. In my school visits, it's now common to see American teachers passing out wireless clickers to students for instant polling. In South Korea—despite a cultural obsession with digital toys—the classrooms are typically "utilitarian and spare" with no digital gadgets.[12] Ripley notes that in Poland, Finland, and South Korea, the board at the front of the classroom is "not connected to anything but the wall....Conversely, giving kids expensive, individual wireless clickers so that they can vote in class would be unthinkable in most countries worldwide. In most of the world, kids just raise their hands and that works out fine." She concludes that "Americans waste an extraordinary amount of tax money on high-tech toys for teachers and students, most of which have no proven learning value whatsoever." In most of the countries that score ahead of us on the PISA, "technology is remarkably absent from the classrooms."[13] After *New York Times* columnist Jessica Grose recently spent weeks meeting with teachers, school administrators, and researchers studying technology in the classroom, she concluded that there is "little or no evidence that the products actually work."[14]

- **Overemphasis on sports:** Ripley describes American schools as emphasizing sports—multiple playing fields, lots of resources for sports, an Athlete's Hall of Fame— over academics. In most of the rest of the world, the first mission of the school is academics. In the United States, at many schools, sports routinely preempt academics. Even at leading schools in the USA, varsity athletes are often excused from class to participate in games. That rarely happens in other countries. "Sports are embedded in American schools in a way they are not almost anywhere else," Ripley observes. "Yet this difference hardly ever comes up in domestic debates about America's international mediocrity in education."[15]

- **Low selectivity in teacher training:** In Finland, the teacher-training colleges are highly selective. Being admitted to a teacher-training program in Finland is as prestigious as getting into medical school in the United States.[16] In the United States, almost any high school graduate can qualify to become a teacher. "Incredibly, at some U.S. colleges, students [have] to meet higher academic standards to play football than to become teachers."[17]

Each of these factors is important, but I would add one more: the culture of disrespect. In Finland, Poland, and South Korea, most children and many adolescents are more likely to value what the grown-ups value, compared with American students. Ripley followed an American high school exchange student, Kim, who spent a year in Finland. At one point, Kim asked the Finnish students the question that had been on her mind: "Why do you guys care so much?" The students in Finland were baffled by the question, "as if Kim had just asked them why they insisted on breathing so much.... Maybe the real mystery was not why Finnish kids cared so much, but why so many of her [American] classmates did not."[18]

I think that's right. In American classrooms, much effort is devoted to making education cool in the eyes of the students. Hence all the screens, all the gadgets. *If kids don't regard education as cool, then they will not be motivated to learn*—I've heard this line from many school administrators in the United States. And if students are not motivated to learn, then classroom management—getting kids to behave—consumes a disproportionate share of the teacher's time and energy.

The solution is not to purchase more and more electronic gizmos so that school resembles a video game arcade. The solution is to change and reorient the culture so that students are more concerned with understanding what the grown-ups are talking about rather than looking cool in the eyes of their peers. To create a culture of respect in the classroom.

The "I couldn't care less" attitude which many American kids now adopt toward school stays with them when they go on to college. We now have evidence that young Americans are studying less at college, and learning less, than they did a generation ago.

Researchers Christopher Huber and Nathan Kuncel reviewed studies of college students conducted between 1963 and 2011, specifically those studies which examined how students' critical thinking skills improved between freshman year and senior year at college. In 1963, students made great strides between freshman year and senior year, but by 2011, those gains had dwindled to only a quarter of the improvement seen in 1963. Studies since 2011 suggest that things have only gotten worse. One recent study of 46 colleges across the United States found that the gains made between freshman year and senior year are now only about one-fifth the gains made by college students in 1963.[19]

Some students themselves may be vaguely aware that they are not learning much at college, but many are not especially concerned. Often, students tell the researchers some variation on "It's not what you know, it's who you know." Many of the students interviewed in another study believed that the main point of college is not academic learning at all but making the right social connections.[20] Small wonder then that so many show little gains on measures of cognitive skill and reasoning.

Combining data from multiple sources, economists Philip Babcock and Mindy Marks found that American college students in the 1960s devoted an average of 25 hours per week to studying. By the early 2000s, the amount of time American college students spent studying had decreased to about 12 hours, roughly half the figure from the 1960s.[21] American students now spend less time studying than students in any European country with the sole exception of Slovakia.[22]

Kevin Carey, director of the education policy program at the New America Foundation, observed in an essay for the *New York Times* that the vaunted reputations of America's leading

universities are due largely to the accomplishments of their leading researchers, not to their success in teaching introductory
courses. "A university could stop enrolling undergraduates with
no effect on its score" on most international rankings because
those rankings are based on metrics such as the number of Nobel
Prize winners, numbers of patents awarded, etc. with no input
from any measure of undergraduate education. Carey asserted
that the quality of the actual education received by undergraduates at most American colleges and universities is mediocre.[23]

One reader of Carey's article who has worked outside the
United States agrees. If you compare American college graduates
with college graduates outside the United States, "You may be
shocked, as I am, at how good they are in their chosen field, and
how literate and cultured a tech worker can be. The Brits write
technical design docs like they were English Lit majors at university. The average European software engineer has command of
several spoken and written languages and approaches software
engineering as what it is, Computer Science. Not slinging code.
Something you no longer see in US graduates unless they have a
masters or PhD. You can see why this is [so] when you spend time
with their families. Getting an education is a more serious enterprise than it is in the US. Their kids spend…more time doing
homework, and less time complaining about what a drag school
is, than American students."[24]

Which school is the best school for your child? What should
you be looking for in a school?[25]

As you know, I have visited more than 500 schools over the past
23 years: urban, suburban, and rural; affluent, middle-income,

and low-income; public, private, and parochial. I have led workshops for teachers and spoken to parents. I have learned that many middle-income and affluent parents now define "the best school" as *the school most likely to get my child into Princeton, Stanford, MIT, or another highly selective university.* When considering a school, even a kindergarten or pre-K, the first question these parents are likely to ask is, *Where do these kids go after they graduate?*

We now have long-term longitudinal cohort studies in which researchers have followed students for up to 50 years after graduation, investigating the effect that different school types have on different outcomes. We also have extensive research on the effects that different schools have on parameters such as anxiety and depression. The results are surprising.

Forty years ago, when I was earning my PhD in psychology at the University of Pennsylvania, the research seemed clear. Studies back then showed that kids who attended schools in low-income communities were at higher risk for substance abuse, anxiety, and depression, compared with kids who attended schools in more affluent communities. Suniya Luthar, then at Columbia University, was among the first to document a change. Beginning in the late 1990s, she found that the previous association had flipped. In a seminal study published in 1999, Luthar and her Yale colleague Karen D'Avanzo documented that affluent kids were now at higher risk for substance abuse, and scored higher on measures of anxiety and depression, compared with low-income kids.[26] Multiple subsequent studies, including several authored by Luthar, replicated and extended this finding.[27] In 2009, researchers at New York University coined the term "affluenza" to describe this new phenomenon: upper-middle-income and affluent kids now at greater risk for psychiatric disorders and substance abuse compared to their low-income peers.[28]

Subsequent research, however, led to a significant revision in our understanding of what's going on. In 2018, Luthar and her colleague Nina Kumar published a detailed study showing that the risk associated with affluence derives not from household income per se, but from the school.[29] They found that schools which prioritize getting into top universities, schools which place a premium on superior academic and extracurricular performance—so-called "high-achieving schools"—are the schools most closely associated with increased risk of anxiety, depression, and substance abuse. The risk of these schools is separable from household income. Low-income kids who attend high-achieving schools are at increased risk, just as their affluent peers are. Affluent kids who attend schools that are *not* "high-achieving" are not at risk. The toxicity comes from the school, not from the income bracket.

So the research seems to suggest that you don't want your child or teenager to attend a high-achieving school, a school which encourages superior academic and extracurricular performance. But that doesn't sound right. Aren't we *supposed* to encourage kids to strive for excellence?

In a recent review of the research—bluntly titled "High-Achieving Schools Connote Risks for Adolescents"—Luthar and her colleagues summarize the findings: kids attending high-achieving schools are indeed much more likely to become anxious and/or depressed compared to kids who don't attend such schools.[30] Luthar and coworkers also look at what characteristics of a high-achieving school are responsible for the toxicity. They highlight *social comparison*. These schools, intentionally or not, typically foster a competitive environment in which kids are constantly comparing themselves with one another. *Did you hear about Vanessa?! Perfect GPA. Got a 5 on her AP Physics exam. Captain of the girls' soccer team. And she started her own nonprofit to feed the homeless! Accepted to Stanford. And MIT. And Princeton. Wow. Just wow.* And instead of parents shielding their kids from the stress of comparison, "both generations buy into the pursuit of doing ever more to achieve." When a child or teen's sense of self-worth depends on the magnificence of their accomplishments, that kid becomes fragile.

When I share this research with parents, some respond, *Well, that's the price of success. You have to be tough in order to succeed. I'm willing to accept the risk of some stress in the short term if that increases the odds of my child's success in the long term.* Those parents are assuming that attending a high-achieving school predicts better outcomes later in life: more wealth, better health, and greater happiness. But the research contradicts that assumption. Affluent kids are more likely to become affluent adults than low-income kids are, that's true. But after controlling for household income in childhood and adolescence, attending a high-achieving school does *not* increase the long-term odds of success. On the contrary, when researchers tracked down high school students 11 years and then 50 years (!) after graduation, they found that attending a high-achieving high school was associated with *lower* educational and occupational achievement, compared to students with the same household income who attended schools with average achievement profiles.[31] Citing this research, Luthar and colleagues note that "continual social comparisons with mostly high-achieving peers may explain the long-term negative effects of participation in the high-achieving school race-to-the-top."

If getting good marks at a high-achieving school does not predict good outcomes long term, what does? We will take a deeper dive into this question in Chapters 8 and 9, but let me give you the short answer now: the answer is Conscientiousness. Conscientiousness—meaning honesty, helpfulness, and self-control—predicts health, wealth, and happiness long term. Boys who were rated as helpful by their kindergarten teacher were earning more money 30 years later compared to boys rated less helpful in kindergarten.[32] Children who exhibited better self-control at age 11 were much more likely to be healthy and doing well financially when investigators tracked them down 21 years later, at age 32.[33] Young people who are more Conscientious are less likely to be divorced 30 years later; conversely, young people who are less Conscientious are more likely to die prematurely.[34] Getting good marks at a high-achieving school does not predict health, or wealth, or happiness long term; but Conscientiousness predicts all three.

It follows from this research that if you want your child to be healthy, well-off, and happy as an adult, your top priority should *not* be to enroll your child in a high-achieving school; instead, your first priority should be to teach your child to be honest and Conscientious.

How to do that, exactly? I asked Suniya Luthar this question when she and I spoke via Zoom.[35] She recommends explicitly prioritizing character and Conscientiousness over performance. Tell your child, "I would rather you get a 'C' on the test honestly than cheat and get an 'A.'" She also suggests that you should "watch for [your] children becoming overextended and exhausted and help them to reduce commitments if necessary." Many middle-income and affluent kids are immersed in a toxic culture that pushes them to perform. Parents may have to intervene to limit activities and commitments and ensure that kids are not overextended. In Chapter 11, we will talk more about the importance of scheduling time off to do fun things with your kids.

I want you to know that I have skin in this game. For nine years, beginning in pre-K, my daughter attended a highly selective, high-achieving private school in Bryn Mawr, an affluent suburb of Philadelphia (we couldn't afford a home with a back-yard in Bryn Mawr, so we drove thirty minutes each way every day from our home to the school).[36] This particular school boasts many graduates who go on to Princeton, Yale, Stanford, etc. Although my daughter was doing well academically, my wife and I made the decision in 2019—before the pandemic—to move her to a less academically competitive school, a school with a serious religious commitment. Sarah is on track to graduate from high school next year, and all of us—I, my wife, and my daughter—agree that the change of school has been a huge change for the better. Less stress. Less drama. More focus on who you *are*—Are you kind? Do you give people the benefit of the doubt? Are you a good friend?—rather than on what you *do*.

I recognize that my daughter's chances of going to Yale may have diminished as a result of the change of school. But I am convinced that her chances of being healthy and happy in ten or twenty or thirty years have improved. And she agrees.

American parents used to be able to assume that their kids were getting a good education if the family lived in a good neighborhood with good schools and if the child went on to attend a selective university. That assumption may no longer be valid. As a result, you need to be involved in your child's education. Don't let the culture of disrespect poison your child's attitude toward learning. Remember Lil Nas X singing *You can't tell me nothin' / can't nobody tell me nothin'*? Unlike Lil Nas X, you want your child to be open to learning everything.

4

Medication

Trent is 8 years old. In my office, he is happy. He giggles when I wag my Daffy Duck puppet over my head and use my Daffy Duck voice. But his parents tell me that if Trent doesn't get his way, or some little unexpected thing goes wrong, then he erupts in a temper tantrum. "He just goes totally berserk," his mom says. "He screams. He cries. He throws things. But then 5 minutes later he's laughing again." Before I can say anything, mom continues, "I went online and Googled it, and I'm thinking maybe he's bipolar. Rapid cycling."

Hmm, I nod sagely.

After a thorough evaluation of Trent, it's clear that he doesn't have any form of bipolar disorder, rapid cycling or otherwise. He has mood swings. He's happy one minute and angry the next. He gets mad when he doesn't get his way. That's within the range of normal for an 8-year-old. But his parents seem helpless to guide his behavior or to respond appropriately to his outbursts. I begin to wonder, *How do I break the news to this mom that there is no role for medication here?* The problem lies not in Trent at all, but in his parents' reluctance to recognize that his mood swings are normal behaviors which require good parenting to help their son to govern himself, rather than a symptom of a brain-based pathology to be treated with a medication.

As I mentioned earlier, a big part of your job as a parent is to teach the rules of our culture, Fulghum's Rules: *Play fair / Don't hit people / Put things back where you found them / Clean up your own mess / Say you're sorry when you hurt somebody.* In the four decades between the mid-1950s and the mid-1990s, parents could rely on the kindergarten classroom and the most popular programs on television to teach these rules. In that era, even those parents who didn't work terribly hard at parenting could usually take for granted that kids knew and accepted these rules. But not anymore. In many American kindergartens today, as I said earlier, the first priority is more likely to be teaching diphthongs rather than teaching respect and courtesy and manners.

Parents today must explicitly teach Fulghum's Rules and everything that goes with them. But many parents don't do that, for at least two reasons. First, they may not realize that they need to. Their own parents didn't preach to them on these topics 20 or 30 years ago, so why do they have to teach this stuff to their own kids? Second, parents today are less comfortable asserting authority than parents in previous generations.

I now regularly encounter parents like Trent's mom, parents who wonder whether their young child might have rapid cycling bipolar disorder or some other brain-based psychiatric explanation for bad behavior. I explain to those parents that it's normal for an 8-year-old to swing through different moods in half an hour. Sometimes in just five minutes. That's not rapid cycling bipolar disorder. That's being 8 years old. I say it over and over again: *The job of the parent is to teach self-control.* To explain what is acceptable and what is not acceptable. To establish boundaries and to enforce consequences.

Three decades ago, that was common sense. Not anymore.

Prior to the early 1990s, pediatric bipolar disorder was rarely diagnosed in the United States or anywhere else. In that era, most experts agreed that bipolar disorder was characterized by episodes of depression alternating with episodes of mania. A person experiencing a manic episode is typically euphoric and energetic, often going without sleep. Episodes of mania can last days or weeks; episodes of depression can last weeks or months.

Beginning in the mid-1990s, a group of researchers led by Dr. Joseph Biederman at Harvard Medical School published a series of papers claiming that bipolar disorder in children is different. In children, Biederman and his colleagues argued, bipolar disorder isn't episodic at all. It is rapid cycling, with the phases lasting minutes instead of weeks or months. And Biederman argued further that mania in childhood doesn't look like mania in adults. Manic children are not energetic and euphoric, according to Biederman and his Harvard colleagues; instead, they are irritable.[1]

The children Biederman was describing are so different from adults with bipolar disorder that one might reasonably question whether Biederman was describing any kind of bipolar disorder at all. But Biederman insisted that this was indeed bipolar disorder and that it should be treated with the same powerful antipsychotic drugs, such as Risperdal and Seroquel, that are used for bipolar disorder in adults.

There were skeptics. One of them was Dominick Riccio, a New York City psychotherapist. Riccio believed that Biederman and colleagues were "making a diagnosis of bipolar because a child has mood switches. If a child goes from happy to sad and has impulsive outbursts, it's characterized as bipolar. But children have mood swings. To characterize this as mental illness is a serious flaw."[2] Psychiatrist Jennifer Harris agreed. Harris found that "many clinicians find it easier to tell parents that their child has a brain-based disorder than to suggest changes in their parenting."[3]

That's the situation I was in with Trent and his mom. Trent was having mood swings. When his parents didn't buy him the toy he wanted, he would scream in the toy store. But his parents had never taught him the rules of good behavior. They had not taught him Fulghum's Rules. They had not told him that he should be in control of his emotions, rather than his emotions controlling him. His behavior was what you would expect of an 8-year-old kid who has never known consistent discipline.

Trent's mom had read a cover story in a major magazine featuring Dr. Biederman and his Harvard colleagues. The article repeated Biederman's assertion that doctors are missing bipolar disorder in children.[4] I could understand mom's frustration: I, Leonard Sax, am just a local family physician. Who am I to dispute Dr. Biederman, the nationally renowned Harvard psychiatrist and researcher?

Trent's mom wanted me to tell her that Trent had a chemical imbalance that could be fixed by Risperdal or Seroquel, the drugs championed by Dr. Biederman. I told mom that Trent didn't need those medications. Trent needed parents who had the confidence and the authority to teach Fulghum's Rules.

Mom left the office in a huff.

L ess than three weeks after that mom stormed out of my office, Dr. Biederman and two of his Harvard colleagues admitted to receiving more than $4 million from Johnson & Johnson (the manufacturer of Risperdal), AstraZeneca (the manufacturer of Seroquel), and other drug companies. The payments were discovered in the course of an investigation launched by US Senator Charles Grassley and conducted by the staff of the Senate Judiciary Committee.[5] To be clear, Biederman and his colleagues broke no law. There is no law prohibiting doctors from accepting millions of dollars from drug companies. But Dr. Biederman's action was unethical, in my judgment. I think Dr. Biederman should have disclosed that he was getting more money from the drug companies than he was getting from his job at Harvard; that he was, in fact, acting as a paid spokesperson for the drug companies. But he kept the money a secret, or at least he tried to.[6]

Psychiatric social worker Elizabeth Root observes that parents are "satisfied with the quick fix" that the medications offer, and parents then don't want to do the hard work to get to the bottom of the problem.[7] Child psychiatrist Elizabeth Roberts goes even further: "Psychiatrists are now misdiagnosing and overmedicating children for ordinary defiance and misbehavior. The temper tantrums of belligerent children are increasingly being characterized as psychiatric illnesses. Using such diagnoses as bipolar disorder, Attention Deficit Hyperactivity Disorder (ADHD) and Asperger's, doctors are justifying the sedation of difficult kids with powerful psychiatric drugs that may have serious, permanent or even lethal side effects."[8]

Kids need authority, guideposts, structure. When parents abdicate their authority, a vacuum results. Nature abhors a vacuum.

The doctor, armed with a prescription pad, steps in, or is sucked in. Medication fills the role of regulating the child's behavior, a role which ought to have been filled by the parents.

For many American parents, it is now easier to administer a pill than to reprimand a child. That's a shame. And that, in my view, is a major factor driving the explosion in the prescribing of these medications in the United States.

Some aspects of this phenomenon are peculiar to North America. German researchers found that during roughly the same time period in which diagnosis of bipolar disorder was exploding for children in the United States, the proportion of children diagnosed with bipolar disorder in Germany actually *decreased*.[9] In Spain, likewise, the rate of diagnosis of pediatric bipolar disorder did not increase during the same interval when it was exploding in the United States.[10] Likewise for New Zealand.[11]

The Germans observed, dryly, "There is no compelling reason to presume that the frequency of bipolar disorder in children and adolescents is actually much higher in the U.S. than in Europe. Therefore, there is considerable European skepticism about the high prevalence rate of bipolar disorder in children in the U.S. The diagnosis of bipolar disorder in youngsters is fairly rare outside the United States.... In Germany, a diagnosis of bipolar disorder in childhood is still extremely rare."[12]

Researchers compared diagnoses for children in the United States with children in England, using comprehensive national databases for both countries. They found that—after adjusting for overall population—for every one child in England discharged with a diagnosis of bipolar disorder, there are 73 children in the United States discharged with a diagnosis of bipolar disorder. In both countries, teenagers are more likely to be diagnosed with bipolar disorder than young children are. But in the United States, a 6-year-old is substantially more likely to be diagnosed with bipolar disorder than an English teenager.[13]

Let me tell you about another patient. Dylan had been a good student throughout elementary school, with many friends. But something changed when he started middle school. He lost interest: in school, in most of his friends, and in his sports. His circle of friends narrowed. He now spent most of his free time with a few other boys who shared his interest in video games. He became defiant and disrespectful toward grown-ups, including his parents. He began refusing to eat supper with the family. Instead, he would stay in his bedroom and play online video games.

His parents made an appointment for him to see a board-certified child psychiatrist. The psychiatrist talked with Dylan and his parents and reviewed the ADHD rating scales which several teachers at the school had filled out for Dylan.

The psychiatrist initially considered the diagnosis of depression but rejected it. Instead, the psychiatrist made two diagnoses: Oppositional-Defiant Disorder and ADHD. He recommended a stimulant medication such as Adderall, Vyvanse, or Concerta. He was confident that Dylan would show improvement once he began treatment with one of those medications.

"The medication really has helped," Dylan's mom Sofie told me later. "With some things. He has started paying attention in school again. He seems to listen better at home. And he's started eating supper with us again, or at least sitting with us at suppertime. He doesn't really eat much. His appetite has been terrible ever since he started taking the medication. And something else is different. There used to be a twinkle in his eye, a spark, a mischievous spark. I don't see that spark anymore."

Sofie brought Dylan to me because she was concerned about Dylan losing that spark. "Do you think Dylan gets enough sleep?" I asked mom.

"Yes, I do," she said. "We make sure he's in his bedroom no later than 9 at night, and we wake him up next morning at 6 a.m. to start getting ready for school. So that's nine hours. That's enough, don't you think?"

"Do you have a video-game console in your bedroom?" I asked Dylan.

"Course," Dylan said. "Doesn't everybody?"

"Were you playing video games last night?"

"Sure," Dylan said.

"Which games?" I asked.

"RDR2 mostly."

"An excellent game," I said. "Truly a masterpiece. How late were you up playing last night?"

He shrugged. "Don't know, maybe 1:30, 2?"

"*Two AM?*" Sofie asked.

And this was Dylan's routine. Mom had no idea how much time Dylan spent playing video games because his door was closed, and he played his video games with the headset on.

I concluded that Dylan was sleep-deprived. I advised no devices in the bedroom. No TV. No cell phones. No video-game console. He could play video games up to 40 minutes a night on school nights, and one hour a day on other days, but the console had to be in a public space such as the living room, not in his bedroom.[14]

I also recommended that we taper and discontinue his stimulant medication. The stimulant medication "worked," I explained, because it's a powerful stimulant: it compensated for his sleep deprivation. The sleep-deprived child will have trouble paying attention not because he has ADHD, but because he is sleep-deprived. Sleep deprivation mimics ADHD almost perfectly. The usual screening tools for ADHD, such as the Conners Rating Scales, cannot distinguish the child who is not paying attention because he is sleep-deprived from the child who is not paying attention because he truly has ADHD. Medications such as Adderall and Vyvanse are amphetamines: they are "speed." Dylan's behavior improved on the stimulant not because he has ADHD but because the amphetamines compensated for the sleep deprivation. The appropriate remedy for sleep deprivation, I explained to Sofie, is not Schedule II amphetamines such as Vyvanse and Adderall. The appropriate remedy for sleep deprivation is sleep. And that means no video-game console in the bedroom.

One of the basic duties of a parent is to ensure that the child gets a good night's sleep rather than staying up late playing games. That's not a new idea. But 30 years ago, we didn't have Internet-enabled devices making it easy for kids to play games online with other kids at 2 in the morning. Now we do. That means that parents have to be more assertive of their authority than in previous decades. But many American parents have abdicated their authority rather than asserting it. The result is boys playing video games at 2 a.m. and girls staying up past midnight texting their friends or posting selfies to Instagram.

Sleep deprivation is one reason why American kids today are more likely to be diagnosed with ADHD, compared with American kids from 1979 (more about that below). The failure of parents to assert their authority is a big part of the reason why American kids are getting less sleep than they used to.

Dylan regained his spark soon after he stopped the medication. But other problems were not so easily solved. He had been devoting most of his social time to hanging with other gamers: kids who spend almost all their free time playing video games. His parents calculated that Dylan had been spending 20 hours or more a week playing video games, an average of nearly three hours per day. Once his parents restricted his time playing video games and enforced that restriction, he decided to stop playing altogether. "Forty minutes a night? That's barely enough time to get online and see what's going on," he complained. "I don't see the point." He stopped hanging out with his gamer friends. But his old friends from his life before video games were not quick to take him back. They had moved on. Dylan became something of a loner, although—to his parents' amazement—he actually became something of a scholarly loner. His grades soared and his relationships with his teachers improved.

I was sorry to hear that Dylan was not able to reestablish his previous friendships. Kids do need same-age friends. When I speak to parents about the importance of prioritizing family over same-age friends, some parents will respond, "But don't kids need friends their own age?" Of course they do. But here we should take a tip from the financial planners: *diversify*. If you find that all your kid's friends share one particular interest, that's not healthy. If your daughter is a soccer star and all her friends play soccer, then what will happen when your daughter sustains a complete rupture of the ACL and can't play soccer again for six months, or a year, or ever? I have seen such a girl essentially abandoned by almost all of her friends. She struggled to find a new identity that wasn't bound up with the game of soccer. If her parents had encouraged her to diversify her activities, had connected her with other opportunities to make friends—perhaps at the church or synagogue or mosque, perhaps at the barn (this girl used to ride horses), or even just with the neighbor girl down the street—her life would not have seemed so bleak when she couldn't play soccer anymore.

Likewise for Dylan. His parents saw what was happening. They saw how his other friendships were withering away as his obsession with video games became more severe. But they felt powerless to intervene. American parents today often think they are meddling, or hovering like "helicopter parents," when they try to influence their child's friendships. And I agree that it accomplishes very little to say, *Jacob is such a nice boy. Why don't you invite him over?* But I think it would have been perfectly reasonable for Dylan's parents to restrict his video games much earlier in the sequence, before his other friendships had withered. Such a restriction might have helped Dylan to choose for himself which friendships—friendships that didn't involve gaming—were worth hanging on to.

What was going on in the United States with regard to ADHD a generation ago? In 1979, the best estimate was that only about 1.2 percent of American kids—12 out of 1,000—had the condition we now call ADHD.[15] But among kids 11 to 17 years of age, more than 18 percent—nearly one in five—have now been diagnosed with ADHD.[16]

Why such an increase? Why is ADHD so much more common in the USA today than it was in 1979?

I see several factors in play. First of all, some kids are being diagnosed with ADHD when they don't actually have ADHD. As

I mentioned above, sleep deprivation can perfectly mimic ADHD of the inattentive variety. If more kids are sleep-deprived, more kids will be coming home from school with notes saying they weren't paying attention and maybe they should get an evaluation. The doctor says, "Let's try Vyvanse and see if it helps." And it helps!—because Vyvanse is a mix of amphetamines, and amphetamines compensate for the sleep deprivation.

Another factor is what I have called "the medicalization of misbehavior."[17] Instead of correcting our kids' misbehavior, we parents today are more likely to medicate our kids in hopes of fixing the behavior with a pill. We parents are no longer doing our job of enculturation, as I explained that job in Chapter 1. Neither we the parents, nor the schools, nor the TV shows, nor the Internet are adequately teaching Fulghum's Rules such as *Play fair / Don't hit people / Put things back where you found them / Clean up your own mess / Say you're sorry when you hurt somebody.* As a result, kids are now more likely to be treated with powerful medications which may indeed control their bad behavior. But instead of teaching the child to control his or her emotions, we are teaching the child that their behavior is due to a psychiatric disorder which must be controlled with medication. The unintended message: *You are helpless to govern yourself. You need these pills instead.*

Today, American parents are hungry for brain-based explanations. Instead of removing the cell phone and the laptop from their kids' bedrooms so they can get a good night's sleep, many American parents are medicating their kids with Adderall or Concerta or Vyvanse or Metadate to compensate for their sleep deprivation, often without any awareness that sleep deprivation is the underlying problem. Instead, the kid's failure to pay attention

has been misdiagnosed as ADHD. Likewise, instead of acknowl-
edging that their kid misbehaves and/or is disrespectful, many
American parents would prefer that a doctor diagnose an imbalance in brain chemistry and prescribe Risperdal or Seroquel or
Adderall or Concerta.

You remember Dylan, the boy I described a few pages back.
A board-certified child psychiatrist concluded that Dylan had
both ADHD and Oppositional-Defiant Disorder. But the psychiatrist was mistaken. Dylan has neither ADHD nor Oppositional-
Defiant Disorder. The main cause of Dylan's lack of attention was
not ADHD, but sleep deprivation. And Dylan was sleep-deprived
because his parents were not aware of the time he was wasting
playing video games in his bedroom. When that problem was
fixed, Dylan's situation improved without medication. Dylan's
case illustrates how the abdication of parental authority led to a
psychiatrist prescribing medication. I see that sort of thing often.

Recall the story I shared in the previous chapter of my adult
patient who was bitten by a student, a 12-year-old boy, who
had been diagnosed as being on the autism spectrum even though
my patient questioned that diagnosis. Autism is not a new diagnosis. There have always been autistic children. Some autistic
children struggle to control their impulses. That's not new either. But 30 years ago, a high-functioning autistic child who bit
a teacher would have been reprimanded. The parents would have
been called in to take their son home for a three-day suspension,
at a minimum. I know this because I was involved in some of
these cases firsthand. The parents would have been reminded to
teach their son the first requirement to stay in school: don't bite
the teacher.

Imagine an 8- or 10-year-old boy who misbehaves. He talks back to teachers. He is deliberately spiteful and vindictive. He doesn't listen. He seems to have little or no self-control. Thirty years ago, perhaps even 20 years ago, the school counselor or the principal might have said to the parent, "Your son is disrespectful. He is rude. He exhibits no self-control. You need to teach him some basic rules about civilized behavior if he is going to stay at this school." Today it is much less common for an American school counselor or administrator to speak so bluntly to a parent. Instead, the counselor or school administrator will suggest a consultation with a physician or a psychologist. And the physician or psychologist will look at the reports from the school and talk about Oppositional-Defiant Disorder or Attention Deficit Hyperactivity Disorder or Pediatric Bipolar Disorder or the autism spectrum.

What's the difference between saying, "Your son is disrespectful" and saying, "Your son may meet criteria for a psychiatric disorder"? There's a big difference. When I say, "Your son is disrespectful," the burden of responsibility is on you, the parent, and on your child. With that responsibility comes the authority to do something about the problem. But when I say, "Your son may meet criteria for a psychiatric disorder," then the burden of responsibility shifts away from the parent and the child to the whole medical/psychiatric/therapeutic/counseling complex. And the reasonable next question from the parents is not "What should we do to change his behavior?" but rather "Should he begin taking a medication?"

The medications work. They do change the child's behavior. That's what I find so scary. These medications are being used as a means of behavior modification.

The most popular medications now used to control temper tantrums and other acting-out misbehaviors in American kids are the second-generation antipsychotics, especially Risperdal, Seroquel, and Zyprexa. These are the same medications which psychiatrists use to treat schizophrenia. They are called second-generation antipsychotics to distinguish them from the older, first-generation antipsychotics such as Thorazine and Mellaril.

The most dramatic and obvious side effects of the second-generation antipsychotic medications are metabolic: kids who take these medications are much more likely to become obese and to develop diabetes.[18] This risk is greater for children than for adults, and the younger the child, the greater the risk.[19] Stopping the antipsychotic medication does not reliably reverse the metabolic consequences.[20] And yet when I meet with parents whose kids are on these medications, I find that few have been seriously counseled regarding these risks.

Aside from the side effects which these medications can cause, I see a deeper problem: a shift of authority away from the parents and to the prescribing physician. When the child subsequently misbehaves, many parents say, *He can't help it; he has a psychiatric disorder.*

I saw this firsthand at a school in St. Louis, in a second-grade classroom. The students had just returned to class from recess. The teacher was trying to bring the class to order, but one boy was ignoring the teacher, running around the room making buzzing noises.

"Jason, I need you to sit down and be quiet so we can begin the lesson," she said. He ignored her. "It's really not fair to the other students for you to keep buzzing around like that. How would you feel if you were trying to concentrate, and somebody else was running around the room making buzzing noises?" Still no acknowledgment. "I have to ask you please to sit still and be quiet. Or else."

"Or else *what?*" the boy said in a jeering tone, pausing for a moment.

"Or else I will *make* you sit still," she said.

"I'd like to see you try," the boy said. When the teacher tried to grab him, he bit the teacher's wrist, then ran out of the room, laughing. The bite was deep. It drew blood.

The teacher called the boy's mother. When the teacher told mom what had happened—that the boy had bit her wrist, drawing blood—the mother did not apologize. She did not even express surprise. "Well, you know that he is on multiple medications, he has an IEP, he has a 504," the mother said, using the jargon for documents certifying that a child has special educational needs. "He probably needs an adjustment in his medication. You should have called the psychiatrist directly. Don't you have his number?"

That's the end result of the medicalization of misbehavior: a shift of responsibility away from the parent, where it belongs, to the prescribing physician.

Teaching self-control is one of the first tasks of the parent and the teacher. But if that child has been diagnosed with a psychiatric disorder and is on powerful medication to control behavior, the child's self-control is undermined. "My son can't help it; he's on the spectrum."

Never use a psychiatric diagnosis as an excuse. Recognize it as a challenge. If your son is truly on the autism spectrum, I get it: it's going to be much harder for him to understand the rules of polite social interaction compared with a child who's not on the spectrum. I understand. But don't use that as an excuse. Step up to the challenge. You and your son are going to have to work that much harder. You, the parent, are going to have to work longer and harder to teach him the rules. But you still have to teach him the rules. Don't rely on medication as a means of behavior control. Teach your son self-control instead.

View medication as an absolute *last* resort after every other possible intervention has been tried. In the United States, medication has become the first resort: *Let's try it and see if it helps.* The result of the medication-first mindset is a generation of kids on powerful psychiatric medications whose long-term consequences are disturbing or unknown.

If you get a report from the school that your son was misbehaving or your daughter was being a bully, don't rush to the child psychiatrist. Ask your child what happened. Talk with the teachers and the school administrators. Do everything you can to teach the rules of good behavior to your children. And enforce those rules. Remember that you—not the teacher, not the coach, not the school administrator—must be the primary authority responsible for instilling in your child the rules of good behavior.

So far we've talked about bipolar disorder and ADHD as well as self-control and the medicalization of misbehavior. But in the years since I wrote the first edition of *The Collapse of Parenting*, there has been an explosion in the proportion of children and teens who feel sad, hopeless, anxious, and/or depressed.

According to the latest report from the CDC, 57 percent of American teen girls now report feeling persistently sad or hopeless, up from 36 percent in 2011. Among boys, 29 percent now report feeling persistently sad or hopeless, up from 21 percent in 2011.[21] That may sound as though the boys are doing great, or at least not so bad, but as we will see in the next chapter, it may be more a reflection of the fact that the boys are playing video games while many of the girls are on social media.

The first prerequisite for a healthy family is that the relationship between the parent and the child is the most important relationship in the child's life, more important than the child's relationships with same-age peers. That's true for young kids, but it's true for teenagers as well. When I say that the parent-child relationship should be the most important relationship in the child's life, I mean that the child should care about that relationship more than about his or her relationships with same-age peers. When children and teenagers care about their relationships with other kids their own age more than they care about their relationship with their parents, that spells trouble because it means that kids are immersed in the culture of their peers, untethered from their parents' culture. In the culture of children and teens, what matters and what doesn't matter, what's good and what's bad, can change from day to day or hour to hour. Your child may be popular today but unpopular tomorrow, and she knows it. Nothing in the world of children or teens is stable. Everything can change in a day, or a minute. As a result, when relationships with same-age peers are paramount, kids are—understandably—anxious. They are trying to find their way in a world in which what's up and what's down change with no notice. In order for you to help your kid through this confusion, you need to understand the emerging worlds of social media and video games as experienced by kids: the world of screens.

5

Screens

Mom brings her son into our office to be seen. The 3-year-old doesn't feel well. He is irritable and whiny. Mom gives him her smartphone and starts the phone playing a *SpongeBob Square-Pants* episode. The boy visibly relaxes, staring transfixed at the screen.

I see this every day that I am in the office: parents using a smartphone to calm a child down. Good idea? Or not?

Researchers at the University of Michigan wanted to find out. They studied children 3, 4, and 5 years of age. Some parents often gave their kids a screen of some kind to help the child calm down. Other parents never did that. Still other parents did it sometimes, but not all the time. The researchers then followed each kid over six months' time to see what effect, if any, the use of devices had on the kids' emotional reactivity.

The results: the more often parents gave the child a smartphone to calm them down, the more the child was subsequently likely—3 or 6 months later—to be irritable and emotionally hyperreactive.

The authors of the study concluded that when kids are stressed, and parents put a screen in front of them, kids are not learning how to deal with stress; they are just distracted by the screen.[1] In another recent study, researchers found that the more screen time a child experienced at 1 year of age, the more likely that child was to be developmentally delayed at 2 and 4 years of age.[2]

Dr. Beth Long, founder of Works of Wonder Therapy, shared with me her experience working with young children.[3] She told me that she routinely advises parents of challenging kids to remove all screens for a period of three weeks.

> *The parents who took handheld electronics away from their children always report a significant decrease in problem behaviors: reduction in tantrums, decrease in physical and verbal aggression, increase in emotional regulation, decrease in sleeping problems, increase in ability to engage with others, increase in contentment, etc. Sadly, less than half of the parents follow our advice. The other parents completely ignore us or lie to us. The only reason we know that parents have followed through on our treatment recommendation is the drastic change observed in their child's behavior. We have never had a family that followed through on the three-week removal of handheld electronics say they regret the process or express an increase in problem behaviors.*

I asked her, how do you know when a parent is lying to you? If a parent says they took the phone away, but they didn't, how would you know? Dr. Long answered that when the parents have taken the phone away, the child

> *almost always addresses me and complains that I made the parents take electronics away. However, the child is usually able to tell me*

what he/she is doing with the extra time. I often ask the parents to play "old fashioned" games with their children when they remove devices and so the families usually tell me all the games they have been playing, the books they are reading, etc.

The parents may be lying, but children are extremely honest. If the parents say they have removed electronics [but didn't], the child almost always tells me the truth when the parents are not in the room. The child often explains that one parent still gives permission to play or that the parents want to "look good" in front of me. Some children even do this when their parents are still in the room.

I was doing a well-child visit for a 9-month-old baby, chatting with the baby's mom, a first-time mother. "I don't know how you guys did it, before smartphones," she said.

"Did what?" I asked.

"Well, like change a diaper," she said.

"You need a smartphone to change your baby's diaper?" I asked.

"Absolutely!" she said. "Liam loves *Teenage Mutant Ninja Turtles*, the TV show not the movies. We haven't watched the movies yet. When it's time to change the diaper, I just put an episode on the phone, and it totally relaxes him."

I paused, not sure how to respond. I was tempted to point out that *Teenage Mutant Ninja Turtles* is really violent. Characters are stabbed, maimed, and killed. Violence is normalized. But I didn't say any of that.

"Changing a diaper is a stress for any baby," I said. "It's a mild stress, but it's still a stress. So it's a great opportunity to bond with your child. You can make funny faces, use weird voices, jiggle your head in a silly way. And all that communicates to your baby *I'm here for you; we can get through this, you and me.* But when you put a screen in front of your child, what message are you sending? You're sending the message, *when you feel stressed, look at a screen.* You don't want to send that message."

Mom's eyes widened. At first I thought she was going to be angry, but she wasn't. "But...all the other moms do it too," she said finally.

"Don't be all the other moms," I said. "I can tell you that all those other moms, by the time their kids are 4 years old, their kids just want to look at screens. Be different. Connect with your kid. Help your kid to connect to *you* instead of to a screen."

We have already discussed how a long childhood and adolescence is a defining feature of our species. Those years of childhood and adolescence provide time for you, the parent, in partnership with other adults, to teach your child everything they need to know in order to fulfill their potential. Screens are OK if they facilitate that process. I have occasionally played video games with my daughter, and I don't see a problem with that, as long as the time spent playing video games doesn't displace real-world experience. But my daughter and I have spent much more time doing real-world activities together than we have spent playing video games, whether that's hiking, riding bikes, sailing, paddleboarding, or just singing songs in the car together.

Kids need hands-on experience of the real world before they are immersed in virtual worlds. If they don't get that real-world experience, they are more likely to become alienated, disconnected, and confused about what matters and what's important. Kids need strong connections with adults, ideally with their parents and with other grown-ups in the community. Video games and social media tend to disconnect the generations. Boys play video games mostly with other boys their own age. Girls engage with and follow other girls on social media, or they follow social media celebrities. As NYU psychologist Jonathan Haidt observes, social media "hijack social learning and drown out the culture of one's family and local community while locking children's eyes on influencers of questionable value."[4] That redirection—away from family, toward online influencers—may be one factor contributing to the rise of anxiety and depression among kids.

Social media is a major factor driving that disconnect between the generations. We need to do a deeper dive into what's going on with social media, how social media can affect your child or your teen, and what you need to do about it.

Anxiety and depression. To repeat the numbers I mentioned at the end of the last chapter: According to the latest national data reported by the CDC, 57 percent of American teen girls now report feeling persistently sad or hopeless, up from 36 percent in 2011. Among boys, 29 percent now report feeling persistently sad or hopeless, up from 21 percent in 2011.[5] These rises weren't caused by the pandemic: they began back around 2012. As Haidt observed, "Covid barely moved the needle. The incredibly rapid rise of mental illness since 2012 basically just charged on almost unaffected."[6] The National Survey on Drug Use and Health assesses the proportion of teenagers reporting a diagnosed episode of major depression in the past year. Since 2010, there has been a 145 percent increase in the proportion of girls reporting an episode of major depression, and a 161 percent increase in the proportion of boys reporting an episode of major depression.[7] Many other national surveys and studies show a remarkable rise in anxiety and depression among American children and teens beginning around 2010–2012.[8] Professor Jean Twenge observes that "the trends are stunning in their consistency, breadth, and size."[9]

The surgeon general of the United States issued a special advisory in 2023 in which he warned that social media pose "a profound risk of harm to the mental health and well-being of children and adolescents."[10] There has been a tremendous rise in the amount of time that kids are spending on social media. In 2012, 48 percent of American teens reported using social media less than once a day, or not at all; 34 percent of teens in 2012 reported accessing social media more than once a day. By 2018, 70 percent of American teens reported accessing social media more than once a day.[11] Five years later, in 2023, more than half of teens reported spending more than *four hours a day* on social media.[12] Those hours often come at the expense of sleep. The surgeon general's advisory found "a consistent relationship between social media use and poor sleep quality, reduced sleep duration, sleep difficulties, and depression among youth."

We now have multiple lines of evidence that the increased use of social media is a major factor driving the rise in anxiety and depression among American kids. The first line of evidence comes from cross-sectional studies and longitudinal cohort studies showing that as social media use by adolescents increases, there is an increased risk of anxiety, depression, diminished well-being, and other adverse mental health outcomes.[13] Girls who are heavy users of social media are three times as likely to become depressed compared with girls who aren't on social media; boys who are heavy users of social media are twice as likely.[14] A subset of these studies explores the mechanisms whereby social media drive adverse mental health outcomes. These studies find that social comparison is one key factor whereby social media exerts toxic effects.[15] (Recall Suniya Luthar's research, discussed in Chapter 3: she found that social comparison was the mechanism whereby high-achieving schools increased the risk of anxiety and depression in students.) Children and teens look at other children and teens posting on social media. *Wow, she's having so much fun*—and from there it's easy for your kid to conclude, *I'm just sitting here not doing anything. My life sucks.* A review of 42 studies found strong evidence linking social media use to poor sleep quality and to anxiety and depression.[16]

A second line of evidence is experimental. When experimenters randomly assign students either to unrestricted use of social media or to restricted use or no use of social media, the students randomly assigned to less use of social media experience significant improvements in measures of mental health.[17] The same result has been replicated in real-world situations, for example where one group of employees lost access to social media but another group of employees at the same company did not lose access: the employees who lost access experienced significant improvement in measures of happiness and well-being.[18] Another real-world "experiment of nature," cited in the surgeon general's advisory, was a study of Facebook's rollout on college campuses in the 2000s. Facebook was introduced on some college campuses earlier than on other campuses. Researchers found that soon after Facebook arrived on particular campuses, student mental health declined; but that decline did not occur at the campuses of comparable colleges where Facebook was not introduced.[19] These researchers also presented evidence that the mechanism whereby Facebook drove the decline in mental health was the social comparison mechanism described above.

Social media promises to offer connection and community, but it doesn't deliver. It can't. Expecting that you can fulfill your need for connection with other human beings by browsing social media is like expecting that you can satisfy your hunger by looking at an illustrated menu and drooling over the pictures. As author and entrepreneur Scott Galloway has observed, "Social [media] creates this illusion that you have a lot of friends, but you don't experience friendship.... We have a series of replacements—fueled by technology—for relationships, mentorships, the workplace, friendships, romantic relationships. And in the short term it sort of fills a void. But it's empty calories, and I think you end up more depressed."[20]

When you talk to your child or teen about the dangers of social media, be prepared for pushback. You may discover that your teen is remarkably knowledgeable about the limited ability of scientific studies of correlation to prove causality. Your teen may point out—quite rightly—that the claim that social media use *causes* an increased risk of anxiety and depression has not yet been proven beyond a reasonable doubt. At this moment, some critics insist that the connection between social media use and adverse psychiatric outcomes may be merely an association, not causally driven;[21] or that the link between social media use and bad outcomes, if present, is so small as to be insignificant or at least is not increasing over time.[22] They note that many teens who use social media are not anxious or depressed. And some kids who are anxious and depressed are not on social media.

My own assessment is that the debate over whether social media is driving the rise in anxiety and depression is missing something important. On the one hand, researchers such as Jonathan Haidt and Jean Twenge have argued that social media per se are driving the rise in anxiety and depression. Other researchers, such as Andrew Przybylski at Oxford and Candice Odgers at the University of California, Irvine, have pushed back, arguing that correlation does not equal causation. Odgers has accused Haidt of "making up stories by looking at trend lines."[23] Professor Amy Orben at Cambridge asserts that concerns about smartphones are "overblown."[24] What all the researchers on both sides of the debate are overlooking, or at least not talking about, is how *changes in the culture* have undermined the parent-child connection. The smartphones and social media outlets spread that toxic culture and exacerbate the breaking of bonds across generations. But maybe we need to recognize that at least some of the blame should fall first not on social media or the smartphone, but on the culture of disrespect.

The culture kids experience has become much more toxic just in the past decade, over the same span of years in which we have seen an alarming rise in anxiety and depression. Fifteen years ago, when I was writing my book *Girls on the Edge*, the girls I interviewed told me about wanting to be, or at least to seem to be, "effortlessly perfect." That world is gone. The girls I hear from today don't want to seem perfect or even normal. Perfection, the lack of major problems, or even simply being normal, is now equivalent to being a "basic white bitch"—which means you are boring and lame. Instead, higher status is accorded to those who have overcome some obstacle or societal prejudice. Lesbian, gay, bisexual, trans (LGBT): all good. BIPOC is better (BIPOC, pronounced "bye-pock," refers to people who are Black, or Indigenous, or people of color). Anxious or depressed or bipolar isn't as good as LGBT or BIPOC, but at least it isn't "basic white bitch." And a psychiatric diagnosis can provide an avalanche of excuses curated by TikTok influencers with millions of views. You're not lazy, you have ADHD. You're not shy, you have an anxiety disorder, which the influencers tell you is due to a chemical imbalance in your brain. It's not something you can control. It's not your fault.

Mary Harrington recently coined the term "normophobia" to describe the growing fear of being normal in our culture, a fear now especially common among young people. She writes, "Normophobia frames everything conventional, average, given, assumed, traditional, and normative—whether its origin be physiological or cultural—as arbitrarily and coercively constructed to support vested interests, particularly those of white, Christian, heterosexual men."[25] In this new culture, today's online culture, there is almost nothing worse than being white, Christian, and straight.

This prejudice is embedded in the terms that social media teaches kids to use. Are you "neuro**typical**" or are you "neuro**divergent**"? Are you gender-**conforming** or gender-**nonconforming**? Normal now means typical. Conforming. And who wants to be typical and conforming? That is so BORING. As Matthew Crawford has observed, normophobia equates "normal" with "unimaginative," "passive," and "lame." Crawford concludes that normophobia "incentivizes healthy people to think of themselves as sick."[26] And the danger of thinking of yourself as sick is that it can actually make you sick. As C. S. Lewis wrote 70 years ago, "the trouble about trying to make yourself stupider than you really are is that you very often succeed."[27] Substitute "more anxious" or "more depressed" for "stupider" and you begin to understand what is happening with American kids. The collapse of parenting has set kids adrift in a newly toxic culture in which it's now cool to be anxious and depressed, a culture in which it's totally lame to be normal. Smartphones and social media may exacerbate the problem, but smartphones are perhaps not the root cause of the problem, only the vector. We as parents need to limit the phones and the screens not primarily because phones and screens are intrinsically evil, but because they are spreading a toxic culture, tinged with normophobia.

Take-home message: It's not enough just to say No to the world of social media and smartphones. You have to say Yes to a healthy culture. You have to offer your child a culture in which it's cool to be healthy and sane, ideally in collaboration with other like-minded families, in opposition to the ambient culture of normophobia and disrespect in which it's cool to be anxious and depressed.

Exposure to inappropriate content. In one study, researchers created social media accounts for fictitious boys and girls 13 to 17 years of age. Within hours, the accounts began receiving unsolicited content from adults. The "boys'" accounts received unsolicited links to sexually explicit material, enticing them to pornography sites. Within two days, all of the boys' accounts had received many similar links. The "girls'" accounts were likely to receive information on crash diets, self-harm, and suicide. A 17-year-old "girl" who expressed interest in losing weight received a deluge of links to pages glamorizing anorexia and encouraging radical weight loss. Other unsolicited pages sent to the girls valorized self-harm and suicide.[28]

A separate team of researchers conducted a similar study and got similar results. In this more recent study, researchers created TikTok accounts for fictitious 13-year-old girls. Once again, the "girls" were instantly bombarded with links promoting radical diets, extreme weight loss, and self-harm. Well, not quite instantly.

But within eight minutes.[29] Other researchers find that girls use social media to recruit other girls to lose weight and to share strategies for extreme weight loss. "Who wants to join the fast?"[30] A recent investigation found that TikTok has actually become more harmful to girls, pushing even more videos encouraging anorexia and self-harm.[31] A spokesperson for TikTok responded that TikTok employs more than 40,000 humans to scan the app for harmful content, removing millions of videos each month.[32] Forty thousand people sounds like a lot, until you consider that 34 million new videos are posted on TikTok *every day*.[33] If 40,000 TikTok employees were to review all the new videos, each employee would have to watch about 850 videos every day. In an eight-hour day, that would require watching almost two videos a minute every minute nonstop all day long—and that doesn't allow any time for any consideration of the video just watched, or any time to take any action. Given that a TikTok video averages 42 seconds, it's not possible.[34] Clearly, many videos are going on the platform without substantive review by humans.

Sextortion. Jordan DeMay was a well-liked student and football player at Marquette High School on Michigan's Upper Peninsula. He received a direct message via Instagram from a girl named Dani Robertts. He had never met her, but the selfies she shared showed a pretty girl, and her messages were funny and friendly. After they had exchanged messages, she asked him for a sexually explicit photo. Researchers find that many American teenage boys will happily share a selfie of their own erect penis if a teenage girl asks for it.[35] So Jordan sent Dani a sexually explicit selfie.

That's when Jordan found out that "Dani" wasn't a teenage girl at all, but a group of three young men who had deliberately

tricked him. They warned him that they had contact information for many of his friends at school. They sent him photos of
his friends, with contact information, to prove that they had done
their homework. They demanded that Jordan pay them $1,000
or they would send the photo to his friends. He paid $300, all he
had. They were not satisfied. Jordan pleaded with the men, saying,
"I'm going to kill myself right now because of you." They taunted
him, daring him to kill himself. Less than six hours later, Jordan
was found dead from a self-inflicted gunshot wound. His parents
gave permission to share his story with the world, in the hope of
preventing similar tragedies. The three men have been arrested
and are facing charges with maximum penalties of up to 50 years
in prison.[36]

Jordan's story is an example of the new crime of sextortion. An
adult pretending to be a teen contacts a teenager on social media.
Some adults are really proficient at pretending to be teenage girls,
or teenage boys, complete with selfies of the teen they are pretending to be. Once they have lured the target into sharing an explicit
photo, the trap is sprung and the adult demands more photos, or
money. The National Center for Missing and Exploited Children
received fewer than ten reports, total, of sextortion as recently as
2020. In 2023 they received more than 12,000 such reports.[37]

Moral confusion. Researchers at UCLA studied the most popular TV shows targeting children and teens from 1967, 1977, 1987,
1997, and 2007.[38] They analyzed the extent to which these shows
prioritized 16 different values, such as fame, achievement, serving
others, etc. They found tremendous consistency among the most
popular TV shows from 1967 to 1997, whether the show was *The
Andy Griffith Show* in 1967, *Happy Days* in 1977, *Family Ties* in
1987, or *Buffy the Vampire Slayer* in 1997. Serving others was the

#1 value—out of 16—in 1967, the #1 value in 1977, the #2 value in 1987, and the #1 value in 1997. In other words: the most popular shows were teaching kids that the most important thing is to do the right thing, to help your neighbor, to tell the truth. Being famous was the 15th most important value—out of 16—in 1967, the 13th most important in 1977, the 15th most important in 1987, and the 15th most important in 1997.

But then, between 1997 and 2007, American culture flipped upside down. The most popular TV shows in 2007—shows such as *American Idol* and *iCarly*—were shows that prioritized becoming famous as the highest value. Fame rocketed to the #1 spot in 2007, these researchers found, while serving others dropped to #11.

Why? What happened between 1997 and 2007 that caused fame to jump from the #15 spot to the #1 spot, while service to others plunged from the top spot down to the #11 position? The authors conclude that **social media** was to blame. Social media transformed American culture. Suddenly the highest priority wasn't serving others, or doing the right thing, or being a good friend; it was getting likes, getting followers, becoming an influencer.

A culture in which the highest priority is serving others is a culture which is fundamentally healthy for children and teenagers. In the words of Dr. Martin Luther King Jr.: "Everybody can be great, because anybody can serve." If service to others is the highest priority, kids have a clear moral compass. They know which way is up and which way is down. As Dr. King said, anybody can serve, so anyone can be successful in their own eyes and in the eyes of the world—if the highest priority is service to others, and if the young person can find the moral resolve to serve others. But as social psychologist Haidt observes, social media now "trains people to think in ways exactly contrary to the world's religious and spiritual traditions: think about yourself first; be materialistic, judgmental, boastful, and petty; seek glory as quantified by likes and followers."[39]

A culture in which the highest priority is to become famous is a culture that is fundamentally toxic to children and teenagers, if only for the simple reason that the overwhelming majority of people who strive to be famous will not succeed, no matter how hard they try. Here's one example. Lorenzo Mitchell was earning a computer science degree at college but dropped out in hopes of becoming a social media influencer. He gained 52,000 followers on his TikTok account, but he has earned less than $70 total from all his efforts on social media.[40] His most successful video has been viewed nearly two million times and earned him about $25. He earns most of his money as a busboy at a local restaurant. Tensor Social, a social media analytics firm, estimates that there are more than one million TikTok accounts with more than 52,000 followers.[41] Of those million-plus accounts, fewer than 100 will yield a social media career that can support someone lasting five years or more, according to Sarah Peretz, a social media analytics expert. A TikTok video with 100,000 views will earn about $2.[42] More than 50 million people right now are trying to become influencers on social media platforms such as YouTube and TikTok.[43] In one survey, 86 percent of young Americans said they would like to become social media influencers, and 12 percent claimed that they already *are* social media influencers.[44]

Even the winners are often losers in the new culture of social media. Verity Johnson was 21 years old when she unexpectedly won the position of female anchor on a morning TV show. In a short time, she went from zero to more than 8,000 followers on her social media platforms. "I became convinced that I was so fascinating. It's also the most numbly exhausting job I've ever done. You get trapped in your own triviality, in the mind-numbing packaging and distribution of the minutiae of your day. It's a real joy killer. Normally you take a photo because you want to capture a great moment, right? But as an influencer you have to manufacture those moments.... But the very worst, most dangerous part of Instafame in your 20s is that it totally messes up your character development. Not only did it make me self-obsessed, but it indulged my very worst qualities.... Staying Instafamous relies on you mining the depths of your own narcissism. The problem is that in your 20s you're busy working out who you want to be. A big part of that process is managing and squashing down the dark parts of yourself to make more room for your better parts. But Instafame fed my own vanity and insecurity until it became almost impossible to control them and make space for my better self." So she quit. "I realized in order to stay Insta-famous I'd have had to nurture the most pathetic parts of my own psyche. And honestly, no amount of free ombre activewear is worth that."[45]

This cultural upheaval—in which *becoming famous* is now the highest value—has consequences. When sociologists interviewed young people, 34 percent of their interviewees "said that *they simply did not know what makes anything morally right or wrong*. They had no idea about the basis of morality. Tellingly, many of these stumped interviewees could not even understand our questions on this point. No matter how many different ways we posed them, our very questions about morality's sources did not or could not make sense to them. They replied to our inquiries by saying things like 'I just don't understand, like, what do you mean?'"[46]

Even among the 66 percent of young people who were able to say why some things are right and other things are wrong, these researchers found many respondents who said that *what other people think* was their primary guide to right and wrong. For example, one young man, when asked what was the basis of morality, answered, "I want to be looked at as the dude who...was a good man, a decent man." The researchers noted that the opinions of others are not a firm foundation for morality. It doesn't take much imagination to recall recent historical eras in which the majority approved of actions or convictions which we now regard as wrong—for example, the internment of Japanese Americans during World War II. As recently as 1969, 80 percent of Americans disapproved of interracial marriage; that figure is now down to 6 percent.[47]

A culture in which fame and the opinion of others are the highest priorities is a culture without a moral compass. The end result of a culture in which most teenagers are on social media is moral confusion for many.

Part of your job as a parent is to teach your kid what's right, what's wrong, and why. Your parents didn't have to do that, at least not to the extent that you do, because the popular culture 30 years ago or 50 years ago taught kids that service to others is the highest priority, as we saw for example in that UCLA study of popular TV shows which I just cited. In today's culture, a culture that prioritizes being famous above everything else, kids will be adrift if you don't step up and do the heavy lifting of teaching right and wrong.

I'm not saying you have to teach the culture of *The Andy Griffith Show*. I'm saying you have to teach *something*, whether that is orthodox Judaism, evangelical Christianity, left-of-center

Catholicism, Sunni Islam, enlightened humanism, or any of the dozens of other moral frameworks available. I'm saying it is not reasonable to expect your child to be an Aristotle or Saint Paul or Friedrich Nietzsche, working out a new moral system almost entirely on their own. If you don't provide your child with a moral framework, they will look to the society in which they live for guidance. And if they have a device with Internet access, they are likely to learn the contemporary culture in which being famous is the ultimate goal, and in which the opinion of others is the primary judge of morals. And the result of your neglect will be your child's moral confusion.

Pornography. This chapter is about screens, so we have to talk about pornography. Many parents are clueless. I visited a boys' high school in the United States. Almost all the parents of the students at this school have earned a college degree. The school leaders were concerned because so many of the boys were openly looking at pornography on their phones while waiting for their ride home after school, sharing the photos and videos with others. "There was no sense of shame or embarrassment about looking at porn," one administrator told me. So the principal decided to commission a survey. All the parents were asked, "How often does your son look at pornography?" The options were Never, Less than once a month, Less than once a week, About once a week, More than once a week, or Every day. More than 90 percent of parents answered Never. Then the students, all high school boys, were surveyed. More than 80 percent of the boys answered More than once a week or Every day. The boys were asked, "On what device are you looking at porn?" More than 90 percent said they were looking at porn on their phone. What proportion of parents were taking any steps, such as installing a parental monitoring app, to limit their son's access to porn? Only 4 percent.

I am aware of many claims regarding the hazards of pornography. I have read the famous study which suggests that pornography literally causes the brains of young men to become "unglued."[48] I know there's good evidence that pornography leads to decreased satisfaction with real-world romantic relationships.[49] I know that pornography can become a morally corrosive addiction.[50] I am aware that 17 US states have declared that pornography is now a public health emergency.[51] But my concerns are somewhat different. As a family doctor, I have seen firsthand how pornography *undermines real-world motivation.* Let me give you an example.

Mom confronted her son one day. "What's the story?" mom asked. "You wake up late every day. You work a few hours a week at the coffee shop. You're *twenty-eight years old.* You don't have a real job. You don't even have a girlfriend. When are you going to get a life?"

Her son laughed. "Well, I *used* to have a girlfriend, but then she found out I only work a few hours a week at Starbucks, so she dumped me."

"Well, duh," mom said. "What woman wants to be with a man who has no ambition beyond earning a few dollars for his video games?" She insisted that he come into my office and talk to me. He was fine with that.

I asked him about his girlfriend. "She was fat," he said dismissively. "And she wanted me to take her places, do stuff with her. $19.95 a month," he said.

"Wait, I don't understand," I said. "$19.95 a month? What's $19.95 a month?"

He mentioned a porn site. "It's $19.95 a month and it is EX-CELLENT," he said with emphasis. "The girls are amazing. Way prettier than any of the girls around here."

"Wait," I said again. "Those aren't girls. Those are pictures on a computer screen. Pixels. Wouldn't you rather be intimate with an actual woman rather than masturbate over pornography?"

"NO," he said with a snort. "Absolutely NOT. Are you kidding?"

This man is not alone. He is not even unusual. The pop star John Mayer told *Rolling Stone* magazine that he is "the new generation of masturbator."[52] Old school men preferred actual sex with real women, according to Mayer, but he is the new generation of masturbator, by which he means that he *prefers* masturbating over pornography rather than being intimate with actual women. In a subsequent interview with *Playboy* magazine, the reporter asked him, Why? You're rich, you're famous, you're good-looking. You could have all kinds of amazing girlfriends. You've *had* all kinds of amazing girlfriends. (Mayer's previous girlfriends include Taylor Swift, Jessica Simpson, Jennifer Love Hewitt, Katy Perry, and Jennifer Aniston.)[53] Why do you prefer masturbation over actual intimacy with a woman? Mayer answered, "I'm more comfortable in my imagination than in actual human discovery."[54] That's becoming the new normal. In a 2023 report of a nationwide survey of 1,358 teens, 76 percent of teenage boys 13 to 17 years of age said that they look at pornography more than once a week.[55]

For most of human history, men's sexual desire has motivated them to real-world achievement. By achieving great things, a man could impress a woman: *Look at me! I will be a good provider. You will lack for nothing. I can protect you.* More than 80 years ago, the bestselling American author Napoleon Hill observed that a man's sex drive promotes "keenness of imagination, courage, willpower, persistence, and creative ability" otherwise unavailable to that man.[56] And I think there's considerable truth to that.

Pornography diverts and undermines that drive. A man no longer has to achieve in the real world. He can satisfy himself with an infinite number of women chosen according to his taste, and now refined by artificial intelligence to perfections literally impossible for an actual human female,[57] or with AI-created virtual girlfriends built to the boy's specifications,[58] or with AI-created pornographic images of real women he knows, so-called "deep-fake porn."[59] The young man who met with me seemed perfectly content, as near as I could tell, with the limitless pornography available to him online. I asked him about wanting personal connection. Friendship. "I'm friends with other guys," he said. "I don't really relate that way to women. Never have." Maybe that's true. At least now it is true. But he has been masturbating over pornography since early adolescence. Maybe if he had tried harder to have a relationship with a girl, or a woman, he might have developed another aspect of his character. He might have had a chance at a romantic relationship with a woman. And maybe he would have tried harder if he hadn't been looking at porn since he was in middle school. We will probably never know.

When I speak to parents about the hazards of pornography, occasionally a parent asks about girls using pornography. I have read scholarly reports of young women who describe themselves as being addicted to online pornography.[60] But I just have not seen it firsthand. I regularly encounter teenage boys and young men who are addicted to porn, who prefer pornography to actual intimacy with real women. I have never encountered a girl or woman who told me that she would rather masturbate over pornography than engage in actual intimacy with another human. Maybe there are such girls and such women. Maybe I haven't encountered them because they prefer to consult female doctors. That's possible. My recommendations here are based on my experience with actual boys and men.

You need to speak to your son about the hazards of pornography. You need to make sure he understands the risks of becoming addicted to porn, of the unrealistic expectations created by porn, and of the negative impact of porn on romantic relationships. But you also need to tell him that you will not allow him to look at porn. You will install a parental monitoring app on any device with Internet access to block his access to porn. Explain that you will be disappointed if he tries to get around this prohibition, for example by looking at a friend's phone. Remind him that pornography degrades not only the woman who is depicted but also the man who consumes.

This is where some parents push back hard. "By prohibiting it, you're just making it more desirable," one parent said. "All the boys are looking at it. That ship has sailed," another parent said. "I looked at porn when I was younger, and I don't think it damaged me," said one father. OK, pornography existed 30 years ago—or so I have been told by reliable sources. But 30 years ago, the pornography was tame by modern standards. As French researcher Pascal-Emmanuel Gobry observes, 30 years ago soft-core pornography—the most popular kind at that time—meant "something similar to *Playboy* and lingerie catalogues."[61] The traditional porn industry of 30 years ago—if we can use the word "traditional" to describe the porn industry—has largely collapsed, with performers who used to earn $3,000 a shoot now earning just $600 a shoot, forcing sex workers into "extreme acts of degradation" as violent porn has become the new norm.[62] The trend toward deviance in online porn is now so pronounced that many young people today think it's normal for the man to choke the woman during sex.[63]

And 30 years ago, it was unusual for boys to boast of their collection of pornography. In that era, boys might boast of their actual sexual exploits, real or imagined. Porn was for losers, for boys who couldn't get the real thing. Also, in that era, boys had to go to an actual adult bookstore to buy hard-core pornographic magazines, and those bookstores had signs prominently warning customers: "adults only." (Soft-core porn magazines such as *Playboy* and *Penthouse* were sometimes available at drugstores and newsstands, often behind a discreet shield.) Online porn videos weren't widely available until the late 1990s.[64] Today, as Gobry notes, "online porn provides literally infinite novelty with no effort.... You can have a new clip—what your brain interprets as a new partner—literally every minute, every second. And with laptops, smartphones and tablets, they can be accessed everywhere, 24/7, immediately."[65]

One more word about parental monitoring apps. When I advise parents to install a parental monitoring app on their teen's smartphone, it's common for parents to respond, "I don't think that will work. My kid will just Google '*how to get around parental controls on NetNanny.*'" As it happens, I have spoken to employees at NetNanny. They have told me they have colleagues whose full-time job is to Google the query *how to get around parental controls on NetNanny* and every possible variation on that query. If they find that some kid has found a hole, they patch it, usually within a day or two, and the app will update.

Cañon City, Colorado, is a small town, under 20,000 population, about one hour's drive southwest of Colorado Springs. People there say it's a great place to raise a family. Everybody knows everybody, everybody looks out for everybody else, a high proportion of families attend church every Sunday. But it turns out that more than 100 kids at Cañon City High School were exchanging obscene photos—of themselves. They were sexting selfies, partly or wholly undressed, using a vault app. On the phone, the app looks like a calculator. It *is* a calculator. It can add, subtract, multiply, divide. But if you enter your four- or five-digit password, the calculator vanishes to reveal a vault of the obscene photos the teens were sharing.

In Colorado, if you are 16 years old and you take a photo of yourself naked and send it to your 16-year-old friend, you have produced and distributed child pornography. That's a Class 3 felony under Colorado law. If convicted, you must register as a sex offender anywhere you live in the United States for the next 20 years. There is no exception in the law if the producer of the pornography is the minor child depicted in the photos. When the scandal broke, Thom LeDoux, the district attorney, had to decide whether to bring criminal charges against more than 100 underage teens who had been sharing their photos.[66]

Don't put your kid in that jeopardy. Install a parental monitoring app. (The Ethics and Public Policy Center offers a useful and free online guide to the various parental monitoring apps.)[67] Explain to your kids that the app will see every photo they take, even before they do anything with the photo. If you see that your teen has taken a photo of anything inappropriate—and the app will flag it for you—then your teen will lose their device, indefinitely.

I was doing this talk for a parents' group, making just these recommendations. During Q&A, a father politely voiced an objection. "Dr. Sax, I totally hear what you're saying about the potential dangers of kids sexting, and looking at bad stuff online, and I get it. But the idea of a parental monitoring app—that seems unnecessarily intrusive to me. I'm something of a technology guy myself. I've done some IT work. I look at my daughter's phone regularly, and she knows that I'm going to do that. I check for apps recently installed. I make sure I understand what apps she has. So I agree that parents need to know what kids are doing with their phones, but I'd have to say I don't agree with the idea of installing a parental monitoring app."

I said to this father, "I think it's great that you look at your kid's phone. But the idea that you can just look at a phone, scroll through the apps on somebody's phone, and have any idea how that phone is being used—that's very 2007. It might have been true in 2007. It certainly is NOT true today. The vault apps that the kids in Cañon City were using are designed to be invisible to parents. They won't show up under 'apps recently installed.'[68] Parents are in an arms race and they don't even realize it. The apps are getting better and better, harder and harder to detect if you just look at a phone and check the history. But some parents are still living in 2007. You may know something about IT, but that doesn't mean that you can spot a vault app which is designed to be invisible to you. The professionals who make these parental monitoring apps understand the challenges. The monitoring app will detect the vault apps, and the parental monitoring app will let you know what's going on."

Video games. Let me share another observation from my perspective as a family doctor. The same boy who spends many hours a week looking at pornography is, often, also spending many hours a week playing video games. And again, my chief concern about video games is how they can undermine motivation to succeed in the real world. I had an encounter with another young man, similar to the encounter I described above but with a different emphasis. Once again this young man was in my office at the insistence of his mother. This time the encounter did not go as smoothly. At least the porn addict and I got along reasonably well. But this young man was not happy to be in my office. I struggled to open the conversation. My usual openers—"Tell me about yourself"; "Where do you see yourself in five years?"—got me nowhere. Finally, the young man blurted out, "I'm Guild Master. Do you have *any* idea what that means?"

I was thankful for a recent conversation with a teenage boy which enabled me to answer the question. "I believe 'Guild Master' is a reference to *World of Warcraft*, the online video game. It means that you are master of a guild in *World of Warcraft*."

"I'll tell you what it means," the young man said. "It means that there are people who *worship* me in Singapore, in Johannesburg, South Africa, in Liverpool, England."

"OK," I said.

"I'm level 120," he said. "Do you know what *that* means?"

"Yes," I said. "I believe that's another reference to *World of Warcraft*. It means that you have reached level 120 in *World of Warcraft*."

"It means I'm *the best there is*," he said. "There is no level above level 120."

"OK, but in the real world you're 32 years old, you don't have a job, and you live in your parents' basement," I said.

"So you're saying that accomplishment in the meat world is more important than accomplishment in the virtual world?" he asked.

"Well, if by the 'meat world' you mean the real world, then Yes," I said. "I think that's a fair statement of my position."

It was not a productive conversation. As near as I can tell, this young man is perfectly happy with his 65-inch flatscreen, his 5.1 surround sound, and his 400-watt subwoofer, all paid for by his parents. (He boasted that when a mortar round lands near him in a video game, the vibration from the subwoofer can cause books to fall off the bookshelf.) His parents are concerned. "What will happen when we're gone?" his mom said to me. "He's completely incapable of earning a living. In the real world, he is unemployed and unemployable. He dropped out of college. He has no real-world skills."

As with the sex drive, the *drive to achieve* has been a primary motivator for men in almost every culture for which anthropologists can find substantial records. Video games divert that drive to achieve away from the real world and into the virtual world. When I try to explain that to parents, some parents just don't buy it. "I played *Space Invaders* when I was a teenager, and it didn't do anything to my 'drive to achieve,'" one father said to me. But video games have come a long way since *Space Invaders*. *Red Dead Redemption 2* is an immensely popular video game. You play as Arthur Morgan, an outlaw living in the American West in 1899, a turbulent era as the Wild West frontier is morphing into law-abiding jurisdictions with reliable law enforcement. You can steal a horse, tame it, and win its loyalty and affection by treating it well. You can kill wild animals such as bison and elk, eat the meat, and save the carcass to sell later—but if you forget about it, the carcass will rot, losing value and attracting dangerous predators such as bears. In pursuit of your missions, most of which are violent, you can acquire and fire a variety of firearms as well as a bow and arrow. Your firearms require periodic maintenance to maintain their performance. Along the way, you can play poker, blackjack, and dominoes in utterly realistic saloons created with the assistance of professional historians.

Red Dead Redemption 2 (*RDR2*) cost about $540 million to make.[69] By comparison, the 2009 movie *Avatar*, the highest-grossing movie of all time, cost about $237 million to make. So the budget for *RDR2* was more than twice that of *Avatar*. *RDR2* earned more than $720 million in its opening weekend. To put that number in perspective, *Avatar* earned $77 million in its opening weekend.[70] By many measures, the video game industry is now bigger than the movie industry.

It typically takes a minimum of about 40 hours to complete all the required missions in *RDR2*. When you have completed those missions and the game is done, you feel that you have really accomplished something. "It's just such a great feeling, finally to get there, to finish," one young man told me. "I'm just so proud of accomplishing that." Remember, this game cost more than half a billion dollars to make. No expense was spared to make the gameplay utterly realistic and absorbing. You can go anywhere and do anything, be the hero or the villain.

And that's exactly my concern. The young man who told me how proud he is to have completed all the missions in *RDR2*— in real life, he works for a low wage at a dead-end job with little prospect of advancement. He's fine with that. "I get my sense of accomplishment online [i.e., from playing online games]. The job just pays the bills," he told me frankly.

There are some gender issues here. Boys are more likely than girls to become addicted to video games. Boys are much more likely than girls to become addicted to porn. Girls, on the other hand, are more vulnerable to the toxic effects of social media, more likely to become anxious and/or depressed.

But my point is that too much screen time is harmful, whether you have a son or a daughter. I know a family where the teenage son spends every free minute playing video games and occasionally looks at porn. The teenage daughter spends all her time on social media, primarily TikTok. The daughter is taking medication for anxiety and depression. The boy is happy as a clam with his video games and his porn. He's not depressed in the slightest. But both these kids have problems. Just because the boy isn't anxious or depressed doesn't mean that he is fulfilling his potential. On the contrary, he is doing poorly in school (his sister is getting almost straight As). He has the potential to be an excellent student, but he spends his free time playing video games instead of studying. Both these kids have problems, but they have different problems. Both kids would benefit if the parents cut back on their screen time. But when I suggested to mom that she begin by making sure neither kid has a phone in their bedroom at bedtime, mom said no. "My daughter would totally freak out if I took her phone from her," she said.

OK. In this chapter we have talked about the risks of social media, pornography, and video games. What are you supposed to do about it? Social media isn't going to go away. Neither is porn. Neither are video games. So here's what I recommend:

1. **No devices in the bedroom.** That means no TV in the bedroom, no video-game console in the bedroom, and no phone in the bedroom. This has to be your call, not your

child's call. It is not reasonable, it is not age-appropriate, to dump this decision—whether or not to have a phone in the bedroom—in the lap of your 13-year-old. What is she supposed to say in school tomorrow when her friend says, "Hey, I texted you at midnight, how come you didn't answer?" Is your daughter supposed to say, "Well, researchers have found that the mere presence of a phone in the bedroom diminishes the quantity and quality of adolescent sleep, increasing the risk of both anxiety and depression. For that reason, I give my phone to my parents every night at 9 p.m., and they keep it in their bedroom." It's completely unrealistic to expect a child or teen to talk like that. You have to allow your kid to say, "My evil parents take my phone every night at 9 p.m.! And switch it off and put it in the charger, which is in THEIR bedroom!" And that's what you should do. That's also the official guidance of the American Academy of Pediatrics: no phone in the bedroom, no video-game console in the bedroom, no TV in the bedroom.[71]

2. **No devices at the dinner table**—or anywhere, anytime, when the family is together. Family time is a time for you to talk with your kids and listen to what they have to say. Screens interfere with that. No TV playing in the background either. Likewise, **no use of phones or earbuds in the car.** Time in the car is special. It's private time. When you are in the car, you should be listening to your kid, and she should be listening to you—not scrolling through social media or playing a video game. In the car, you can use your phone to listen to music that you and your kid can enjoy

together. My daughter and I have memorized the lyrics to dozens of songs, from the final movement of Beethoven's Ninth to the Beatles to Bruce Springsteen to Taylor Swift. You shouldn't make a phone call to a friend when your kid is in the car with you—that's sending the message that your friend is more important to you than your kid is. That's the wrong message to send. Exceptions for emergencies only.

3. **No social media.** We have already discussed the many risks of social media. The risks of social media now greatly outweigh any benefits. No social media for any child under 18—that's the rule we followed with our daughter, now 17, and neither she nor we have any regrets. You can listen to a podcast in which our daughter addressed this question in her own words.[72] The interviewer asked her why she doesn't have any social media. She answered, basically, "I have a life." She dances. She hikes. She does crafts. She hangs with friends. She recognizes that social media would take time away from those activities, and she doesn't see the point, or the need.

4. **No pornography.** In the United States, it is unlawful in all 50 states and all United States territories to sell, distribute, or display pornography to a child under 18 years of age.[73] Of course, any kid with a smartphone can view unlimited porn, but that doesn't make it right. We have already considered the evidence that when a kid is looking at pornography beginning in middle school, it can really mess with that kid's head and undermine motivation to make romantic connections in the real world.

5. **Limit video games.** My daughter and I play video games together. It's fun, and it's no big deal. But if video games are displacing your kid's achievement in the real world, then that *is* a big deal. No more than 40 minutes a night playing video games on school nights, no more than an hour a day on weekends, and your minutes do not roll over (please see the chapter on video games in my book *Boys Adrift* for a review of the research supporting these guidelines). No video games until all the chores are done and all the homework is done. No video-game console in the bedroom.

We are at a pivot point in human history. Artificial intelligence platforms are causing many people to wonder what's next. Some tech moguls want us to invest much more of our time and our money in a metaverse of their creation, for their profit. But we now have sufficient evidence to recognize that **kids need to be grounded in the real world, not the world of screens.** To the extent that kids live in the world of screens, they are at increased risk of anxiety and depression (especially for girls), and increased risk of disengagement from the real world (especially for boys).

Don't expect much help with this. The leadership at your local school, no matter how enlightened or informed, can't limit what your kids are doing in their bedrooms on evenings or weekends. That's your job. Some people in government are trying to do something about this. Several states are making it harder for porn sites to promote their wares to kids under 18.[74] The attorneys general of 33 states have filed a lawsuit against Meta, parent company of Instagram and Facebook, alleging that Instagram and Facebook subject "young users to a wave of harmful, manipulative, and addictive content [and] that Meta knowingly designs and deploys features harmful to children on its platforms, while at the same time, falsely assuring the public that those features are suitable for children."[75] But real help from the government isn't likely, at least not anytime soon. And the tech industry certainly isn't going to help. If anybody is going to limit and guide your kid's use of screens, right now and not ten years from now, it's got to be you.

6

Theybies

The leadership of Trinity United Presbyterian Church in Orange County, California—just a few minutes' drive from Disneyland— hired me to lead eight different workshops for parents, on eight different topics, over two days. I have a few diehard fans who attended all eight workshops. That's more than 12 hours of Leonard Sax. Yikes! During Q&A and between sessions, we had a chance to get acquainted. One woman told me how she and her husband had been trying to get pregnant for the past three years and finally succeeded. She was so excited that she shared the news, and the updates, with her coworkers at the local public elementary school where she is a teacher. "Guess what!" she told a colleague at the school. "We just found out! We're having a boy!"

"Don't you think you should let the *baby* decide?" her colleague responded, coolly.

Yup, that's a thing now. Not only in Southern California, but across the United States and Canada, I'm now encountering parents who think enlightened parenting means letting kids decide *everything*, including whether the child will grow up male, or female, or both, or neither. According to these parents, good parenting means you give your kid a gender-neutral name such as Zyler or Kadyn.[1] Then when the kid is three or four, the kid will let you know whether the kid is going to be a girl, a boy, or something else. If the child has male genitalia but announces that he's a girl, then she's a girl. The parents are supposed to change the birth certificate to "female," and the child will begin down the road that leads to puberty blockers, female hormones, and perhaps castration and other surgery.[2]

So let's say that your child is not transgender, perfectly comfortable as a girl or as a boy. Why am I asking you to read this chapter? I think this topic is relevant for all parents, regardless of whether your child might identify as trans, because it illustrates how the authority of parents is being undermined. As recently as 10 years ago, it would have been unthinkable for a teacher at a public school to encourage a 6-year-old boy to transition to being a girl without the parents' knowledge or consent.

But that's exactly what recently happened, allegedly, in a Pittsburgh suburb. According to court documents, Megan Williams, a first-grade teacher in the Mount Lebanon School District and herself the mother of a boy who has transitioned to being a girl, repeatedly encouraged one of the boys in her classroom to transition to being a girl, as her own child has done. Ms. Williams allegedly "explained to her students that sometimes 'parents are wrong' and parents and doctors 'make mistakes' when they bring a child home from the hospital."[3] Ms. Williams also allegedly instructed her students not to tell their parents what she had said. The school district defended itself by saying that parents have no right to be notified when the teacher talks to first graders about transitioning from male to female or vice versa, and no right to opt their children out of such discussions.[4] The district petitioned the judge to dismiss the case without the case even going to trial.

But the federal judge in this case, Joy Flowers Conti, has ruled that the case may proceed. Conti found that the school district's "refusal to recognize any parental rights in a public school setting is contrary to clear, binding U.S. Supreme Court and Third Circuit Court of Appeals authority." She further held that the district's lawyers distorted previous court decisions "holding that parental rights are not absolute to argue that parents have no rights at all."[5]

At this writing, the case is proceeding to trial. A transgender activist group has filed an amicus curiae brief in support of the school district, asserting that the parents' lawsuit is "transphobic" and will have the effect of creating a "hostile school climate" for other transgender students.[6]

What should you do if your 6-year-old son tells you that he is a girl?[7]

Our nation's largest association of pediatricians, the American Academy of Pediatrics (AAP), released guidelines in 2018—which the AAP officially reaffirmed in 2023—for the evaluation and management of children and adolescents who identify as transgender.[8] Previous guidelines recognized that best practice depends on the age of the child.[9] The great majority of 6-year-old boys who say that they are girls will not persist in that conviction; 10 years later, most of those boys will say that they are boys. They may be gay, they may be straight, but they are now sure that they are boys. They no longer want to be girls.

Six-year-olds are not mature adults. They are young children. They may be mistaken about the reality of Santa Claus, the tooth fairy, or their own gender identities.

Expert pediatricians used to understand that. They no longer do. The new guidelines from the AAP explicitly eliminate any role for age in evaluation of the child. According to the new guidelines, *any* child who wants to transition to the other sex should be "affirmed." *Regardless of age.* If a 6-year-old boy tells you that he is a girl, your job is to buy him a dress and change his name to Emily. Any other response is outdated and transphobic. The authors of the AAP guidelines specifically reject any "watchful waiting" for prepubescent children or any children.

These new guidelines are not based in evidence. On the contrary, they contradict the available research. For example, in one study, 139 boys who persistently said they were girls were evaluated around 7 years of age. When researchers tracked down those boys many years later, at least 13 years later, only 17 out of the 139, or 12 percent, still said they were female or had any doubts about their gender identity.[10] This study, and others like it, demonstrate that the majority of boys who say they are girls prior to the onset of puberty will not say they are girls after the onset of puberty.[11] (We don't have comparable long-term studies of prepubescent girls who say they are boys because until just a few years ago, such girls were exceedingly rare.) But the American Academy of Pediatrics is now on record prioritizing the opinion of a 6-year-old over the considered judgment of the child's parents, even suggesting that the pediatrician should take (unspecified) legal action if those ignorant parents refuse to obey their child's wishes to transition to the other gender. In other words, the AAP is saying that a 6-year-old knows better than the child's parents what is best for the child.

Suppose a 6-year-old boy tells his parents that he is a girl. He wants to wear a dress to school and change his name to Emily. Suppose the parents want to adopt a wait-and-see attitude. He can wear a dress for his Halloween costume, but not to school. The AAP now denounces such an approach as "outdated." Even worse: those parents are trying to prevent the child "from identifying as transgender." The AAP guidelines label such an approach as "reparative therapy." According to the AAP guidelines, such therapies have been shown to be unsuccessful. In support of that assertion, they cited a 1994 report documenting the failure of interventions intended to change the sexual orientation of adult homosexual men and women.[12]

Outdated, indeed. A report documenting the failure of efforts to change the sexual orientation of adults is of doubtful relevance to the question of whether a 6-year-old boy named Justin who says that he is really a girl named Emily should be encouraged to transition. Oops! Excuse me for saying "transition." The AAP guidelines advise that we no longer use the term "transition" because we are supposed to "view the process as an affirmation and acceptance of who they have always been rather than a transition." The guidelines also endorse changing the child's birth certificate to erase any trace of Justin's existence; the child's name on the birth certificate will be changed to Emily, and the child's sex at birth will be changed to female. Justin never existed.

What actually happens to young boys who say that they are girls? As I noted above, some grow up to be gay men. Those gay men don't want to be women. They are quite happy to be gay men.

They have no desire to change their name, or to take female hormones, or to be castrated. The physician who truly seeks to do what is best for that young boy must therefore determine, is this boy truly transgender, or is he perhaps a gay boy who hasn't yet figured out that he is gay? Or maybe he is a straight boy who just happens to like ballet and glitter?

How are you to make that distinction if you are dealing with a 6-year-old? It isn't easy. I remember asking my mom, when I was 7 or 8 years old, "If I marry a woman, will I have to take my pajamas off in bed with her?" My mom answered, "Yes, you will, but you will *want* to." I said, "No, I won't! Girls have cooties!" As it happened, I turned out to be a straight man. And I still like ballet and glitter.

It is not developmentally appropriate to ask a 6-year-old about their sexual orientation. Prepubescent children do not have a sexual agenda, nor should they. They are prepubescent children. But if there is no way accurately to determine the sexual orientation of a 6-year-old—and there isn't—then there can be no way to say whether this 6-year-old boy will persist in wanting to be female, whether he is simply a gay boy who hasn't yet discovered his own sexual orientation, or whether he is a straight boy who just happens to love glitter and ballet. Based on the evidence, the most sensible approach to such a boy is to show him love and support, but not for him to transition to the other gender. He wants to study ballet? Great! But he will study ballet as a boy, not as a girl.

The 6-year-old boy who transitions to identify as a girl has taken a major step on a road that may lead to treatment with cross-sex hormones, castration, and infertility. The AAP's guidelines prioritizing the child's impulse over the parent's considered judgment are not only reckless, they underscore how our nation's leading professional association of pediatricians now undermines the authority of parents.

A lmost every enduring culture of which we have any knowledge has taught girls to be women and boys to be men. Exactly what that means has varied from one culture to the next. In Japan during the era of the shogunate, 1603 to 1868, the sons of a samurai would have received instruction in tea ceremony: meticulous care in the preparation and serving of tea. That activity was prohibited to girls.[13] In the United States today, we would think of meticulous care in the preparation and serving of tea as being feminine rather than masculine, but cultures differ in which activities are considered masculine and which are feminine.

Every culture of which we have substantial knowledge has made the distinction between male and female and has taught it to the children. For more than a century, cultural critics in the West have highlighted how gender roles constrain and limit what people can do. When my late mother, Dr. Janet Sax, graduated in 1953 from the Case Western Reserve School of Medicine, she was one of just two women in the graduating class of more than 100. In that era, the 1950s and earlier, young women were told that they could be nurses but not doctors; secretaries but not lawyers; teachers but not principals. There were some exceptional women like my mother who transgressed those barriers, but they were exceptions.

Second-wave feminism from the 1960s onward sought to open more doors for women and did so with considerable success. In the 1970s, 1980s, 1990s, and 2000s, there was a rolling tide of "first woman to . . ." First woman to lead a Fortune 500 company: Katharine Graham, 1972. First woman to be a US Supreme Court justice:

Sandra Day O'Connor, 1981. First American woman to fly in space: Sally Ride, 1983. First woman to lead the National Institutes of Health: Bernadine Healy, 1991. First woman to be secretary of state: Madeleine Albright, 1997. First woman to be national security advisor: Condoleezza Rice, 2001. First woman to lead Harvard University: Drew Gilpin Faust, 2007. First woman to be named a four-star general in the US Army: Ann Dunwoody, 2008. And so on.

That's all great. But in recent years, there has been a peculiar twist. Instead of feminism marching on, the reality of the categories "male" and "female" has come under attack. One example: Go to Amazon.com and sign your kid up for the Amazon Kids+ app. Amazon Kids+ promises "a safe space for kids to explore," with choices carefully curated for your child based on your child's age. If your child is 8 years old, Amazon Kids+ will offer your child *It Feels Good to Be Yourself: A Book About Gender Identity*.[14] Here's a quote: "When you were born, you couldn't tell people who you were or how you felt. They looked at you and made a guess. Maybe they got it right, maybe they got it wrong.... You might feel like a boy. You might feel like a girl. You might feel like both boy and girl—or like neither. You might feel that your gender changes from day to day or from year to year."[15] The book features Alex, who is both a boy and a girl, and JJ, who is neither a boy nor a girl. What determines whether you are a boy or a girl? Whatever you feel yourself to be, which may change "from day to day or from year to year." There is no hint anywhere in the book that every cell in your body is either male or female, or that intersex—a rare anomaly in which a child is truly both male and female (for example an XX/XY chimera)—is observed in fewer than 2 in 10,000 live births.[16] To be blunt: the book is lying to young children. Male and female are biological realities, not feelings which change "from day to day or from year to year."

What does it mean to "feel like a girl"? Did Ann Dunwoody, future four-star general, "feel like a girl" when she was growing up? Her favorite activity was jumping out of a plane with a parachute, an activity we associate more with men than with women. (Dunwoody was the first woman to command a battalion of parachute jumpers in the 82nd Airborne.) Should she have transitioned to the male role? Some parents in Wauwatosa, Wisconsin, were alarmed to hear that their school was encouraging fourth graders to read *It Feels Good to Be Yourself*. Those parents petitioned the school board to remove the book from the recommended curriculum. The school board refused.[17]

The irony is that such policies have the unintended effect of reinforcing gender stereotypes. The girl who wants to be a Marine, the boy who wants to dance ballet and design sparkly costumes, are now asked whether they are transitioning to the other gender, whether they would like to change their pronouns. Journalist and author Nina Power recalls that as a child, she only did boy things, wore boy clothes, insisted on a boy's haircut, and had nothing to do with anything pink or girly. "If you'd have asked me at 11 if I wanted to be a boy, I would have said, 'Yes.'" But now, in her 30s, she is horrified at the idea that she might have been transitioned to the male role, undergone a mastectomy, and taken male hormones. In her article "The Trans War on Tomboys," she writes, "Children must be allowed to grow up without having their normal behavior pathologized. Adults must face up to their duty to protect children and teenagers from their own desires and *not to imagine that their children know best*."[18]

Not to imagine that their children know best. I italicized that phrase because I think it's the key to our discussion here. American popular culture now operates with the implicit (or sometimes explicit) assumption that the child knows best, that the child is better-qualified than his or her own parents to determine where his or her best interest lies. Jessica Bradshaw is a mother in California who discovered that her 15-year-old daughter had transitioned to the male role at school six months previously. School personnel had been addressing Jessica's child using a boy's name, at the child's request, but neither mom nor dad had been informed. When Jessica reached out to the school to ask why nobody had informed her that her daughter was now her son, a counselor explained that the child didn't want the parents to know and that the school had to respect the child's wishes. The child had previously been diagnosed as being on the autism spectrum, as well as having Attention Deficit Hyperactivity Disorder (ADHD), Post-Traumatic Stress Disorder (PTSD), and anxiety. Given the complexities of her child's psychiatric history, Jessica said that the school's decision to conceal her daughter's transition to the male role "felt like a parenting stab in the back from the school system. It should have been a decision we made as a family."[19]

Parents in Eau Claire, Wisconsin, sued their school district, claiming that the district was transgressing on the rights of the parents. Their lawsuit included a photo of a flyer that a teacher posted at school that read, "If your parents aren't accepting of your identity, I'm your mom now." The lawsuit also noted that the district's official training for teachers includes a slide which reads, "parents are not entitled to know their kids' gender identities."[20] In Michigan and in New York, teachers used students' legal names when talking with parents, but used the students' new other-gender names and pronouns in class in order to conceal from parents the fact that the student had transitioned to the other gender.[21] California, New Jersey, and Maryland now have official statewide guidelines in place advising teachers not to inform parents when their child has transitioned to the other gender. ACLU lawyer Jon Davidson said, "Parents don't have a constitutional right to dictate to schools how they should create an optimal learning environment for students."[22]

I understand that in the rare case of an abusive parent, a school may need to conceal some information from a parent. But most parents are not abusive. These new policies assume that parents are the bad guys. The default setting is to keep parents uninformed. These policies deliberately negate the authority of the parent to determine what is best for the child.

The website GoFundMe is the world's largest crowdfunding mechanism, having raised more than $15 billion since its founding in 2010. The website encourages individuals who wish to transition to the other sex to use GoFundMe to raise money for their transition, and it provides free promotion for those web pages.[23] GoFundMe makes no mention of any age limit or any requirement for minor children to have parental consent. The only requirement is that you have to say that you are 13 or older to open a GoFundMe account. And the Internet is already full of stories of teens under 18 boasting of using their GoFundMe accounts to pay for their gender transitions.[24]

True story: A husband and wife had two children, an older son and a younger daughter. The girl had always been a girly girl. She loved Barbie dolls. She insisted on dressing up as a princess for Halloween year after year. She liked to draw colorful landscapes in pastels (I have several of her drawings). But at age 14, she plunged into depression. She found videos on social media promising her that if she transitioned to being a boy, her depression would be cured. She told her parents that she was a boy and she wanted to transition to the male role. They refused. She ran away from home and petitioned the state of Arizona, where the family lived, to allow her to become a ward of the state and to transition to the male role. The state agreed.

The parents sued to regain custody of their daughter. The attorney representing the parents hired me to serve as an expert witness. So I went on Zoom on the appointed date and testified under oath. I explained that lots of teenagers are confused, and a growing number of teenagers are depressed. I noted that many popular videos on social media promise girls that if they just transition to the male role, their depression will melt away. I observed that these videos are often misleading or even promote outright falsehoods. In most such cases—and particularly with a girl who has never manifested any hint of gender dysphoria prior to 14 years of age—it is not in the girl's best interest to begin male hormones and transition to the male role. Evidence-based best practice in this case would be to treat the girl's depression with antidepressant medication and counseling, but not to begin male hormones and not to transition to the male role.

"Is your recommendation in accordance with the guidelines of the American Academy of Pediatrics?" the judge asked.

"No, it is not," I conceded. "The Academy guidelines would recommend that this girl transition to the male role."

"So let me see if I understand you," the judge said. "You, Dr. Sax, are a family doctor in private practice. Is that correct?"

"That is correct," I said.

"And you are asking me to follow your recommendation rather than the guidelines of the American Academy of Pediatrics, published by their experts on this topic, isn't that correct?"

"That is correct," I said.

The judge ruled against the family. The girl has transitioned to the male role and has cut off all contact with her parents. She lives as a ward of the state and is now in foster care.

I attended public schools in Ohio, kindergarten through grade 12. But in my day, a kid couldn't go on a field trip without their parents' consent, let alone change their pronouns from "he" to "she" or "zhe" or "they." Parents today must advocate for their children and insist on their right to know what's going on in their kids' lives. Most teachers and most school leaders are willing and even eager to work with parents. Most primary care physicians and providers correctly regard a good parent-child relationship as essential to a child's well-being. But there are some teachers and some school administrators, and a few medical providers, who have a hostile attitude toward parents, who regard you as the enemy. You have to be on your guard.

7

Fragile

I had the privilege of visiting an outdoor kindergarten in Oberammergau, in the Bavarian Alps. What was most striking to me was the attitude toward risk and danger, which my hosts and other Germans told me was common throughout Germany. I saw 4-year-old girls and boys using sharp knives to whittle sticks they found in the woods. Four- and five-year-old children climbed tall trees without a harness or safety gear, and without help from a grown-up. On this trip and on my previous trips to schools in Germany and in German-speaking Switzerland, I found the general attitude toward risk to be profoundly different from the culture of "safetyism" which is now so prevalent in the United States.

I borrow the term "safetyism" from the book *The Coddling of the American Mind* by Greg Lukianoff and Jonathan Haidt. They describe how many American schools now prohibit any activity which might conceivably result in any injury to any child. The defining rule of safetyism: **if *any* child *might* get hurt, then *no* child**

is allowed to participate. American parents follow suit. Four-year-olds whittling sticks with sharp knives? Not happening.

But researchers suggest that prohibiting children from engaging in risky play, and repeatedly warning kids about the bad things that might happen if they do anything remotely dangerous, may actually increase kids' anxiety and cause kids to become more fragile.[1] Kids who have never climbed a tree, or whittled a stick with a knife, and who constantly hear warnings about the dangers inherent in everyday life, may be more likely to become anxious, sometimes without even knowing *why* they are anxious.

As a family doctor, I have seen how easily young kids can get injured when they play with sharp knives or climb trees. I molded a fiberglass cast to my daughter's right wrist when she broke it after falling from the top of a nine-foot jungle gym at 8 years of age. But it's not the end of the world if your kid cuts her finger with a knife, or scrapes her knee on tree bark, or breaks her wrist. The great majority of such injuries are easily treated, and the child is stronger for the experience. To quote another German: *Was mich nicht umbringt, macht mich stärker.*[2] What doesn't kill me, makes me stronger.

Of course, one of our prime responsibilities as parents is to keep our kids safe. If your toddler is waddling toward a busy street, you stop them. But be mindful in other situations where the tradeoff between risk and benefit is more nuanced. When you are tempted to say, "Don't do that, you might get hurt!"—pause for a moment. Remember that if kids continually hear "don't do that, you might get hurt," the result may be kids who are risk averse, fearful of the world around them, and fragile.[3]

I earned my medical degree way back in 1986. For most of my career as a family doctor, most parents were OK if their kid scraped their knee or sprained their ankle on the school playground. But today, if a kid sustains a minor injury at school or on the playground, parents now often swoop in like attorneys, demanding to know how the school could be so negligent. "I'm not paying all this money on a private school for my kid to come home injured," one mother told me as I examined her 11-year-old daughter's sprained ankle.

I paused, took a breath, and looked mom directly in the eye. "If your daughter gets through elementary school without a sprained ankle or a scraped knee," I said, "that's a deprived childhood. These are the kinds of experiences kids need to become strong. Without them, kids are fragile."

So what led you to suggest that Aaron should try playing football?" I asked Aaron's father, Steve.

"Actually, it was the nurse practitioner at the pediatrician's office who first brought it up. She showed us how his weight percentile was climbing but his height percentile wasn't changing. I remember I asked her, 'What are you trying to tell us?' And she said, 'Aaron is overweight.' She didn't mention football per se. She just said that Aaron needed to be more active, and she suggested after-school sports. Football was my idea. I played football all through middle school and high school and it helped me get into shape. It helped me to get strong. So that's where I was coming from."

"You mentioned that Aaron has always had a talent for video games. How old was Aaron when you first realized that?" I asked.

"Pretty young," Steve said. "I remember. Aaron was 6 years old. We were playing *Madden NFL Football*. You know that game?" I nodded. "Aaron beat me. By some crazy score. I think the final score was 62 to 7."

"He had 62 points, you had 7?" I asked.

"Yep. I was pathetic. I didn't play video games much with him after that," Steve said. "I just wasn't in his league. Plus, I never really saw the point. I'd rather go outside and throw a football around. An actual football."

"So what happened last fall?" I asked.

"I had been nagging Aaron for years about playing football, but he always ignored me. Then some of his friends, guys he played video games with, announced that they were going to try out for the JV team at school. That's the first time that Aaron showed any interest in playing the game. So he and I went to the park and we threw the ball around, did some blocking. I told him that he had potential. I wasn't lying. He's got a few extra pounds on board, but that's not a bad thing if you're playing the line. I told him how the left tackle position is one of the highest-paid positions in the NFL. You can actually earn millions of dollars a year being a big guy, as long as you're strong and you're fast and you don't mind taking a hit. He thought that was pretty interesting."

"What happened last fall?" I repeated.

"Aaron was pretty cocky when he went to the tryouts. He thought that being master of *Madden NFL Football* would give him an advantage. But the coach said he wanted to get a sense of who was in shape and who wasn't. So he had them do some sprints. Then he made everyone run a mile, and every boy was timed. Aaron's times in the sprints were terrible, and he took nearly 12 minutes to run a mile. One mile. He told me the coach said, 'Son, I have no idea whether you're going to be able to play this game or not. You're out of shape. I expect to see you back here tomorrow morning at 7 a.m. with the other kids who are out of shape. You'll run another mile around the track, then we'll go to the weight room.'"

"What happened? Did Aaron go back the next morning?" I asked.

"Nope. He never went back, period. That was his first and last foray into any kind of after-school sport. He said, 'I'm not a jock. I'll never be a jock. I don't *want* to be a jock. I'm a gamer.' I told him that you can be *both* an athlete *and* a gamer. I reminded him that lots of men who play in the NFL are big-time gamers as well. But he wasn't interested. He just retreated into his bedroom, closed the door, and kept on playing the games."

"So what's going on now?" I asked.

"He's just playing more and more. When I ask him what he wants to do with his life, he says he wants to be a professional gamer. He talks about these guys who are earning $100,000 a month, or more, playing video games."

"And you say?"

"What can I say?" Steve said. "Maybe that's his passion. That's what he says he really wants. Who am I to tell him that he shouldn't go after his dream? I just want him to be happy."

Julia always had a competitive streak. She always wanted to be #1 in her class. She may have inherited some of that drive from her parents: her mother is an investment banker, and her father is a surgeon. In any case, her parents were proud of the academic honors she earned beginning in elementary school. She was attending the top independent school in the city, a school which routinely sends graduates to the most selective colleges. And she was #1 in her class at that school, on track to be valedictorian.

She was already taking AP courses in 9th grade and earning As in every one as well as 5s on the Advanced Placement examinations with an occasional 4. When she started 11th grade, she decided to sign up for AP Physics, a course that students at her school usually took in 12th grade.[4] But Julia was already thinking of an independent study program for 12th grade, to do an engineering project at the university. She had decided, on her own, that taking AP Physics in 11th grade would be just the thing to impress the various people who would have to approve her program. She had to get special permission to take AP Physics as a junior. She obtained that permission.

"She has always been at the top, or very near the top, academically," her mom, Jennifer, told me. "But that was just *marginal* superiority. She was earning a 99 when the other kids were earning a 97. She wanted to do something that would catapult her into another league altogether. She wanted something that would set her apart from the rest, not only in the eyes of college admission officers, but in her own eyes. So that's where the idea for the senior year engineering project came from."

"What happened?"

"AP Physics was just way harder than she expected it to be. She had never really had any serious difficulty in school before. Everything always came easily to her. Physics was the first subject where she just didn't understand the concepts the first time around."

"When did she realize there might be a problem?" I asked.

"The first quiz," Jennifer answered. "Prior to that, I think Julia had some notion that maybe everything would be OK, she would be top of the class like always. She was studying really hard. The first quiz destroyed that notion. She got one of the lowest scores in the class, a 74. The teacher met with her afterward and told her it wasn't too late to drop the class."

"What happened?" I asked.

"It was the first week of October. I came home from work. She was in the bedroom with her door closed, which is unusual. Usually she leaves her door open. I went to the bedroom door, and I was about to knock when I heard something I never heard before. Sobbing. I had not heard her cry like that since she was a toddler. Convulsive, gasping sobs."

"What did you do?"

"I rushed into the room without knocking. She was on the bed, face down, crying into her pillow. Can you imagine what went through my mind? I didn't know anything about the physics exam. My first thought, to be honest, was that she had been sexually assaulted, that someone had victimized her. Because I thought, what else could cause her to be so incredibly upset? So I asked her, 'Are you OK? What happened?'"

"What did she tell you?"

"It wasn't easy for her to get the words out, but she managed to explain that she had gotten a low score on the quiz. To be honest, I had to put my hand over my mouth to keep from laughing. I was so relieved. Here I thought she had been the victim of some awful crime, and it was just a low mark on a quiz. But finally I said, 'Oh, honey, that's terrible. You must feel so bad. I understand.'"

"What happened next?"

"I tried to reassure her. I said that we could hire a tutor to help her. She said she didn't want a tutor. It took me a few days to understand why this was such a big deal. If she couldn't ace physics, then she wouldn't be able to do her big engineering project as a senior. Or at least not the way she had planned. She was discovering, maybe she wasn't as amazing a student as she thought she was. So it was pretty wrenching for her."

"When did she start taking medication?"

"Things just snowballed. I thought that she would come to her senses and put things in perspective. We did get a tutor for her, and I think the tutor was helpful. Her score on the next quiz was a 79. Still not great, but better. She could still pass the course. 'But I'll get a C!' she wailed. 'There are worse things in life than getting a C in physics,' I said. 'You don't understand,' she said. And the crying spells continued, except now she told me to get out of her bedroom. She didn't want me to try to comfort her. That's when I took her to see the pediatrician. He prescribed Lexapro, 10 milligrams. He said we should try it, maybe it would help."

"Did it help?"

"A little. Eventually she was able to talk about how she was feeling without bursting into tears. She was able to explain how humiliating it was for her to be near the bottom of the class. But by Thanksgiving she seemed to be slipping back, more withdrawn, moody all the time. So we decided to take her to the psychiatrist. Actually the pediatrician suggested it."

"What did the psychiatrist say?"

"The psychiatrist spent only a few minutes with us. I was hoping for a more thorough evaluation, but he didn't seem to think it was necessary. We had been squeezed in because they didn't have a regular appointment for weeks. He recommended adding Risperdal. He said that when an SSRI like Lexapro doesn't work, he likes to add Risperdal on top of the Lexapro. I looked it up online and I just freaked out when I read the side effects of Risperdal.

Weight gain. Diabetes. That's why I decided to come see you, for a second opinion. I read online that you are really skeptical about some of those medications."

Jean Twenge, a professor at San Diego State University who studies how the generations have changed over time, reports that "Many college faculty and staff report a noticeable fragility among today's students. Some describe them as 'teacups'—beautiful, but liable to break with the slightest drop."[5] I can tell you more stories similar to Aaron's story and Julia's story, stories which have been related to me by parents, or which I have observed firsthand in my role as a family physician. The common thread which connects the story of Aaron the out-of-shape gamer to Julia the would-be engineer is *fragility*. When Aaron came home from the tryout, why didn't he take up the coach's challenge to return, to try harder? When Julia discovered that she wasn't as smart as she thought she was, why did she collapse? My answer in both cases is that these kids are *fragile*. It doesn't take much for them to give up and retreat, as Aaron did, or to fall apart completely, as Julia did.

Fragility has become a characteristic of American children and teenagers to an extent unknown 30 years ago. That's what I'm seeing in the office today—and what I did not see in the office 30 years ago. But besides my observations and experience as a family doctor over the past three decades, several lines of evidence support my claim that young Americans today are more fragile in comparison with young Americans 20 or 30 years ago. The first and most obvious evidence is the extraordinary and continuing rise in the proportion of young Americans who are diagnosed and treated today for anxiety and depression, which we have already discussed.

That line of evidence is relevant in Julia's case since two physicians—a pediatrician and a psychiatrist—treated her with prescription medication for depression. But that line of evidence doesn't pertain in Aaron's case. Nobody has diagnosed Aaron with anything. In fact, Aaron is a pretty happy guy as long as you don't interrupt him while he's playing his video game.

But Aaron and Julia do share something in common. In each case, something inside seems to be missing: some inner strength and resilience which we took for granted in young people a few decades back, but which just didn't develop in these two. How can we quantify that? Can it be measured in statistics?

Maybe it can. In Aaron's story, the end result is a young man who has retreated from the real world into his bedroom in order to play video games. I have seen the same process in young adults—more often young men than young women—who come home from college, or drop out of college, to retreat into the bedroom with a computer screen or a video game. That's an increasingly common pathway I have observed in 20-somethings: young people whose dreams don't come true, who then give up, retreat, and return home to live with their parents or (if their parents have the means) live separately from their parents but remain supported by their parents.[6]

The phenomenon of young, able-bodied adults not working and not looking for work is becoming much more common in the United States. As recently as 2000, it was rare in this country compared to other countries. In the year 2000, young Americans led the world in the proportion of young people who were creating new businesses, and who were either working or looking for work, ahead of countries such as Sweden, Canada, the United Kingdom, Germany, France, Australia, and Poland. But today, the United States ranks *last* among the countries just mentioned.

Here's the listing from the year 2000, with each nation rank-ordered according to the proportion of young people 25 to 34 years of age who were either gainfully employed or actively looking for work, from highest to lowest:

1. **United States**
2. Sweden
3. Canada
4. United Kingdom
5. Germany
6. France
7. Australia
8. Poland

And here is the most recent listing, for the year 2022, with the rank order from the year 2000 shown in parentheses:[7]

1. United Kingdom (was #4 in 2000)
2. Poland (was #8 in 2000)
3. Canada (remained #3)
4. Australia (#7)
5. Germany (remained #5)
6. Sweden (#2)
7. France (#6)
8. **United States** (was #1)

A professor of economics at Harvard called this drop in the young American workforce "a very big puzzle."[8]

In a healthy culture, young adults drive much of the growth in the economy. They start new businesses. They are the most likely to become entrepreneurs. Think of Bill Gates launching Microsoft at the age of 20, or Steve Jobs launching Apple at the age of 21, or Mark Zuckerberg launching Facebook at the age of 19. But contrary to a common impression, the United States has become substantially *less* entrepreneurial over the past four decades. There has been a steady downward trend in the proportion of entrepreneurs in the United States since the 1980s, with no taper in that trend line: it's just heading down and down.[9] And when researchers break down the results by age group, the message is clear: the younger you are, the *less* likely you are to be an entrepreneur. Young adults are now much less likely to be entrepreneurs compared with adults 36 to 50, who are somewhat less likely to be entrepreneurs compared with adults 51 to 64.[10] Researchers have concluded that "the rate of new business formation in the United States has been cut in half over the past 35 years."[11] The decline is pervasive; it is seen in all 50 states; it is seen in all sectors of the economy; and it has become more homogenous across the United States over time. Every region in the USA is affected. As a remedy, researchers suggest "liberalized entry of high-skilled immigrants."[12]

When I share these findings in a presentation, some attendees argue that while the decline in entrepreneurship may reflect a growing reluctance of young people to take risks, a reluctance to take risks isn't the same thing as a marker of fragility. But I disagree. In fact, I think fragility—in the sense I'm using it here—can almost be *defined* as the reluctance to take risks. Think of those children at the outdoor kindergarten in Oberammergau, climbing trees and using sharp knives to whittle sticks or chop cucumbers.

The growing phenomenon of young Americans who are fragile, who give up easily, who no longer have the drive to start new businesses, may have huge economic consequences, but the causes do not lie in economics. The causes lie in American parenting, which now creates fragile kids in at least two different ways. One way is the cult of safetyism just described, which leads kids to be risk averse. The second is the prioritizing of relations with same-age peers over the parent-child relationship.

Prioritizing kids' relationships with other kids over their relationship with their parents results in a shift from an adult frame of reference to a kid's frame of reference. Often a child or teen just is not that concerned about what her parents think. She's more concerned with what her friends think.

You can see that dynamic in play with Aaron the would-be football player, the boy who gave up after the coach told him he was out of shape. Aaron wants to look cool in the eyes of his friends. When he's playing video games, he's top dog. His friends are impressed by how great he is at the video game. If he returned to the football field, he would be at the bottom of a totem pole, with the athlete at the top and chubby Aaron huffing and puffing far below.

Julia is concerned about her friends' opinions, but she is mortified by her own self-assessment. She has constructed a self-concept which is all about being amazing. Her struggles in physics have punctured that bubble, leading to an existential crisis. "If I am not the amazing student I thought I was, then who am I?" she asks herself, and she has no answer.

My assessment is that one cause of the fragility in Aaron's case, as well as Julia's case, is the failure to prioritize the parent-child relationship. Aaron and Julia would be the first to tell you that they love their parents. But they don't really care much what their parents think. Or more precisely: Aaron is more concerned about what his peers think than what his parents think. Julia is more concerned about her inflated self-concept than about what her parents think. *Kids need to value their parents' opinion as their first scale of value*, at least throughout childhood and adolescence. (Of course, this rule cannot apply if the parents are incompetent or pathological or absent. My assumption in this book is that you are a caring and concerned parent. If that assumption isn't valid, then this book is not for you.) If parents don't come first, then kids become fragile. Here's why:

A good parent-child relationship is robust and unconditional. My daughter might shout at me, *"I hate you!"* But she would know that her outburst is not going to change our relationship. She would know that my wife and I both still love her. That won't change.

Peer relations, by contrast, are fragile by nature. Emily and Melissa may be best friends, but both of them know that one wrong word might fracture the relationship beyond repair. That's one reason why Emily is so frantic about checking her text messages every five minutes. If Melissa sends a text, and Emily does not promptly respond, Emily is afraid that Melissa may misinterpret her silence as indicating a lack of enthusiasm. In peer relations, everything is conditional and contingent. Everything can change in a minute.

Aaron doesn't want to look incompetent in the eyes of his peers, not for a week, not for a single day. So he will not risk the humbling experience of being the least-fit player. Julia can't bear the thought of being anything other than a top student. So she will not, cannot, risk the humbling experience of being below the class average in her physics class. From the adult perspective, she did take a risk by enrolling in AP Physics a year earlier than usual. But from her perspective, that wasn't a risk, just another manifestation of her bloated self-esteem. Her self-concept *depended* on being #1. When she is no longer #1, or close to #1, her self-concept crumbles. I agree with the two other physicians who evaluated her that she meets formal criteria for the diagnosis of depression. But the question those other doctors failed to ask is, *Why* is she depressed? The answer is that the bubble of her self-concept has been pricked by the rough burr of reality. And the appropriate remedy for Julia, I believe, is not Risperdal or any other psychiatric medication, but rather for her to construct a different self-concept—one rooted not in extraordinary academic achievement but in the *unconditional* love and acceptance which her parents are ready to offer to her.

Children and teenagers need unconditional love and acceptance today no less than they did 30 years ago or 50 years ago. But they cannot get unconditional love and acceptance from their peers, or from a report card. That's one factor driving the explosion in the prevalence of anxiety and depression among American teenagers as they frantically try to secure their attachment to other teens, as they try to gain *unconditional* love and acceptance from sources which are unable to provide it.[13]

Many American parents accept this situation as an inevitable consequence of 21st-century life. But they are mistaken. In my own practice, I have seen that when teens have a strong relationship with their parents and really care what their parents think, those teens are much less likely to be anxious or depressed than the typical American teen who is more concerned about what the other kids think.

All of us, as parents, need to establish the primacy of the parent-child relationship over the peer-to-peer relationship, over academics, over other activities. How to accomplish that?

One simple strategy is to schedule vacations just for the family. When your daughter asks whether her best friend can come along on the family vacation, the answer must be NO. If the best friend comes along, then your daughter will spend a significant portion of time on the vacation bonding with her best friend. The main purpose of the family vacation should be to strengthen the bonds between parent and child, not to give the kids an expensive play date. Even simpler is to create rituals, such as a once-a-week parent-daughter or parent-son visit to the coffee shop or casual restaurant. Taking a walk together to the coffee shop, if a shop is within walking distance, is a good opportunity to talk and to listen to whatever your daughter or son has to say. The family supper, the family trip to the movies, even a ride in the car—all should provide opportunities to strengthen these bonds.

In all your arrangements for your child, try to make connecting with adults a higher priority than connecting with your child's same-age peers or academics or after-school activities. Prioritize your extended family and your close adult friends in the life of your child. If you have the opportunity to move closer to your child's aunts, uncles, and grandparents, do it. When you are planning a vacation, look for opportunities for your child to connect with her aunts, uncles, and grandparents. You want to give your child a different perspective. You want to connect her to your culture. That task is arguably more difficult today than at any previous time in history. Today, the default for most American kids is a primary attachment to same-age peers.

There is another important element in Aaron's story, and that is his involvement in social media, linked to his online video games. As recently as 20 years ago, I can recall boys who were in situations similar to Aaron's. They failed to make the team, so they worked harder, got in shape, went back the next week or the next season, and they made the team. Those stories were common 20 years ago. They are rare today. How come?

I think the online world is part of the answer. Twenty years ago, the Internet was slow. Online video games were painfully sluggish. But today's online world provides Aaron with an alternative culture created mostly by other young people. His parents regard Aaron's immersion in the world of video games as unusual. They wonder why Aaron is not more concerned about being out of shape physically. But Aaron's reference point is not the real world of his parents, but the online world where he hangs with his gamer friends. He is in touch with literally hundreds of other people who are roughly his own age and whose priorities are similar to his. Video games come first. In his online world, his unconcerned, laid-back style is the norm, not the exception. If he were to express an earnest desire to get in shape so that he could play sports rather than spend all his time with a game controller and a video screen, he might get a derisive response from his online peers. Or they might think he was joking.

Aaron's father isn't sure what to do. He said to me, "Who am I to tell him that he shouldn't go after his dream? I just want him to be happy." That's a common response. The kids themselves often say something along the same lines. Another young person in a similar situation said to me, "I'm just doing my own thing.

Whatever floats your boat, you know?" That notion—*whatever floats your boat; if it feels good, do it*—is now pervasive.

The parent-child attachment has to be the first priority. The irony here is that the majority of middle-income and affluent American parents know about attachment. Some of them have even read books about "attachment parenting." They know all about offering their newborn baby unconditional love and acceptance. By 6 months of age, a baby who is born to middle-income or affluent American parents is likely to be surrounded with nurturing and love. At one year of age, American toddlers are just as competent as toddlers in the Netherlands or New Zealand. But after the second birthday, American parents begin to go astray.

Your parenting style has to change as your child grows up. Think of a high school cheerleader. Now think of a varsity high school coach. When your child is an infant or toddler, you play the role of the cheerleader. When your toddler stumbles and falls, then clambers back up again, you say, "Good job! Way to go!" But as your child gets older, your role must shift. Less cheerleader, more coach.[14] You have to correct. To redirect. To point out shortcomings. If your teenage son can't think of any better career objective than playing video games, then you need to turn off the devices and get him outdoors, into the real world. You have to teach your child your values rather than allowing him or her to adopt by default the values promoted by the contemporary culture.

The main mechanisms by which contemporary American culture today asserts its primacy in the hearts of American kids are social media, high-speed online games, and the smartphone. None of these existed in the lives of American kids 30 years ago. But today, it's common to see an American 4-year-old playing with an iPad, complete with Internet access. That's particularly true in affluent communities. And it's becoming common to see an American 10-year-old with her own smartphone.

When a 10-year-old is given her own smartphone, and she spends more time looking online to see what other kids are doing, the more likely she is to look to them for guidance about what matters and what doesn't. It's crazy for a 10-year-old kid to look primarily to other kids for guidance, but that is what is happening. And the phone separates you from your child.

The technology and the devices spread a toxic culture that divides the generations and undermines parental authority. The kids are more likely to understand the technology than the adults are. The 9-year-old easily conquers the vagaries of Instagram and TikTok. Her 40-something parents may struggle. Or they may not see the point. Your daughter and her friends are more likely than you are to know how to upload a photo from a smartphone to an Instagram page, complete with digital special effects. That's one reason why your daughter may come to value her friends' opinions above yours. Her friends seem to know more about important things than you do. And the more time she spends on Instagram, the more likely she is to think that knowing about Instagram is important.

Some countries have traditions which help to maintain parent-child bonds. In the Netherlands, the majority of elementary schools close at noon every Wednesday so that kids can enjoy some quality midweek time with their parents.[15] Many Dutch employers give their employees Wednesday afternoons off, or all day Wednesday off. Throughout German-speaking Switzerland, most elementary schools close for two hours at lunch, every day, so that kids can go home and eat lunch with a parent.[16] Many Swiss employers accommodate that tradition by giving their employees 2½ hours off for lunch so that a parent can be at home with the child.[17]

We used to do something similar in this country. Growing up outside Cleveland, Ohio, in the 1960s and 1970s, I remember walking home from school for lunch every day.[18] For me, it seemed pointless because my mom had to work and I was walking to an empty home. (My parents were divorced; my father lived in Los Angeles.) My mother's employer didn't give her a two-hour lunch break so that she could be at home with her kids.

So what are we supposed to do? American employers aren't going to give us, the employees, two hours off for lunch. They're not going to give us every Wednesday afternoon off. So we have to fight for supper with our families. Fight for time with our kids. Cancel or forego early-evening after-school activities, if need be, in order to have more evening meals together. Your kids can't attach to you if they hardly ever see you. And turn the devices off.

In Chapter 1, we considered Dr. Gordon Neufeld's observations on the disintegration of the parent-child bond over the past 20 years. Dr. Neufeld's main idea is that many of the problems we see with North American kids today—the defiance, the disrespect, the disconnection from the real world—can be traced to the lack of a strong attachment between parents and their kids. Or more precisely, to the fact that kids now form their primary attachment with same-age peers rather than with parents. As Dr. Neufeld writes, "the waning of adult authority is directly related to the weakening of attachments with adults and their displacement by peer attachments."[19]

The results are often downright weird. The wrong attachment style in childhood and adolescence results in the wrong attachment style in early adulthood. The key to healthy child development is to do the right thing *at the right time*. Throughout childhood and adolescence, the primary attachment of a child should be to the parent. If a child has a strong primary attachment to a parent from infancy through adolescence, then when the child becomes an adult, that bond will break naturally, as an acorn breaks open naturally at the right time so that a new tree can grow. Such a child, once she becomes an adult, is ready to head out confidently into the real world as an independent young adult. But increasingly, Dr. Neufeld and others are finding that young people across North America are not ready to step into the adult world. The same girl who refused to talk with her mom at 13 years of age is now texting her mom five times a day at age 24. The acorn, having broken open too early, does not have the strength to become a tree.

Earlier in this chapter I wrote that "Kids need to value their parents' opinion as their first scale of value, at least throughout childhood and adolescence." When I say that to parents, I often get pushback. A parent may say, "I think my child needs to develop her own values, independent of what I think." And of course that's true—*at the right time*. But it's not true at age 9 or even age 15. The result of parents letting kids make all the big decisions at age 9 or age 15 is young adults at age 25 or even 35 desperately calling their parents for help because the young adult is clueless. When kids value their parents' opinion at age 15, they are more likely to be confident of their own judgment at age 25 or 35. That's what I have observed as a family doctor over the past 30+ years.

Parents have to regain the central place in the lives of their children. Same-age friends are great for your child. But your child's first allegiance must be to you, not to her best friend. The contemporary culture of texting, Instagram, YouTube, TikTok, and online video games has twisted this fundamental reality, promoting and accelerating the premature transfer of allegiance to same-age peers.

Why are American kids today so fragile? One fundamental change driving this fragility is the breaking of the bonds across generations so that kids now value the opinions of same-age peers, or their own self-concept, more than they care about the good regard of their parents and other adults. The result is a cult of success because success is the easiest way to impress your peers and yourself. But the cult of success just sets the kid up for catastrophe when failure arrives, as we saw in Julia's case. And failure will always arrive, sooner or later.

We all experience failure. The *willingness to fail*, and to move on with no loss of enthusiasm, is a mark of character.[20] The opposite of fragility, as we have discussed fragility in this chapter, is the willingness to fail. When kids are secure in the unconditional acceptance of their parents, then they can find the courage to venture and to fail. When kids value the good regard of their peers, or their own self-concept, above the good regard of their parents, then they lose the willingness to fail. They become fragile.

PART TWO

Solutions

8

What Matters?

Which one of the following, measured when a child is 11 or 12 years of age, is the best predictor of health, wealth, and happiness 20 years later, when that child has become an adult 31 or 32 years old?

A. Emotional stability
B. Grade point average
C. Self-control
D. Openness to new ideas
E. Friendliness

The correct answer is C, self-control.

Until fairly recently, the answer to this question would have been a matter of opinion or guesswork. Different people had different theories of parenting and child development, each of which had a different scale of value for what characteristics might predict good outcomes. But in the mid- to late-20th century, teams of researchers in North America and around the world embarked on long-term longitudinal cohort studies in which children were recruited early in life and then followed throughout childhood, into adolescence, and into adulthood. Such studies, launched 20 or 30 or more years ago, have now borne fruit, allowing us to determine what characteristics of a child that you can influence best predict the child's health, wealth, and happiness as an adult.

For many years now, researchers have been studying correlations between personality traits and outcomes, taking care to separate these outcomes from other factors such as IQ, household income, race, and ethnicity. When these correlations are studied over years and decades—when we consider how a trait possessed by a child at age 10 predicts that individual's health and wealth at, say, age 38—then we can begin to move from statistical correlation to causal inference. That's a fancy way of saying that we can move from saying that A and B are associated to saying that A *caused* B. We can start to say, with some confidence, *what matters*. We can begin to answer the question: What should we be doing as parents in order to improve the likelihood of good outcomes for our children?

In one study, researchers looked at American adults nationwide who came from a wide range of backgrounds: affluent and low-income, Black and White and Asian and Hispanic. They recorded how much money they had earned in the past year, how happy they were, how much wealth they possessed overall, and how satisfied they were with their life. The researchers correlated those outcomes with personality traits, and separately with intelligence. Not surprisingly, they found that intelligence predicts both income and wealth. People who are more intelligent earn more money and have a higher net worth, on average, compared with people of below-average intelligence. But intelligence does not predict happiness. Smart people are not happier or unhappier, on average, compared with less-intelligent people. Nor does intelligence predict life satisfaction. Smarter people might have more money compared with less-smart people, on average, but they are not any more satisfied with their lives overall.

You might reasonably wonder whether *any* individual trait can predict happiness, *and* wealth, *and* life satisfaction. There is only one trait that does: it is Conscientiousness. Conscientiousness comprises a constellation of traits including self-control, honesty, and reliability. Individuals who are more Conscientious earn more money and save more money, even after researchers adjust for intelligence, race, ethnicity, and education. Individuals who are more Conscientious are also significantly happier than individuals who are less Conscientious, and they are substantially more satisfied with their lives.[1] Other studies have shown that Conscientiousness predicts better health and longer life.[2] People who are more Conscientious are less likely to become obese,[3] less likely to develop Alzheimer's disease,[4] more likely to live longer and happier lives,[5] and more likely to be satisfied with their life.[6] Teenagers who are more Conscientious are less likely subsequently to use drugs or alcohol and less likely to engage in risky sexual behaviors.[7] Although it's true that more-Conscientious individuals enjoy higher socioeconomic status on average compared with less-Conscientious individuals, the benefit of Conscientiousness with regard to health can't be attributed to socioeconomic status, for two reasons: first, the researchers in all these studies controlled for socioeconomic status; second, the magnitude of the health benefit of Conscientiousness is more than three times the benefit associated with socioeconomic status.[8] No other trait can pull off this hat trick. No other trait predicts significantly greater wealth, *and* health, *and* happiness among those who possess it compared with those who do not.

In some ways, this is not a new insight. Nearly 300 years ago, in 1735, Benjamin Franklin wrote, *"Early to bed, early to rise, makes a man healthy, wealthy, and wise."* Going to bed early—i.e., deliberately abstaining from the temptations of the night—and getting up early—i.e., resisting the temptation to sleep in late—are good measures of *self-control*, and self-control is the characteristic most emblematic of Conscientiousness. We can update Franklin's maxim in 21st-century English as follows: "Exercising self-control in terms of when you go to sleep and when you wake up is associated with improved health, greater wealth, and greater academic achievement." And that's a true statement. But Franklin's version is catchier.

When I ask parents whether their kids are on the right road, many respond by mentioning something about grades and/or test scores. Parents often assume that if their kid is above average as measured by grades and test scores, then their kid has an above-average chance of achieving happiness and success. Conversely, if their kid is below average in academic achievement, many parents are frantically searching for an explanation and a remedy, perhaps medication for ADHD, etc.

In other words: Many parents *act as if* good grades and test scores are the best measures of achievement and the most reliable key to future happiness. But they are mistaken. If you want your child to be healthy *and* wealthy *and* wise, then your first priority should not be to boost your child's grades or test scores, but to teach your child to be Conscientious: to be honest, to be reliable, to be self-controlled.

et's take a closer look at the data, starting with drugs and alcohol. Addiction to drugs and alcohol in adulthood can be measured. If Ted has been in drug rehab three times, and Ted tells you that he is still struggling with addiction, and Ted's friends agree that he is struggling, then it's a good bet that Ted has a problem.

Grades and test scores at 11 years of age don't accurately predict whether that individual will grow up to be an alcoholic or a drug addict. The best predictor of whether your 11-year-old will grow up to have a problem with drugs or alcohol is Conscientiousness, and the best single measure of Conscientiousness is self-control. Researchers found that children who scored high on measures of self-control at 11 years of age were much less likely to report problems with substance abuse at 32 years of age—and their friends gave reports which confirmed the same trend. But kids who scored low on measures of self-control at 11 years of age were much more likely to have problems with substance abuse two decades later, at 32 years of age.[9]

Again, some parents push back when I share this finding. If a child is an outstanding student or artist, a real prodigy, those parents often assume that their child's gifts will protect him or her from drug addiction. That's when I find that stories of real people are helpful. I sometimes mention Jim Morrison, lead singer for The Doors. Morrison was an outstanding student whose high school teachers were awed by the depth and breadth of his scholarship. And Morrison's artistic gifts as a composer and musician are beyond dispute. Morrison died in 1971, addicted to heroin, at 27 years of age.[10]

The same relationship holds for overall physical health. Kids who scored lowest on self-control at 11 years of age were most likely to be in poor physical health at 32 years of age. Likewise, kids who scored highest in self-control at 11 years of age were least likely to be in poor physical health at age 32.

Let's talk about money. What factors at 11 years of age predict who's going to be earning the most money at age 32? Who's going to be in financial distress? (Incidentally, those are two separate questions. How much money you earn is not an infallible predictor of whether you will be in financial distress. People earning $600,000 a year are somewhat less likely to be in financial distress compared with people earning $60,000 a year, but only somewhat. Regardless of income, it's often a struggle for people to live within their means.) Once again, self-control as measured in childhood predicts outcomes with uncanny accuracy. Kids who had the most self-control at age 11 had the highest income and the best credit score, and were least likely to be struggling financially, at age 32. Conversely, kids with the least self-control at age 11 were, at age 32, the most likely to be struggling financially and the least likely to have a good credit score.[11]

This information is important because you can help your child to become more Conscientious: to be more honest, to be more trustworthy, to have better self-control. There are many things you can't change. You can't change the color of your child's eyes. You can't change how tall they will grow up to be. Many other parameters which influence long-term outcomes in these studies, such as household income, also are not easily changed. Likewise, some aspects of personality are harder to change than others. But there is good evidence that you can boost your kid's Conscientiousness—including honesty and self-control—in a matter of weeks without spending any money.[12]

How do you help an 8-year-old build self-control? You say, *No dessert until you eat your vegetables.*

How do you help a teenager build self-control? You say, *No video games until you've done all your homework and all your chores.*

As a family doctor, I have personally witnessed a child change from impulsive and out-of-control to self-controlled within six weeks. Without medication. All it takes is for the parents seriously to implement a simple program that builds self-control. You already know how to do this. *No video games until the homework is done. No use of the cell phone until you do your chores.*

Let me give you a tip. If you want to become a more authoritative parent, if you are going to insist on your child being honest and self-controlled, then sit down with your child and say so. Every household has rules, most of which are unspoken. They are matters of habit. If you are going to change the rules, tell your child what you are doing and why. Parents who explicitly announce, *Things Are Changing As Of Today,* then enforce the new rules and are not cowed when their child yells, *You are totally ruining my life—I hate you!* are consistently surprised by how dramatic the change is. Not in one day. Not in one week. The first week can be really difficult. But after six weeks of consistent enforcement of the rules, your child will be more respectful of you and other adults, and everyone in the family will be enjoying life more.

Your child's Conscientiousness is not hardwired. It is not determined at birth. It is learned. You must teach it.

One key point: If you are making a change, announcing, "New Rules For The Household Starting Today," then it's crucial that both parents be on the same page. The big announcement has to come from both parents and should come only after both parents have agreed on every item of substance. I have seen too many homes where one parent is the strict parent and the other is the permissive parent, creating a "good cop / bad cop" dynamic which the kids exploit to play one parent against the other. Don't let your kids see you arguing this topic. Work out any differences you have with your spouse or partner privately, out of earshot. Always present a united front to your kids. (This can be crazy difficult for divorced parents who share custody, as I have seen.)

What is true of self-control is true of the other aspects of Conscientiousness, such as honesty, responsibility, reliability, and industriousness. There is one truth you can't escape: *you must teach by example.* You can't expect your child to exercise self-control if you stay up past midnight streaming Netflix or surfing the Web or scrolling through TikTok. You can't expect your child to be responsible if you don't keep your word. And you can't expect your child to be industrious if you yourself are looking for the easy way out.

To become a better parent, you must become a better person.

Let's look at another study in which researchers followed kids from birth through adulthood. In this study, the researchers enrolled every child born at local city hospitals, more than 17,000 babies in all. Then they followed those 17,000+ babies at regular intervals, right up through 38 years of age.[13] Dr. James Heckman is a Nobel laureate in economics at the University of Chicago who analyzed the data on that large cohort of 17,000+ babies. Dr. Heckman writes, "Numerous instances can be cited of high-IQ people who failed to achieve success in life because they lacked self-discipline, and low-IQ people who succeeded by virtue of persistence, reliability, and self-discipline."[14] Dr. Heckman's analysis of the cohort data has led him to conclude that grades and test scores "are poor predictors of success in life because they measure only one skill—cognitive achievement....Far too much credit is given to cognitive skills....Character skills play pivotal roles."[15]

So: One of your most essential duties as a parent is to teach Conscientiousness. Let's talk more seriously about how to do that. I find some parents who act as though their job is simply to teach their child to parrot the usual clichés: *If at first you don't succeed, try again. If you try hard enough, your dream will come true.*

By the age of 6, most American kids know these slogans and can produce the right answers when requested. So the parent thinks the job is done.

The job isn't even started.

Teaching Conscientiousness requires a different approach than teaching kids to be smart. Let's start with smart. What's the secret to raising smart kids? Stanford professor Carol Dweck thinks she knows the answer. Her secret, in one sentence: never tell your child that he or she is a smart kid (identity); instead, praise them for working hard (behavior).[16] Many parents who have never heard of Carol Dweck have nevertheless heard of her famous experiment in which she randomly assigned children to two groups. Each group was given the same math quiz, which was easy. Most students earned a perfect score. In the first group, children were told, "You got a perfect score! You are so smart!" (identity). In the second group, students were told, "You earned a perfect score! You must have *tried really hard!*" (behavior). Then children in both groups were given a more difficult math quiz. The students in the first group, who were praised for being smart, did badly on the harder quiz. They gave up too easily. But the students in the second group, who were praised for trying hard, did much better: they kept working on the harder problems until they succeeded in solving them.

Professor Dweck believes that if you praise a child for being smart, that child develops a "fixed mindset" that they have a certain amount of intelligence, that their IQ is fixed. If the child then encounters a problem they can't solve, the child may think, *I'm not smart enough to do this*, and the child gives up. Professor Dweck recommends that you instead praise the child for trying hard. Teach them that your intelligence is not a fixed quantity, but that your intelligence instead depends on a *growth mindset*. If you try harder, you can become smarter.

In other words, Dr. Dweck says that you should praise kids not based on their identity (smart / not smart), but based on their behavior (trying hard / not trying hard). In the realm of cognitive achievement—motivating kids to learn stuff in school—there is good evidence to support Professor Dweck's belief.[17]

But teaching the virtues of Conscientiousness may be different. The students at my daughter's school were asked to bring a dollar to school to buy a special pencil. My daughter's friend forgot to bring her dollar. So my daughter gave her the dollar that she had brought to school to buy the same pencil, which meant that my daughter came home without the coveted pencil. Should I say to my daughter, *That was a very kind thing you did*, or should I say, *You are a very kind person*? Does it make any difference? If Professor Dweck's rule applies in the realm of virtue, then praising the behavior—*that was a very kind thing you did*—would be a better strategy than making a statement about identity: *you are a very kind person*. But there is now good evidence that when it comes to teaching virtue, Professor Dweck's approach is precisely the wrong way to go.

When it comes to teaching virtue, identity seems to work better than behavior. *You are a very kind person* works better than *That was a very kind thing you did.* In one study, students were less likely to cheat when they were told that the researchers were studying the prevalence of *cheaters.* The proportion of students who cheated more than doubled when researchers instead said that they were studying the prevalence of *cheating.*[18] Words make a difference. Saying "don't be a cheater" (identity) is a more effective instruction than saying "don't cheat" (behavior).[19] Apparently kids are more comfortable cheating if they don't see themselves as cheaters. Likewise, researchers have recently found that young children are more likely to help with a project if they are encouraged to "be a helper" rather than merely asked "to help."[20]

In a study of American high school students, more than 60 percent admitted to cheating on homework or on tests in the past year. In the same study, more than 80 percent of the same students said that their own personal ethics were "above average."[21] In the minds of many American students, ethical behavior no longer requires "not cheating on tests." They do not see themselves as "cheaters" even though they did, in fact, cheat. They see themselves as nice kids who occasionally cheat. But they aren't cheaters.

Teach your child that there is no escape from reality. What you *do* influences who you *are.* Behavior influences identity and eventually becomes identity. If you cheat, over and over, you are—or will soon become—a cheater. Your actions will, over time, change your character. These are some of the moral fundamentals which parents used to teach, but which many parents no longer do.

Cheating isn't new. But before roughly 1995, the kids who were most likely to cheat on tests or homework were not the academic high achievers. Today that's no longer the case. Today, the cream of the academic crop is just as likely to engage in cheating compared with students lower down the academic totem pole.[22] Howard Gardner is a professor at Harvard who has been studying academic integrity since the early 1990s. He has said that in recent years, "the ethical muscles have atrophied." The attitude which he now finds at the most selective universities—and which he did not find there 20 years earlier—is, *We want to be famous and successful, we think our colleagues are cutting corners, we'll be damned if we'll lose out to them.*[23] More than 25 percent of the Harvard class of 2023 admitted to cheating on a closed-book test or homework assignment, including 20 percent of those who said that they had a perfect 4.0 grade point average. Those numbers may be an understatement: in the same survey, the same students estimated that "about half" of their classmates had cheated during their time at Harvard.[24]

Stanford University has traditionally relied on an honor system: students promise not to cheat, and there are no proctors in the exam rooms. Stanford faculty, aware of widespread cheating, recently voted to change the honor code, to allow proctors in exam rooms during exams. Students protested, asserting that the proposed change implied a lack of trust in students, and that the presence of proctors in the exam rooms would damage students' mental health. The faculty backed down.[25]

In defense of today's American teens: they are immersed in a popular culture which preaches that self-control is the one remaining sin in a world which has otherwise been washed free of guilt and responsibility. "If It Feels Good, Do It" and "Whatever

Floats Your Boat" define 21st-century American popular culture. Exercising self-restraint in today's teen culture is downright
un-American.

In the opening chapter, I introduced you to Bill Phillips, father
of four sons (remember the Breathalyzer?). Andrew is the oldest of the four. Andrew is also one of the most talented athletes
I have ever met in more than three decades as a family doctor.
Early in the summer after 10th grade, Andrew attended a week-
long football camp at the University of Maryland. At the end of
the camp, the head coach of the Maryland football team called
attention to Andrew as the most outstanding player at the camp.
Coach Friedgen publicly announced that he would offer Andrew a
full scholarship to play football at Maryland at the earliest allow-
able moment under NCAA rules. "I want you to come play with
us. I want you to be a Terrapin," the coach said to Andrew.

Andrew told me that he was flying high at that moment. It's
pretty special when the head coach of an NCAA Division I football team calls attention to how great you are when you still have
two years of high school left.

When Bill Phillips arrived to pick up his son and heard about
his son's new celebrity status, he made an unexpected announcement. "I don't think I mentioned this to you," Bill said to Andrew,
"but you'll be heading up to Maine next week. Your summer job
for the rest of the summer is going to be working on a fishing
boat." Bill Phillips didn't ask his son, "*What would you think of
working on a fishing boat this summer?*" He just told Andrew that
Andrew would be working on a fishing boat.

Sure enough, one week later, Andrew was in Portland, Maine,
cleaning dead fish guts from the deck of a rusting fishing boat.

(Bill Phillips owned a fishing business.) Andrew's coworker was a convicted felon who had just been released from prison after serving a 15-year sentence for selling drugs. "And he was Mexican, and he had become a born-again Christian while he was in the penitentiary," Andrew told me. "So there I was on the deck of this dilapidated boat, listening to this Mexican ex-convict telling me about selling hard drugs, and getting busted, and coming to Jesus. Definitely not the kind of guy I would meet at my high school." Andrew was attending an elite private high school in Maryland.

Bill Phillips didn't preach to his son about Conscientiousness and the virtues of hard work. He didn't say anything. He just put his son to work at a tough summer job. Andrew learned the lesson well. At the time, though, Andrew wasn't happy. "I did feel a little resentful. Other guys were having all kinds of fun adventures and camping trips, and there I was on this dumb boat cleaning fish guts off the deck. But now I understand why my dad made me do it. To give me a taste of the real world. To show me something about how other people live."

That's how you teach the virtue of hard work. That's also how you teach empathy: not by asking, "*How would you feel if you were that man?*" but rather by insisting that the adolescent spend a summer alongside someone from a different background so that they can learn the stories firsthand.

You don't teach virtue by preaching virtue. You teach virtue by requiring virtuous behavior, so that virtuous behavior becomes a habit.

There is a notion prevalent among American parents that kids need to be convinced or persuaded that an action is right before the child should be asked to do it. If you want kids to act virtuously, according to this assumption, you must first persuade your child of the rightness of virtuous behavior. That sounds logical. It might even make sense, in some circumstances, if we're talking about grown-ups.

But even for grown-ups, there is strong evidence that the arrow of causality points in the other direction. Behaving virtuously leads people to become more virtuous, as a rule. Again, this insight is not new. More than a century ago, the American psychologist William James observed,

> Common sense says we lose our fortune, are sorry and weep; we meet a bear, are frightened and run; we are insulted by a rival, are angry and strike.... [But] this order of sequence is incorrect.... The more rational statement is that we feel sorry because we cry, angry because we strike, afraid because we tremble, and not that we cry, strike, or tremble, because we are sorry, angry, or fearful, as the case may be.[26]

There is a 2,000-year tradition along the same lines with regard to virtue. If you compel children to *act* more virtuously, they actually become more virtuous. In the biblical Book of Proverbs, which scholars tell us was written more than 2,500 years ago, we read, *Train up a child in the way he should go, and when he is old he will not depart from it.*[27] In other words, if you compel a child to behave virtuously, then when he is an adult he will continue to behave virtuously.

What does the published research have to say about such an approach?

I think a fair summary of the empirical research would be that the Book of Proverbs is too optimistic. There are no guarantees. But we can tweak that line from the Book of Proverbs so that it does align with contemporary research. The line, tweaked, would read something like this: *Train up a girl or boy in the way they should go, and when they grow up and go away to college, you will have* **improved the odds**. There are no guarantees. But if you instill habits of good behavior and self-control in your son or daughter throughout childhood and adolescence, then the research strongly suggests that you have improved the odds that your child will continue to do the right thing when they move away. Conversely, if you subscribe to the 21st-century American notion that parents should let kids be free to do pretty much whatever they want ("good parenting means letting kids decide, right?"), and your son is spending hours a night masturbating over pornography—which has become very common for American boys[28]—and your daughter is spending hours a night editing her pics for her Instagram or scrolling through TikTok, then what are the odds that when they arrive at college they will say, *Ah, now that I have arrived at college and behold, my peers are spending so much time on social media sites and playing video games, I will nevertheless turn over a new leaf and become a more virtuous person?* Not very likely.

The Western tradition in parenting is to inculcate virtuous habits into children. Again, this goes way back. In the *Nicomachean Ethics*, Aristotle wrote that a person becomes virtuous by doing virtuous acts. Behavior becomes identity. The historian Will Durant, commenting on Aristotle, observed that "we are what we repeatedly do. Excellence, then, is not an act but a habit."[29]

The Western tradition begins not only with the Greeks and the Romans, but also with Judaism. For that reason, I will ask your permission to quote one more time from the Hebrew Bible, this time from the book of Deuteronomy. God has just given the

commandments at Mount Sinai, and the text says וְשִׁנַּנְתָּם לְבָנֶיךָ
V'shinantam l'vanecha. Those two Hebrew words are usually
translated into English as *Teach them diligently to your children* or
something along those lines. But that's not what the Hebrew says.
It would be easy to say that in Biblical Hebrew: the verb would be
lamad, to teach. But the verb is not *lamad*, it is *shanan*. *Shanan*
doesn't mean "to teach." It means to incise, or to chisel in stone, or
to cut with a knife.[30] So a better translation would be something
like "Inscribe these laws, incise these laws, in the hearts of your
children." "Teach them diligently" is watered down.

You teach virtue by requiring children to behave virtuously. In
other words, you ask kids to pretend that they are virtuous before
they really are. As psychologist Adam Grant observes, "People
often believe that character causes action, but when it comes to
producing moral children, we need to remember that action also
shapes character."[31]

As I have already noted, this is not a new idea. Aristotle wrote
about it more than 2,000 years ago. In the mid-20th century, C. S.
Lewis put the same idea this way:

> The pretence leads up to the real thing. When you are not feeling
> particularly friendly but know you ought to be, the best thing you
> can do, very often, is put on a friendly manner and behave as if you
> were a nicer person than you actually are. And in a few minutes,
> as we have all noticed, you will be really feeling friendlier than you
> were. **Very often the only way to get a quality in reality is to start
> behaving as if you had it already.**[32]

*Very often the only way to get a quality in reality is to start be-
having as if you had it already.* Those words were written more

than 70 years ago. They expressed wisdom which was common knowledge then, but no longer.

How you act, what you do day to day, influences the kind of person you are and the kind of person you are becoming. If you act virtuously, day in and day out, you become more virtuous. But this process works the other way as well. Former Yale professor William Deresiewicz interviewed graduates of elite American universities who had little sense of what they wanted to do with their lives. So, some of them decided to get a job working for a Wall Street investment bank or management consultancy. If you don't know what your passion is, or what you really want to do, then—as Deresiewicz's interviewees told him—"you might as well go to Wall Street and make a lot of money if you can't think of anything better to do."[33] And I have heard similar comments from other young college graduates. Nobody has ever taught them that *what you do influences the kind of person you will become*. After a year or two in the culture of Wall Street, working hard for companies which are all about making money, many of these kids will absorb that culture, which after all is well-aligned with American popular culture: *Get what you can while the getting is good*. These attitudes, once formed, are hard to change and will likely influence that young person's choices long after she has left Wall Street.

The 21st-century assumption is that if you give kids a choice between right and wrong, and you show them why they should make the right choice, then they *will* make the right choice. This assumption is not based in evidence. It's based in a 21st-century guess about human nature.

And that guess turns out to be wrong, most of the time. Recall our earlier discussion of kids' eating choices in this context: the more reliable and effective approach is to *require* kids to eat the healthier food, for years, to inculcate healthy habits—as well as educating the child in the virtues of healthy eating. But merely hoping that kids will eat foods which are not their first choice is not likely to be effective in a culture that teaches kids that their own desires should be paramount. "Whatever floats your boat."

A longtime columnist for the *New York Times*, Jennifer Finney Boylan, published an essay in which she asked these questions: What is school for? What does "getting an education" actually mean? What *should* it mean? Here is her answer: "Education means enlightening our children's minds with the uncensored scientific and artistic truth of the world. If that means making our own sons and daughters strangers to us, then so be it." According to Boylan, a good education should be like putting kids in a "witness protection program. If the person who comes out is easily recognizable as the same person who went in, something has gone terribly, dangerously wrong."[34] In other words, the better the education, the less your child will share the values you taught them when they were young.

That may sound brave and noble to some. It is certainly vintage 21st-century American. But the moment you begin to unpack it, questions arise. What precisely is the "artistic truth of the world"? Is the music of Mozart and Beethoven and Brahms closer to the "artistic truth of the world" than the music of Drake or Bruno Mars or Cardi B? Are the ethics of Lehman Brothers circa 2007 better or worse than the ethics of Mother Teresa circa 1977? Who gets to decide? If one simply sets kids loose in the fragmented chaos of 21st-century culture in the hopes that they will discover the "artistic truth of the world," what those kids will discover is most likely the popular culture of TikTok, online video games, and pornography. They will have no standard by which to judge Drake or Bruno Mars in comparison with Stravinsky or Mahler, no standard by which to compare the accounting gimmicks at Lehman Brothers with the altruism of Mother Teresa, because no authoritative teacher will have instructed them about a scale of value.

Conscientiousness is not innate. Self-control is not innate. Honesty is not innate. To restate: These virtues have to be taught. You must teach them.

In fact, the abdication of authority which is put forward as enlightened wisdom by Boylan and others is not wisdom at all. It is a dereliction of duty. It is a retreat from adult responsibility. I am not singling out Boylan personally. On the contrary, I have heard the sentiments she expressed presented at leading universities across the United States, at school board meetings in the United States, and from the heads of school at leading public and private schools across the United States and Canada.

As University of Virginia professor Talbot Brewer recently observed,

> We would be astonished to discover a human community that did not attempt to pass along to its children a form of life that had won the affirmation of its elders. We would be utterly flabbergasted to discover a community that went to great lengths to pass along a form of life that its elders regarded as seriously deficient or mistaken. Yet we have slipped unawares into precisely this bizarre arrangement.[35]

Courtesy of Silicon Valley and social media and online video games, our kids are now at risk of being indoctrinated into the "artistic truth of the world" as promoted by the most popular influencers on TikTok, Instagram, and Twitch.

Reject the notion of "hands-off" parenting promoted by Boylan & Co. Think carefully about the virtues you want your child to possess, and teach them diligently and incisively: which means, among other things, that you yourself must demonstrate the virtue you want your child to have. Teach your child self-control and restraint, which is no easy task in a culture where the billboards scream "Live for Now." Teach your child that the real world matters more than the world of screens, which may require you to put down your own smartphone and go for a walk with your child. Teach your child that virtue and character matter more than fame and wealth. The stakes are high: the health and happiness of your child. This matters.

9

Misconceptions

When I meet with parents, some questions come up again and again. Parents want to do the right thing, but they are sometimes reluctant to try because misconceptions get in the way. We now have the foundation in place to address each of these misconceptions.

Here's the first:

*I'm worried about a rebound effect. If I try to be the kind of parent you describe, and I **force** my child to behave "virtuously"—whatever that means—then when she goes away to the university and she's on her own, I'm worried she will do all kinds of crazy things which she wouldn't have done otherwise because I have prevented her from doing stuff she wants to do. She won't have learned how to make good choices on her own.*

Longitudinal studies, such as those we considered in the previous chapter, are helpful in answering this question. Those studies show that, in general, well-behaved kids are more likely to grow up to be well-behaved adults. Kids raised by more permissive parents are more likely to get into trouble as adults: trouble with alcohol, trouble with drug abuse, trouble with anxiety and depression.

Investigators in the United States launched an ambitious study in 1994 of more than 20,000 American kids, drawn from every part of the country: urban and rural, Asian/Black/Latino/White, affluent and low-income, East Coast and West Coast, Midwest and South, etc. They gathered data when most of these kids were 12 to 14 years of age, and then periodically for 14 more years.[1] Researchers who have analyzed these data have found that the children of authoritative parents did better in school, were less likely to get drunk, and were less likely to engage in unsafe sexual practices—not only in their early teenage years but also in their 20s—compared to the children of parents who are less authoritative.[2] They went on to have healthier, happier romantic relationships in young adulthood.[3] As adults they had healthier babies, even after adjusting for demographic variables such as race, ethnicity, and household income.[4]

The late psychologist Diana Baumrind, who conducted research at the University of California, Berkeley for 58 years, from 1960 until her death in 2018, established the modern field of parenting research. Before Baumrind, guidance for parents was based primarily on the beliefs of the person giving the advice, without much hard evidence to support that advice beyond that person's own experience. Baumrind and her colleagues carefully and systematically assessed how parents interacted with their kids when the children were young, spending at least 30 hours with each family observing how the parents related to their children. Baumrind's team then studied outcomes for each kid many years down the road. Baumrind divided parenting styles into four categories, which we can refer to as Too Hard, Too Soft, Just Right, and Not There. Baumrind herself used the terms "authoritarian," "permissive," "authoritative," and "neglectful." I have always found it confusing that Baumrind used two similar-sounding words— "authoritarian" and "authoritative"—to describe two very different parenting styles.[5]

Too Hard (authoritarian) parents rarely show any kindness or love to their child. They often make unrealistic demands. The children of these harsh parents are more likely than others to become abusive parents themselves 20 years down the road. The children of Too Hard parents are also more likely, when they become adults, to have difficulty sustaining romantic relationships.

Too Soft (permissive) parents are good at expressing love and affection for their child, but not so good at enforcing the rules. The children of Too Soft parents are more likely, as adults, to have problems with drug and alcohol abuse; more likely to struggle financially, regardless of their actual income, because they find it difficult to live within their means; more likely to be anxious and/ or depressed; and more likely to be convicted of a felony.

Just Right (authoritative) parents communicate their love for their child, but they also enforce the rules fairly and consistently. The rules may bend on occasion, when necessary, but they don't break. Over Dr. Baumrind's more than five decades of research, she accumulated overwhelming evidence that the healthiest parenting style is the Just Right style, the authoritative style. The children of Just Right parents are the most likely to have good outcomes, no matter which outcome you look at: they are the most likely to be gainfully employed, the most likely to have lasting romantic relationships, the most likely to be in good physical and mental health and not to be addicted to drugs or alcohol. Just Right parents are strict, within reasonable bounds, and also loving.

By the year 2000, there was broad agreement among researchers that authoritative parenting, Just Right parenting, yields the best outcomes for kids.[6] But in the years before her death in 2018, Baumrind was concerned that the term she had invented way back in 1966—"authoritative parenting"—was being watered down. "The wide endorsement of authoritative parenting has been accompanied by a definitional drift away from its original meaning," she wrote.[7] Many parents—and even many researchers—had begun to act as if there is a tension between "strict" and "loving": that you can be *either* strict *or* loving, but not both. But Baumrind's research proved that notion to be wrong. The parents whom she found to be Just Right parents were *both* strict *and* loving.[8] The mistake being made by many parents, and even by many researchers, Baumrind wrote, was in "equating high control with low love and positioning authoritative parenting midway between love and control."[9] On the contrary, authoritative parenting as defined by Baumrind is characterized by being *both* "power assertive" (her phrase) *and* high in love, unconditional love. She criticized researchers who believed that unconditional *love* means unconditional *acceptance*.[10] You can love your child unconditionally, she insisted, while still correcting your child's mistakes and insisting that your child abide by the rules. If you are not enforcing the rules—if your kids regard you as loving but not strict—then you are Too Soft. Baumrind was concerned not only that there had been a shift in American parenting from authoritative to permissive—from Just Right to Too Soft—but also that parenting researchers themselves had softened and misunderstood authoritative parenting as she had observed it and as she had defined it.

It might be helpful to look at a graph. Baumrind wrote, "Misunderstanding of parental authority and of the authoritative construct is fostered when parental control and love are represented as opposite ends of the same continuum rather than as two independent dimensions."[11] Here's what she means by one continuum, with low control / high love at the left end of the spectrum and high control / low love at the other end of the spectrum:

Permissive ------------- Authoritative ------------- Authoritarian

According to Baumrind, that's the wrong way to think about parenting styles. Love and control are not on the same dimension; they are, as Baumrind wrote, two independent dimensions:

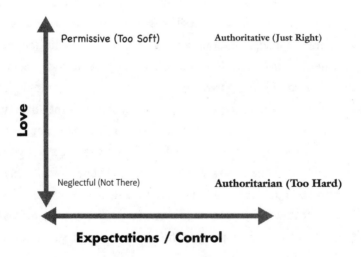

(You will find no discussion in this book of the Neglectful "Not There" parent. Neglectful parents don't buy parenting books. You are not a neglectful parent. Neither am I. That is not our temptation.)

The key point Baumrind is making is that there is no contradiction between loving your child and having high expectations, exerting parental authority, and being strict. The authoritative parent, the Just Right parent, loves her child and shows her love for her child while also setting the rules, enforcing consequences, and having high expectations.

Are you Too Hard? Too Soft? Or Just Right? When I present these three categories—either one-on-one when I am counseling a parent, or in a workshop for parents—almost every parent says that they want to be "Just Right." But what they consider "Just Right" is different from what their parents would have considered "Just Right." Over the past 30 years, the American notion of "Just Right" has shifted steadily away from authoritative to permissive. That's what concerned Baumrind in the years before her death.

This shift helps us to understand the question from the parent who is concerned that her daughter's behavior will "rebound" if the parent enforces a virtuous code of behavior while the daughter is in middle school and high school. Many parents today believe that stricter parenting now will result in a "rebound" into degenerate behavior when their kids go away to college. Sometimes this belief is an after-the-fact rationalization for Too Soft parenting. In other words, it's a way of justifying what the parent is going to do anyhow. When I ask parents *why* they believe that stricter parenting now will result in more reckless behavior by their child a few years down the road, they often respond by citing a movie about a teenager who had puritanical parents, or by mentioning something they saw a few years back on a TV show.

I answer these parents by pointing out that the research provides no support for this notion. Indeed, the research flatly contradicts it. But rather than harp on the scholarly studies, I ask the parents to consider whether this same notion would make sense in any other context.

Suppose you are hiring a new employee, and you have to choose between Sonya and Vanessa. Sonya's previous employers tell you that Sonya always shows up for work on time, never cheats or steals, and never uses company time for personal chores. Vanessa's previous employers tell you that Vanessa often shows up an hour or two late for work, she has stolen office property and then lied about it, and she often scrolls through TikTok when she is supposed to be working. Would you say, *I'm sure Vanessa has gotten rid of all her bad impulses, so now is the time to hire her*? Would you say, *I won't hire Sonya because she is so repressed, odds are good that she is going to "rebound" sometime soon*? No, you wouldn't.

In this example, the prospective employer is following a rule which used to be well-known to American parents: **virtue begets virtue, and vice begets vice.** The employee who has a record of being honest and virtuous in the past is more likely to be honest and virtuous in the future. In the workplace, Americans understand this.

But at home, they forget. This notion of "rebound" is based not in evidence, but in the popular culture of the early 21st century— not a reliable source of information. And this notion is propagated, I believe, in part by the desire of at least some parents to justify to themselves their own Too Soft parenting style.

Don't accept this notion of "rebound." Don't believe it. As I said in the previous chapter, if you train your son or daughter in the way they should go, then when they grow up and leave home, you have significantly improved the odds that they will behave wisely. Virtue begets virtue. Vice begets vice.

Next question.

I'm worried that if I follow your advice, my child will be an outcast. He will be the only one who isn't allowed to play Grand Theft Auto *or* RDR2. *I'm worried that he will be unpopular, and he will blame me for that. And he will be right. I'm trying to find the right balance here.*

I was a guest on the *TODAY* show alongside Dr. Meg Meeker, author of *Strong Fathers, Strong Daughters* and *Strong Mothers, Strong Sons*.[12] Dr. Meeker is also an experienced pediatrician who happens to have four kids of her own, three daughters and one son, Walter. The best part of being on *TODAY* that day wasn't being on the show, but hearing the stories Dr. Meeker shared with me while we were waiting in the green room. She related to me how she told Walter, beginning at age 12, No more video games. No video game devices. You're not wasting your time on that. (Her daughters didn't have much interest in video games.)

Walter complained. "All the other boys are playing *Call of Duty*. I'm the only one who isn't allowed to."

Mom said, "Too bad."

When Walter turned 18, he said, "I'm an adult now. I have money that I have earned from my jobs. I'm going to go and buy an Xbox and some video games."

Mom said, "Fine."

One year later, near the end of his freshman year at college, Walter called his mom. "I just made $400! Guess how I did it?"

Mom said, "No idea."

"I sold my Xbox and all my video games. They were just gathering dust anyhow," Walter said. He continued, "Mom, you would not believe it, there are so many guys at college who expect you to be really impressed that they can kill eight aliens in ten seconds in *Halo*. And I'm like, 'Dude, you can't even talk to girls.'" Walter explained that he saw so many other guys at college who had started playing these games many hours a week at 10 or 12 or 14 years of age. These boys defined themselves as gamers. Their sense of self was tied up with their proficiency at playing video games.

But Walter had a different perspective. During those crucial adolescent years when he was not allowed to play video games, he had developed a wide array of hobbies and interests, as well as people skills, which the gamers were less likely to have.

I have been counseling addicts of every kind for more than 30 years. One robust truth about addiction is that the younger you are when you become an addict, the harder it is to kick the habit. If you start smoking one pack a day around age 25, it will be easy to quit. But if you start smoking a pack a day at age 13, it will be very difficult to quit. Age matters. If a boy starts playing video games 10 or 15 hours a week when he is 9 or 12 or 14, those games may "imprint" on his brain in a way that won't happen if the boy starts playing when he is 18. Once the process of puberty is fully complete—once the boy becomes a man, once the girl becomes a woman—the areas of the brain responsible for anticipating consequences and thinking ahead are stronger.[13]

Now let's return to the question at hand: Do the benefits of restricting what video games your son plays outweigh the (assumed) costs of his being less popular as a result?

I gave a presentation to parents in which I shared recent research on video games. I focused on longitudinal research in which investigators followed a large cohort of kids over several years to see how and whether the kids changed as a result of the kinds of video games they played, after adjusting and controlling for all other variables.[14] This research strongly suggests that kids who spend many hours a week playing violent video games such as *Grand Theft Auto* and *Call of Duty* become more selfish, less honest, and less patient. Not right away, not after a week or a month, but after years of playing these violent games.

After reviewing multiple studies on the long-term outcomes of playing first-person-shooter video games such as *Grand Theft Auto,* I recommended banning such violent games from the household. If your son wants to shoot things, help him join a local skeet club instead. And if your child is going over to a friend's house, call the parents ahead of time and ask whether the kids will be permitted to play really awful, violent video games such as *Grand Theft Auto* in which the gamer is rewarded for killing unarmed bystanders and rewarded for killing police officers. If the other parents allow those games to be played, then your child should not be allowed to go to that friend's house. That child can be invited to your house instead, where you are in charge.

This recommendation struck one parent as unduly harsh. She said that my recommendation was "*totally unrealistic. There is no way I can police what my son is going to do at someone else's house.*" In addition, she was worried that if she even tried to enforce a ban on violent first-person-shooter games such as *Call of Duty* or *Grand Theft Auto*, then her son would be less popular because he would be the only boy who wasn't allowed to play those games. "*I'm worried that he will be unpopular, and he will blame me for that. And he will be right. I'm trying to find the right balance here.*"

Let's unpack the multiple assumptions which are driving this parent's concerns:

Assumption #1: *It's important for my child to be popular.*
False. Being popular in the United States in the 21st century

often entails unhealthy behavior and attitudes, beginning with disregarding the authority of parents. Evidence suggests that being popular in the United States at age 13 today may actually be a major risk factor for bad outcomes in early adulthood.[15] You need to be clear in your own mind about what's important. Helping your child to become kind, well-behaved, and self-controlled is important. Your child being popular with lots of kids his own age is not important.

Assumption #2: *It's unrealistic for me to hold my child responsible for behavior outside my home.* Also false. I have observed many Just Right parents closely and firsthand over the past 30 years, in my medical practice in Maryland and more recently in Pennsylvania. Every Just Right parent I have known expects their child to behave outside the home as they do when they are at home. There is a word for that consistency of behavior: the word is Integrity, and it is one of the traits linked to Conscientiousness. Just Right parents do not hesitate to call or even occasionally to drop in without warning at their kids' friends' homes to check on what their kids are doing. That's one way to teach Integrity.

Assumption #3: *Parents should find a balance between Too Hard and Too Soft.* True, but misunderstood. The parent who asked this question had accepted the contemporary American notion that parents have to choose between being strict *or* loving. As a result, she thinks it's unrealistic to try to be strict *and* loving. She is mistaken.

This particular parent was asking about video games. But the same analysis applies across different domains. If your daughter spends too much of her free time touching up her selfies for her

Instagram, or if your son spends all his free time playing video games, then it's your job to unplug the device and get your child or teen reconnected to the world of real experience—whether that experience is talking with another human being face-to-face, or playing field hockey, or going for a walk in the park.

A parent in Sandy, Utah (near Salt Lake City), told me that she didn't allow any of her children to have cell phones, period, right through high school. "I just never saw the need for it," this mom told me. And the other kids didn't have a problem with it. Not really a big deal. "You know, her mom is the weird mom who won't let her have a phone." But the other *parents* gave this mom a hard time. They would confront her in public. Some were actually hostile. "Why are you making your daughter the odd girl out? Don't you realize this is what girls do today?"—that's what the other parents would say to her. This mom told me she thought that the other parents were uneasy about how much time their own kids are spending on their devices, so they take their unease out on her, the one mom who won't play along. She upsets them because she shows that another path is possible.

Whether you live in Utah or California or British Columbia or New York: Do what's best for your child. Don't be too concerned about what other kids, or other parents, might say.

Next question.

I want my child to be independent. So when she talks back to me or is disrespectful, I try to see that in a positive light, as a sign that she is becoming more independent. And I support that.

It is never acceptable for your child to be disrespectful to you. That doesn't mean she has to agree with you. It's fine for her to say, *I don't agree. I think you are making a mistake.* But it is never acceptable for her to say, *Shut up. You don't know what the f*** you're talking about.* Yet that sort of language has become commonplace in the United States and Canada, in affluent communities as well as in low-income communities. Disrespectful language has also become common on the most popular TikTok videos, YouTube videos, and #1 hit songs. Don't allow such language in your house.

But independence of thought is useful. How to cultivate that independence without encouraging disrespect? Most of the Just Right parents I have known are able to accomplish this feat. One strategy revolves around suppertime conversation. Long rides in the car are also a good opportunity. Help your kid to find her voice or his voice. For younger kids, it could be by talking about a favorite food, or movies that you have seen recently with your kids. Ask them to talk about their favorite movie among those they have seen recently and why it's their favorite. Describe how and why your opinion differs. Explain that two people can disagree about preferences for one movie over another, or about taste in food, without disrespecting each other or disliking each other.

For teens, you might choose a controversial topic from the news. Ask your teen to express an opinion about nuclear power versus conventional power versus solar and wind. Or ask your teen a question about the Palestinian-Israeli conflict. Listen carefully and respectfully to their position. Then state how your opinion differs, and why you don't agree with their position. For purposes of this exercise, stay away from personal topics such as whether your child should be allowed to stay up late at night playing video games. The point of the exercise is to develop the skill of disagreeing respectfully, to build independence without hostility.

Once that skill is developed, you and your child or teen will be able to navigate real disagreements with less likelihood of the disagreement degenerating into anger.

Next question.

I just want my son to be happy. What makes him happy is different from what makes me happy. I'm thinking I may just have to accept that.

This mom has a teenage son who typically spends at least 20 hours a week playing video games. For months she had been trying to restrict his time playing video games to refocus his attention on academics. He's doing OK in school but not as well as he could be. She kept saying things like, "If you want to get into a top college, you need to do better in school. I know you can do better, but you're wasting too much time on video games. You should spend more time on schoolwork and less time playing video games."

Finally, one day he exploded. "I DON'T GIVE A S**T whether I get into a top college!" he yelled. "I don't want to GO to college. I am a gamer. That's worth something. It's worth a lot. I can monetize that. I don't care about trigonometry or Spanish or American History or any of the rest of that crap they teach at school. I. DON'T. F***ING. **CARE**. So just leave me alone, will you?"

Mom was stunned into silence. It had never previously occurred to her that her son might value achievement in virtual online worlds more than he values achievement in the real world.

In the weeks between her son's outburst and her conversation with me, she had come to question her own position. The contemporary world is different from the world of 20 years ago, she reflected. Twenty years ago, online video games were barely visible, clunky, and slow to play. Twitch, one of the dominant online venues where gamers earn money, was not launched until 2011. Last year, more than seven million professional gamers were streaming on Twitch, trying to earn money from their habit.[16] So maybe she should stop worrying about her son's suboptimal academic achievement and instead support him in whatever he wants to do? "I just want him to be happy," she said to me, more than once.

I told mom that she was confusing *happiness* with *pleasure*.[17] That's a common confusion today. A trip to the video-game arcade may be a source of pleasure, but it will not give lasting and enduring happiness. This mother's son derives pleasure from playing video games, but playing video games in an online world is unlikely to be a source of real fulfillment. The pleasure derived from a video game may last for weeks or even months. But it will not last many years, in my firsthand observation of many young men over the past two decades. The boy either moves on to something else, or the happiness undergoes a silent, insidious, and malignant transformation into addiction. The hallmark of addiction is decreasing pleasure over time. Tolerance develops. Playing the game becomes compulsive, almost involuntary. And it no longer gives the thrill and pleasure it once did. But the addict can no longer find pleasure in anything else.

Pleasure is not the same thing as happiness. The gratification of desire yields pleasure, not lasting happiness. Happiness comes from *fulfillment*, from fulfilling your potential, which means more than playing online video games.

You must limit, govern, and guide your son's involvement with video games. Again, this recommendation doesn't just apply to video games. The same considerations apply if your child or teen says that they are happiest when they are uploading photos to Instagram or scrolling through TikTok. Part of the task of the parent is, and always has been, *educating desire*: teaching your child to desire and enjoy things which are higher and better than cotton candy. Video games and social media are the cotton candy of popular culture today.

Our popular culture today puts a premium on the satisfaction of personal desire. "Live for Now." "Whatever floats your boat." You are trying to teach Conscientiousness: honesty, self-control, and responsibility. You are battling the culture.

It's a challenge to raise a child in opposition to the culture in which you are living. As columnist David Brooks observed, "We all live within distinct moral ecologies. The overall environment influences what we think of as normal behavior without [us] being much aware of it."[18] The assumption which today pervades American culture is the belief that your child's personal fulfillment is roughly equivalent to the fulfillment of your child's desires. A child presumably knows her own desires better than her parents can possibly know. If the key to human fulfillment is the mere satisfaction of desire, then the authority of the parent becomes subordinate to the whim of the child.

As I said, one of the assumptions which now drives American culture, as experienced by kids born and raised in this country, is, *If it feels good, do it. Inhibitions just hold you back. Whatever floats your boat, go for it.* Arthur C. Brooks, former president of the American Enterprise Institute, wrote about the American slogan *If it feels good, do it.* He said that this slogan is good advice if you are a protozoon, not so great if you are a human.[19]

We are human beings, not protozoa. Being a human being means more, and *should* mean more, than mere gratification of desire. Service to others, mastery of the arts, faith in something greater than oneself, discipline in pursuit of a higher goal—all these and more have traditionally been recognized as the proper aims of human life. Gratification of desire—"if it feels good, do it"—has historically been seen as a distraction, a temptation to stray from the goal of true fulfillment, not the goal itself. The result of the cultural acceptance of this notion—"Live for Now"—is the infantilizing of American culture, compounding the cult of youth which is already one of our greatest weaknesses.

The solution is mindfully to create an alternative culture. To build a subversive household in which the dinner table conversation is actually conversation, with the screens switched off. To value family time together above time that kids spend with same-age peers. To create a space for silence, for meditation, for reflection, so that your child can discover a true inner self that is something more than the mere gratification of desire.

It's not easy to battle against the culture, to create an alternative culture in your home. But it can be done.

Another misconception:

If I love my child, then that means I also trust my child, right? If she says she didn't cheat on the test, and if I love her, then I have to trust her, right? You can't have love without trust.

This girl was taking a test at school. The teacher caught the girl looking at her cell phone during the test and copying answers from the cell phone. The teacher confiscated the cell phone and sent the girl to the principal's office. The girl insisted that the teacher had made a mistake. The phone just happened to be in her lap, but she wasn't looking at it. So she said.

The principal supported the teacher's decision to mark the test a zero.

The parents went ballistic. The father charged in like a defense attorney. "It's just the teacher's word against the word of our daughter," the father said. "Our daughter said she didn't do it. And our daughter would never lie to us."

Mom had a more reflective, less adversarial tone than her husband. That's when she said, "If I love my child, then that means I also trust my child, right? If she says she didn't cheat on the test, and I love her, then I have to trust her, right? You can't have love without trust."

Short answer to mom's question: **the rules for love between parent and child are different from the rules between adults.** Maybe it is true that love between adults requires blind trust. But that is certainly not true for the love a parent has for a child. The father in this case said, "Our daughter would never lie to us." I don't know that family well, but I know that father is wrong. Any parent who says such a thing is wrong. **Your daughter (or son) is more likely to lie to you than to anyone else** because they don't want to disappoint you. They don't want to let you down. And your daughter or your son wants you to think well of her or him, even if they may value their peers' opinions more highly than yours.

Which brings us back to cheating. In the previous chapter we discussed the rise of cheating among American kids, including among "good" kids who work hard and get good grades. Among

American kids, cheating today is usually no big deal. Many kids believe that almost everybody else is doing it. But many kids also have an uneasy feeling—which happens to be correct—that their parents were raised in a different era, an era in which good kids did not cheat. So the temptation to lie to parents about cheating is very strong.

A generation ago, there was an alliance between parents and the school. If the teacher and the principal notified the parents that the student had been caught cheating, the parents would likely impose penalties at home to reinforce the school's discipline. In the United States today, that alliance is in tatters. Today, when a student is caught cheating and the school seeks to impose some semblance of discipline, the parents often act as adversaries, challenging the school's authority.

I spoke on this topic at a middle school in Menlo Park, California, an affluent community in Silicon Valley. There were more than 300 parents in the audience. A woman in the front row raised her hand. I called on her. She said, "Dr. Sax, I would like to share a story with everyone here. Last year I caught a girl cheating on a test, very similar to the situation you just described. I reprimanded her for cheating, in front of the class, and I marked her test a zero. But it turns out that her parents are venture capitalists worth millions of dollars. They have friends on the school board. They have donated to the school, lots of money. After I reprimanded their daughter, they made some phone calls. About two weeks later, I was called into the principal's office. I was told that as a condition of my continued employment, I would have to apologize to this girl, in class, in front of all the other students. So that's what I did. I can't afford to quit, and I don't want to move.

212 THE COLLAPSE OF PARENTING

"So do you want to know what I did this fall, when the new school year began?" the teacher continued. "I told all my students, *Go ahead and cheat if you want to. I'm not even going to try to enforce the rules because I have learned that the school doesn't want me to. I hope you won't cheat, but if you do, I won't say a word about it.*"

I have heard stories like the one this teacher told me many times in recent years, across the United States, especially in affluent neighborhoods. But usually the stories are whispered to me. Once a teacher actually pulled me into the janitor's closet and closed the door in order to tell me her story. What was unusual about the story the teacher shared in Menlo Park is that this teacher had the courage to tell her story out loud, to an audience of more than 300 of her neighbors.[20]

Don't say, "My daughter would never lie to me." In more than 30 years of clinical practice, I have found that whenever a parent says, "My daughter [or son] would never lie to me," you can be pretty sure that the daughter [or son] is lying to the parent.

Another misconception:

I'm worried that if I follow your advice, my child won't love me anymore.

Read your job description. Your job as a parent is to raise your child to be the best person she or he can be. Your reward comes from knowing that you have done your job well. As wonderful as it is to receive a loving touch or a spontaneous and unasked-for "I *love* being with you" from your own child, receiving such shows of affection can't be your main objective.

Many parents are in marriages or long-term relationships which have frayed. Other parents are single parents without a loving partner. The parent without a partner, or the parent whose partner is unloving, may look to the parent-child relationship in hopes of receiving warmth and affection. I understand that. My own mom was a single mom who spent the last half of her life looking for the right partner. She never found him. In my adult patients, I see the loneliness of the single parent, or of parents who are stuck with partners whom they no longer love, or who no longer love them.

But trying to get your own child to give you the affection you should be getting from an adult partner throws the parent-child relationship out of whack and undermines your authority as a parent. In a relationship between two adult partners, everything is negotiable. Your adult partner is your equal. You can't give orders to him or her, and he or she can't give orders to you. Your relationship with your child is different. You have to set the rules and enforce them, even if your child doesn't agree that vegetables should come before dessert. It's confusing to everybody involved if one moment you are trying to be the affectionate "cool parent," and the next moment you are trying to be the Just Right parent. The most common result is that parents slip from being Just Right to being Too Soft because they don't want to jeopardize the affection they hope to gain from their child.

Abigail, a mom in Tampa, Florida, shared with me a story which I think illustrates the right priorities. Her 14-year-old daughter, Kasey, wanted to go to Cancún for spring break with her friends. But parents were not invited. Her mother pointed out that Cancún has become a popular spring break destination for

American college students. And although Kasey was 14, she could easily pass for 18—she was a physically mature young woman. "How is a young man supposed to know that you are underage?" mom asked.

"Mom, stop being so paranoid," Kasey said. "We will be totally fine. We will stay together. We'll have our cell phones."

"I don't think it's safe," mom said.

"It's totally safe," Kasey said.

"I'm sorry. You're not going," Abigail said.

"Mom! You are going to, like, totally *ruin* my whole *life*! All my friends are going! Everybody is going!"

"You're not going," Abigail repeated.

"I hate you!" Kasey screamed. "I hate you! You are going to, like, totally ruin my whole life!"

"Well," Abigail answered, "to be honest, sometimes I'm not so fond of you either. But I'm your mother. That means my #1 job is keeping you safe. And I know more than you do about the behavior of drunk young men. You're not going."

And Kasey didn't go.

Over my three decades as a family physician, I have been involved professionally in a handful of cases of sexual assault. In one case, my only involvement was to sit with mom after the fact. "I knew I shouldn't have let her go," this mom said to me. "She's just 15 years old. It was a fraternity party at the college. I knew I shouldn't have let her go."

One part of me wanted to shake the mom and yell, **THEN WHY DID YOU LET HER GO??** But of course I didn't do that. Because I already knew the answer. This mom wants to be her daughter's best friend. And a friend cannot command. A friend cannot say, "No, you're not going to the party. I will not allow it."

If you are doing your job as a parent, sometimes you will have to do things which may upset your child. If you are concerned that your child won't love you anymore, that concern may keep you from doing your job.

Do your job.

IO

Humility

When I meet with parents, I sometimes ask, in regard to their children, *What is most important to you? What are you trying to help your child to become?* Parents often answer, *I want my kid to grow up to be happy, to be successful, to be kind.*

That's great, I say. But then I ask, *How are you going to help your child get from here to there? What will it take for your child to reach that goal?*—and many parents aren't sure how to answer. Parents are likely to confuse fulfillment with success. The assumption seems to be that if the child goes to a good college and gets a good job, then personal fulfillment is assured. When I point to the evidence that professional achievement is no guarantee of fulfillment, or life satisfaction, or happiness, many parents don't know what to say.

What do you need to teach your child to best ensure your child's life satisfaction and happiness as an adult? My answer: the first job of the parent today has to be to teach humility.

Why humility? Because humility is the best antidote to the core toxicity in the popular culture right now: the assumption that being famous and/or wealthy are the highest goods and the most worthwhile goals. Whenever your kid is on TikTok or Instagram, or watching TV, or going to see a movie, they are likely being indoctrinated into that culture, into that mindset. And because 99.99 percent of us will never be truly famous or fabulously wealthy, kids who grow up in that culture are much more likely to see themselves as failures, to end up anxious, depressed, and/or disengaged—which is just what we are seeing. A culture which prioritizes wealth and fame above everything else is a toxic culture. Humility is the best defense against that toxicity. (There is some evidence that the fabulously wealthy are as likely or perhaps even more likely to be miserable than the rest of us, but that is a topic for a different book.)[1]

It is not easy to teach humility. The first problem is that many kids now have no idea what the word "humility" even means. I was invited to speak to students at a Catholic school. The school leaders asked me to do a short talk for the kids built around a passage from the Bible. I chose Micah 6:8. I explained to the students that in the sixth chapter of the book of Micah, the prophet is asking, "What does the Lord require of you?" Do you have to dot all the i's and cross all the t's? No, I answered. According to Micah, here is what the Lord requires. It's simple: "Do justice, love kindness, and walk humbly with your God."

"But what does that mean?" I asked the students. "What does it mean to walk *humbly* with your God? Raise your hand if you think you know what the word 'humility' means and you are prepared to share your definition with your classmates."

A boy shot up his hand. I called on him. "Humility means trying to convince yourself you're dumb when you know you're smart," he said.

I shook my head. "Not quite," I said. "That's not humility. That is psychosis: a detachment from reality. How about if we define humility as *being as interested in other people as you are in yourself*?" The kids all looked at me blankly. They had never heard this definition before, or indeed any formal definition of humility. It had never been taught to them. And this was at a school with quotations from the Bible literally chiseled into its stone walls.

But I don't blame the boy. How should he know if he has received no instruction? He's immersed in a culture which is all about walking tall, standing proud, and winning it all. And the parents are often just as clueless. I was speaking to parents at another school about the virtue of humility. During Q&A at the end of my talk, a mother objected. She said, "I don't want to teach my daughter to be *humble*! I want her to have *high* self-esteem—so that when that big job opportunity comes along, she will go for it! I don't want her to be *humble*."

I answered, "Mom, with all due respect, you are confused. You are confusing being humble with being timid. But 'humble' and 'timid' are not the same thing. True humility is very nearly the opposite of being timid. And the virtue you want for your daughter in that situation, when there's a big job opportunity on the line, is not high self-esteem. The virtue you want your daughter to have in that situation is *courage*. Courage means that you know your weaknesses, your inadequacies, your failures, your shortcomings, and you find the strength to push forward anyhow."

That's the definition I offer: Humility means being as interested in other people as you are interested in yourself. Humility means that when you meet someone new, you try to learn something about *them* before giving them a spiel about how incredible your current project is. Humility means really listening when someone else is talking instead of just preparing your own shtick in your head before you've really heard what the other person is saying. Humility means making a sustained effort to get the other person to share their view before trying to inundate them with yours. Humility means taking the time to look up at the sky instead of looking only in the mirror.

Researchers distinguish between self-transcendence, which means looking outward at others and at nature, and self-enhancement, where the priority is on maximizing one's own achievement and prestige. Self-transcendence is linked empirically with prosocial behavior and with empathy.[2] Self-enhancement is linked empirically with selfishness.[3]

How to promote humble self-transcendence rather than proud self-enhancement in a culture which is all about proud self-enhancement? One study suggests one small way that you might begin. In this study, researchers randomly assigned undergraduates to one of two conditions. In one condition, undergraduates spent one minute outdoors looking up at towering, 200-foot-tall eucalyptus trees. In the other condition, undergraduates spent one minute outdoors looking up at a tall building. Looking up at tall trees did indeed lead to feelings of awe, as the researchers expected, whereas looking up at the tall building did not lead to feelings of awe. The students who had looked at the tall trees were subsequently significantly more likely to help the experimenter after a carefully staged accident in which the experimenter spilled a dozen pens on the ground. And the students who had looked at the trees felt significantly less entitled, less likely to agree with statements such as *"I'm just more deserving than others."* After just one minute of tree-gazing![4]

One lesson I take home from that study: spend more time with nature. Forty years ago, I was dating a young woman whose father was a devout Christian. He had lived on a farm in the western Maryland countryside all his life, surrounded by other farms, the nearest big city several hours' drive away. I had lived all my life in the city or the suburbs: Cleveland, Boston, Philadelphia. My girlfriend and I traveled to his farm for a visit over the Christmas holiday. I decided to challenge this man. I asked him, "Why are people way out in the country more likely to be religious, but people living in the city are more likely to be atheists?"

He paused for a moment, smiled just a bit, then answered, "People in the city are surrounded by things that *men* have made. People in the country are surrounded by the things that *God* has made."

I think there's some truth to that. We now have good evidence that more time outdoors, whether in the park or in the forest or in the mountains, leads to improved mood, better self-control, and even better memory.[5] To teach humility, start by spending more time outdoors. And by "outdoors" I don't mean walking on the sidewalk from one store to another. I mean outdoors in nature. If you live in the city, find a park. When you are planning the big family vacation, forget Disneyworld. Cancel Universal Studios. Delete Legoland. Plan a trip to a national park instead.

The opposite of humility is inflated self-esteem. I visited an elementary school where the third-grade students were each required to write five words to describe how amazing they are. Each student was then supposed to attach the words to a big cut-out of their own name. Everything was posted on the bulletin board for everybody to see. I took a photograph of one boy's work. He chose these words to describe himself:

- Marvelous
- Awesome
- talented
- exellent (*misspelled*)
- a Geenius (*misspelled*)

I don't mean to pick on this boy. After all, he was just doing the assignment. I share this story to illustrate how little awareness there is in some schools of the way in which a puffed-up ego at age 8 or age 14 can lead to resentment at age 20 or 25. (I will explain how egotism leads to resentment in just a moment.)

I took another photo at a different school, of a flowery poster with the words "Dream until your dreams come true." That's bad advice. That advice cultivates a sense of entitlement, implying that all you have to do in order for your dreams to come true is to dream. Better advice might be **Work** *until your dreams come true.* That might not sound as appealing, but it would be one notch closer to the truth. An even truer statement would be *Work in pursuit of your dreams, but realize that life is what happens while you are making other plans. Tomorrow may never come or may be unrecognizably different.*[6]

I had the privilege of giving the keynote address at a gathering of public charter school administrators.[7] We all agreed that school should be about more than grades and test scores. We all agreed that teachers should do more than teach math and science and

English and history. We all agreed that part of the mission of the school should be to teach character and virtue.

But which virtue? What sort of character? That's where the conversation gets interesting.

School administrators fall into two camps. One camp wants to talk about grit, passion, and perseverance. *Go for it. Start your own company. Move fast and break things. Have a growth mindset. You can do anything if you try hard enough.* Their role models are often men like Elon Musk and other billionaire entrepreneurs.

The other camp talks about service and self-sacrifice. *Treat others the way you would like to be treated yourself. Love your neighbor. Everybody can be great because everybody can serve.*[8] Their role models are Mother Teresa, Dr. Martin Luther King Jr., and, often, Abraham Lincoln.

As you know, I have visited a great many schools. I have observed that a school can be either an Elon Musk school or it can be a Mother Teresa school. But it can't be both.

One school administrator (not at the conference) put it bluntly. "I don't think it's our job to teach kids about loving your neighbor and all that stuff," he said to me. "That's the parents' job. Our job is to give each kid the skills they need to make their dreams come true. So yeah, if I have to choose, I would say we are more about Elon Musk than Mother Teresa, definitely."

Elon Musk or Mother Teresa? This choice influences every aspect of what a school does. At one school I visited, where every student has an iPad, each fifth grader was assigned to make a commercial on his or her iPad to show how amazing he or she is. That's an Elon Musk school. At a Mother Teresa school, the students would have been assigned to make a commercial about a great American, such as Dwight Eisenhower, Martin Luther King Jr., or Amelia Earhart. Someone other than themselves.

Charlene, a high school student, attends an Elon Musk school. She told me that she hopes and expects to be a famous novelist someday. She's a teenager who has experienced the usual slings and arrows of adolescence and has used those experiences as grist for her fiction. Her teachers have praised her writing. She has sent manuscripts to literary agents but has received only rejection notices.

Charlene has very high self-esteem. I don't think that's necessarily a good thing. Her high self-esteem at age 15 is setting her up for disappointment and resentment at age 25. I have witnessed this trajectory many times. Soaring self-esteem in childhood and adolescence, carefully nurtured by parents and teachers, often leads to a crash after college, typically about two to five years after graduation, when it slowly dawns on the young adult—the same adult who had been so talented as an adolescent—that she's actually not as talented as she thought she was. She discovers that just because she was repeatedly told that she is amazing does not mean that she is, in fact, amazing.[9] Or she may hang on to that high self-esteem and continue to believe in her own amazingness as her self-esteem curdles into resentment. *I'm way more talented than that woman who was on the* TODAY *show talking about her novel. My novel is **so** much better. Why her? Why not me? It's totally not fair. Why should I have to work for a low wage in a cubicle while she's on the* TODAY *show talking about how great she is?*

Put bluntly: **bloated self-esteem leads to resentment**. If I am so wonderful, but my talents are not recognized and I'm still nobody at age 25, then I feel envious and resentful of those who are more successful.

The right kind of humility helps you to recognize your own shortcomings. To correct your deficiencies. To become better prepared. To understand the risks. And to take those risks courageously, when necessary.

The antidote to the culture of bloated self-esteem is the culture of humility. If I am humble, then I rejoice at the success of others and I am happy with my portion. **Humility leads to gratitude and contentment.** And contentment is the key to lasting happiness.

This conclusion is now grounded in some compelling research. Investigators have recently found that if an individual has a grateful attitude toward life, they are more likely to be satisfied with their life, more contented, and happier—as well as having more of a sense of being *in control* of their life.[10]

Again, this is not exactly a new insight. Traditionally, American parents taught this truth to their children with sayings such as "count your blessings" and "be grateful for what you have." It's less common to hear American parents say such things today, except as consolation after their child isn't picked to star in the school play, or when their high school senior gets the thin envelope from Stanford.

The sequence of events matters here. Many of us regard gratitude as a *result*. Santa Claus brings the child an unexpected, wonderful present, and the child is grateful to Santa Claus. But researchers are discovering that a grateful attitude is a *cause* of happiness, psychological well-being, and a sense of personal mastery.[11]

Humility, gratitude, and contentment. These are key virtues which American kids today are unlikely to possess after years of indoctrination in their own awesomeness. These are the virtues you want to teach your child or teen *before* disappointment comes.

I understand that this may rub some of you the wrong way. I
went through an Ayn Rand phase myself when I was a teenager.
(Ayn Rand was an author who won fame for writing novels such
as *The Fountainhead* and *Atlas Shrugged* which featured strong,
selfish protagonists who pursued their own self-interest relentlessly and without apology. When I looked at those novels again
as an adult, I noticed that not one of the major protagonists was
the parent of a child. Rand herself never raised a child.) Such a
phase can be a normal part of adolescence, part and parcel of
the relentless egocentrism of the young. But as you mature into
adulthood—and certainly when you become a parent—you realize that the world is, and should be, bigger than you are. It's not
about you. And once you realize that and accept that, gratefully,
you can breathe a sigh of relief.

Think back to Aaron and Julia, the two kids whose stories I
shared in the chapter on fragility. Aaron was the gamer who gave
up on football after just one day of tryouts. Julia was the star student whose self-concept crumbled when she struggled to understand AP Physics. Think how different their experiences might
have been if their parents had taught them something about humility beforehand. Freed from the pressure to be The Greatest,
and comfortable with being just OK, Aaron might have learned
to persevere, might have gotten in shape, might have made the
team—which in turn might have grounded his self-concept in
something more real than the world of video games. Julia might
have crafted a self-concept which was more mature, less about her
personal awesomeness. She might also have gotten closer to figuring out whether she was taking AP Physics as a junior because
of a genuine interest in physics, or because she wanted to impress
people by taking AP Physics as a junior.

In every era and in every culture, warnings abound regarding the errors to which that culture is least prone. In puritanical eras, pastors preach about the dangers of indulging the flesh, when perhaps they should be talking more about the dangers of self-righteous asceticism. In indulgent eras like our own, TV talk-show hosts warn about the dangers of puritanism when it might be more helpful to acknowledge the risks of giving in to every impulse—"if it feels good, do it"—without considering long-term consequences.[12] In our era of "walk tall" and "stand proud," it takes courage to teach humility. And it won't earn you many friends.

How do you do it? How do you teach your kid to walk *humbly* in an era when every other parent you know is trying to boost their kid's self-esteem?

I think the answer begins early, in the first two years of life. Many parents, tasked with the challenge of preparing supper with a toddler in the home, tend to put the toddler in a safe place where the child can play with toys or watch a screen, out of harm's way. But that sends an unintended message to the child: *Your job is to play while Mommy and Daddy's job is to make supper for you.* And this pattern continues year after year. Then, maybe around 8 years of age, the parent invites the child into the kitchen to help prepare supper. The child refuses, even throws a tantrum when the parent goes to turn off the video game. No surprise there. The child has had eight years to learn that it's the parents' job to do the chores and prepare the meals while the child plays. Once that rule has been in force for eight years, a speech about how "now you're old enough to help around the house" is unlikely to change the child's ingrained understanding of the world. It will seem unfair and just plain *wrong* to the child to upend the rule which has been one of the foundations of life for the past eight years, for the child's entire life, which is *I play while Mommy and Daddy make supper.*

Don't let that rule creep into your home. When your child is 6 months of age, get a front-facing papoose and carry your baby around the kitchen as you prepare supper. Talk to your child as you work. Explain what you are doing and why. "Now I need to chop these onions. Next, I have to get a head of lettuce out of the refrigerator."

Anthropologist David Lancy has found that around 18 months of age, almost all toddlers around the world want to help their parents. And in most societies outside the developed West, the parents integrate the young ones into the work that is required to keep the household running. In most families that have ever lived, across time and in different places, young children want to help in the house, and their help is welcomed. And in those families the unspoken rule is not *I play while Mommy and Daddy do all the chores* but rather *I am part of the household, I help Mommy and Daddy with the chores.* Lancy and other researchers find that in traditional societies that have always followed this practice, kids of every age pitch in and help with every aspect of household life: preparing and serving meals, cleaning the house, making repairs. They don't have to be asked. They see what needs to be done and they do it. And they don't expect to be paid for doing it.[13]

Granted, it's not easy to do that with an 18-month-old. You will need to plan meals that a toddler can help with. Some of the ideas that I have used, or that I have learned from other parents, include:

- Peeling the husks off fresh ears of corn
- Tearing a head of lettuce into little pieces for salad

- Mashing up chickpeas with a potato masher to make homemade hummus, or mashing bananas to make banana bread
- Stamping out cookie dough with a cookie cutter

"Learning towers" are available to help your 2-year-old work alongside you at the kitchen counter. A learning tower is basically a stepstool with a crib-like structure so that a 2-year-old can safely stand alongside you without falling.

This really works. In families that have employed these strategies, parents tell me that their 4-year-old is chomping at the bit to help prepare the meal, the 11-year-old is making his own lunch for school, and the 15-year-old is washing the dishes after supper. Without being asked.

As kids get older, I find that some parents prioritize their kids' academic achievement (and sometimes their athletic achievement) above everything else. As one mother said to me, "My daughter's job is school. We can afford to hire a housekeeper. She's doing so many activities and she has so much homework, we don't want her to waste what little free time she has doing household chores. Her job is school." That parent is sending an unintended message: *Your time is too important to be wasted on chores*, which easily morphs into *YOU are too important to be bothered with chores*. It's the very opposite of teaching humility. That unintended message puffs up the bloated self-esteem and narcissism which now characterize many kids.

Don't send that message. Insist that your kids make their beds. Wash the dishes. Mow the lawn. Feed the pets. Set the table. Do the vacuuming.

I have previously mentioned the late Bill Phillips, his wife, Janet, and their four sons. Bill Phillips was a prosperous businessman and, separately and simultaneously, a successful Washington lawyer and lobbyist. His family enjoyed an affluent lifestyle. But he and his wife insisted that their four sons devote several hours every week, most often on Sunday, to household maintenance.

His oldest son, Andrew, explained it to me this way. Their usual Sunday morning routine was to go to church as a family. After church they had brunch. After brunch, they changed into work clothes and everyone went outside to do chores. The family's large estate near Potomac, Maryland, required lots of maintenance.

"It literally required an army to keep that place running," Andrew told me. "Typically there would be one major task for the day. I remember doing things like moving piles of brush, felling trees, removing bushes, rebuilding fences, cleaning and maintaining the pool, mulching, power washing, planting flowers, weeding, painting, cleaning vehicles, moving debris, weed whacking, replacing bricks from our walkway, etc. My dad had a hard line policy of *'if you're here on a Sunday, you're working.'* I remember several occasions where friends of ours would have spent the night, but they didn't because they didn't want to have to do the chores the next day. My dad made it clear that having a friend over was not an excuse for missing work on Sunday. Frankly, it made for some awkward interactions with friends who were clearly less than excited at the prospect of spending two hours mulching before their parents picked them up. In fact, very few things would get you excused from Sunday chores. I have distinct memories of us all trying really hard to get out of stuff with, 'But I have SO much homework!' and similar excuses."

Janet and Bill could have afforded a landscaping service. Most of the families living on large estates around Potomac employ professional landscapers. Why didn't Janet and Bill just hire a landscaping crew? I posed that question to Janet. Here is her answer:

It would have been easier, for sure. Writing a check and leaving all that work to professionals would have been easier than leading the boys to do it. But I thought understanding the value of labor should be a major part of their upbringing, as it was for me. I grew up working every Sunday on a family "project."

Remember, I grew up in a small town in southwestern Minnesota. My dad was the local town lawyer. Every Sunday after church our entire family would go into town. We lived on a small farm on the edge of town, and we'd pile into the family station wagon and head into dad's small office. As a family we cleaned his office. It never struck me as odd. I thought that's what all practical families did. But I hated it! "Time to go to town" would interrupt our usually great game of kick-the-can on our front field. I so hated this family ritual that once I hid in our chicken coop hoping that mom and dad would think I was kidnapped and head into town with the rest of the crew and forget about me. No such luck. I learned that if you resisted, you got assigned the worst job—mopping the tile floor, which during mud season was torture. I was embarrassed that my friends would see us. I was worried that if dad's clients saw us cleaning, and not employing "professionals," they'd think he wasn't a good lawyer.

Eventually my dad became a local judge, and I remember being so relieved we didn't have to clean the municipal building after he was elected.

As I grew up, I realized what I learned from those Sunday afternoons together. First of all, I learned how to clean. That left me with a life-long appreciation for clean spaces and those who keep them so. I also remember thinking that our family could always survive if the world got turned upside down because we knew how to do things. My parents taught me not to rely on others unless it involved an electrical current. Our family Sundays were also the source of many, many of our favorite family stories because we were all together.

I wanted my boys to know the same strength. Life is not so scary if you know how to do things, even simple things.

I first met Beth Fayard, her husband, Jeff Jones, and their children almost 30 years ago. Beth and her husband are Just Right parents, in my judgment—a judgment based on many years of observation in my role as both their family physician and their neighbor. Beth and Jeff are both strict *and* loving. And they are keen observers with real insight into what has happened in American culture, at least in suburban Maryland just outside Washington, DC, where I practiced for 19 years.

I met with Beth and her oldest daughter, Grace, to ask their thoughts about some of the issues I raise in this book. Grace told me, "My parents taught me early on that I wasn't going to be the cool kid. And I didn't mind that much because what really mattered to me most was not what other kids thought about me. What mattered to me most was what my parents thought about me."

Beth chimed in, "For an American girl to be 'cool' nowadays means dressing in a provocative and inappropriate way, disrespecting your parents, and staying out late at night. None of which my girls were allowed to do."

I asked Beth what her policy was about her kids doing chores. She explained that her kids started helping around the house at a very young age. "Even as toddlers, they helped us. Dusting, for example. I would say, 'Watch what I do. This will be your job.' So that by the age of 4, they really can help with the dusting. There's no great mystery to this."

What do other parents in the neighborhood think of your approach? I asked.

"Most of them don't approve," she said bluntly. "Here's something that just happened recently. After my son's game, the other parents wanted all the kids to go out for pizza together. I said no, we can't go out for pizza because we have to go home and clean house. Clean the chicken coop. [The Fayard family has been raising chickens for many years, mostly for the eggs, which they eat. They have 12 chickens.] The other parents said, *Oh come on, Beth, are you going to keep him from his friends? Don't you think you're being a little extreme?* But these chores have to be done. The game was his leisure time."

Different parents will differ on best practice here. Even some Just Right parents might think that Beth is being too strict in this situation. But I think Beth is teaching her kids an important lesson. *The world doesn't revolve around you. You are a member of this family with obligations to this family, and those obligations are paramount.*

The actor Denzel Washington told a story which illustrates this point. "I remember coming home one time and feeling full of myself and talking, 'Did you imagine all this? I mean, I'm a STAR,'" he said. "[My mom] said, 'First of all, you don't know how many people been praying for you and for how long.' ... So then she told me to get the bucket and the squeegee and clean the windows."[14]

I n the chapter on screens, I wrote about how the world of social media pushes kids to promote themselves: *Here I am at the party, having a great time. Here I am getting dressed for the prom. Here I am sticking my finger up my nose.*

Here I am. Look at me. It's all about broadcasting and promoting the self. Now you can see the dangers of social media from a different perspective. One of our jobs as parents is to inculcate humility and gratitude and contentment, an interest in other people, while limiting the inborn tendency to promote oneself. Social media undercuts all that. I have encountered kids whose parents are trying to do everything right according to the guidelines laid out in this book, but the kids are still disrespectful, disengaged from parents, and defiant. Increasingly I am finding that the root cause in these cases is the kids' involvement in social media.

In 1912, John D. Rockefeller was the richest man in the world with a personal fortune equal to 1.5 percent of total US gross domestic product.[15] An equivalent fortune today would be about $380 billion, far beyond even the fortunes of Elon Musk and Jeff Bezos. But when asked how much money it would take for him to have enough, Rockefeller is supposed to have replied, "Just a little bit more." He was not content.

Around the same time, the great environmentalist John Muir told a friend that he, John Muir, was wealthier than Rockefeller. His friend responded that John Muir owned very little. Rockefeller was inconceivably rich. What did Muir mean by his nonsensical comment? "I have enough," Muir said. "Rockefeller doesn't have enough." Muir was content with the mountains and the sky.

I have enough. That's gratitude and contentment. And that's the key to happiness.

Turn off the device and take your child for a walk through the woods or a hike up the mountain. Go on a camping trip. Late at night, when it's absolutely dark, take your child's hand and ask her to look up at the stars. Talk with her about the vastness of space, more than 100 billion galaxies, and the tininess of our planet in the universe. That's reality. That's perspective.

That's humility.

I I

Joy

I see it almost every day I'm in the office: parents who don't really enjoy the time they have with their son or their daughter. Often the parent doesn't have good insight on this point. I say to the parent, "You need to enjoy the time you spend with your child."

The parent gives me a blank look, then says, "But I *do* enjoy the time I spend with her."

"When's the last time you and your daughter did something totally fun together?" I ask. "Something both of you really enjoyed?"

Another blank look. Finally, mom says, "We've just been so busy recently. She has so many after-school activities. And then there's homework. We are going to Disney over spring break though."

Enjoy the time you spend with your child. That advice seems so banal, so trivial, as to be almost devoid of content. But it's not. The surprising truth is that most American parents, especially mothers, do not enjoy much of the time they spend with their children.

When the Nobel Prize–winning economist Daniel Kahneman and his colleagues surveyed working women in the United States, here is how those women rated how much they enjoyed various activities in their lives. The most-enjoyed are at the top, the least-enjoyed at the bottom:

1. Intimate relations
2. Socializing outside of work
3. Supper
4. Lunch
5. Exercising
6. Praying
7. Socializing at work
8. Watching TV at home
9. Talking on the phone at home
10. Napping
11. Cooking
12. Shopping
13. Housework
14. Time with children
15. Working for pay

As you can see, child care was near the bottom of the list—below cooking, below housework.[1]

Kahneman and his team subsequently compared American women in Columbus, Ohio, with French women in Rennes, France. The team "expected to find substantial differences between the determinants of life satisfaction and experienced happiness in the two cities, and were instead surprised by their remarkable similarity."[2] The American women did not differ significantly from French women in how much they enjoyed active leisure, passive leisure, eating, talking, working, or commuting to work. In other words, the women were similar to one another. French culture and American culture are not as different as one might think.

But there was a big difference in how much the women in both countries enjoyed being with their kids. As Kahneman's team summarized their findings, "The American mothers spent more time focused on child care, but enjoyed it less." Time spent with a child was negatively associated with enjoyment for American women but positively associated with enjoyment for French women. Having a spouse mitigated the negativity somewhat for American women, but—Kahneman and colleagues concluded—"the corresponding values when children were present suggest that the presence of the spouse hardly makes American children less annoying to their mother."

"The relative unhappiness of American mothers obviously demands further study," Kahneman's team concluded. "Our French team member suggested that French children are simply better behaved."[3]

I suspect that the French team member is correct.

Note also that Kahneman surveyed only *women* in these studies. In her book *All Joy and No Fun: The Paradox of Modern Parenthood*, Pulitzer Prize–winning journalist Jennifer Senior suggested that men enjoy parenting more than women do. Partly that's because men are more likely to be doing the fun stuff while the women do the less-fun stuff. Dad tosses the baby in the air and the baby laughs. Mom changes the diapers. Dad takes his daughter to a father-daughter dance. Mom irons the dress for the dance.[4]

Mothers used to spend much more time with kids than fathers did, but that gender difference is diminishing somewhat. Between

1975 and 2022, the amount of time American fathers spent with their kids nearly tripled—from 2.4 hours per week in 1975 to 6.9 hours per week in 2022—though that's still far below the mothers' average of 11.8 hours per week.[5] And there's still a big gap in *how* fathers and mothers spend time with their kids. As Jennifer Senior observes, fathers typically spend more time *playing* with their kids, while moms spend more time doing routine activities such as toothbrushing, bathing, and feeding. "Ask any parent which type of child care they prefer," Senior writes.[6] That may be part of the reason why American fathers may enjoy parenting more than moms: because the dads are playing, not working.

But Jennifer Senior highlights another, more fundamental reason why American moms don't enjoy parenting. American mothers multitask. They try to be a mom at the same time that they are trying to do housework or professional work. The men interviewed by Ms. Senior were less likely to attempt this multitasking. Senior notes that women with children are more than twice as likely to feel rushed "sometimes or always" compared to women without children. But American fathers are no more likely to feel rushed compared to American men without children.[7]

Senior's accounts of women who try to integrate housework or professional work with parenting strike a chord with me, because I have heard so many similar accounts from women in my own practice and when I have spoken with parents across the United States. They tell me how they're trying to get something accomplished in their adult lives at the same time that they're trying to do stuff with their child. They're trying to answer a text message from a friend, or an email from work, at the same time that they're playing *Candyland* with their child.

Don't do that. It's no fun. When you are with your child, devote yourself completely to your child. When I am on duty to watch my daughter, I try to do something outdoors, partly so that I won't feel the temptation to steal a look at a screen for an email. When my daughter was 8 years old, I insisted that she and I go play miniature golf. She had never played miniature golf before, and she did not want to go. "I hate miniature golf," she said.

"You have never played miniature golf," I said. "How could you possibly know?"

"When I was in Heaven, before I was born, I saw people playing it, and I didn't like it," she said with an absolutely straight face.

But I insisted. We drove to the miniature golf course, with her protesting all the way there. But once there, we had a great time. One month later, she and I took a walk through some nearby woods and pretended that we were marooned far from civilization.

"We don't have anything to eat. We don't have anything to drink," she said.

"Yes. We're probably going to die," I said. We jumped up and down and waved our arms, trying to signal for help to an imaginary helicopter.

We had a great time.

Sometimes it's not easy to enjoy time with your child. Sometimes your child may not even want to be with you.

Kayden was 4 years old when his parents divorced. His mother won full custody in part because Kayden's father, James, had been convicted on charges of selling illegal drugs several years earlier. Four years later, when Kayden was 8, Kayden's mother was arrested and convicted on charges of selling illegal drugs herself. The social worker called James and told him that the court was giving full custody to him, the father.

From the first day Kayden came to live with his father, Kayden was unhappy. He missed his mother. For four years he had heard from her what a terrible person his father was. He resented his father. "Every day was difficult," James told me. "No matter what I did, nothing worked. If I tried to be nice, he ignored me. If I tried to be the tough guy and speak firmly, he would start screaming so loudly that I was worried the neighbors would hear. And he could tell I was worried about that.

"So about three weeks after he came to live with me, I said, 'We're going tubing.' He said, '*What?*' He didn't know what tubing was. When I explained that we would go down a snowy mountain in a rubber tube, he yelled that he didn't want to go. But I said, 'Too bad, you're going.'

"It's about an hour's drive to Blue Mountain. The first 20 minutes or so he was yelling and crying about how he didn't want to go. The next 40 minutes he didn't talk at all. But when we got there, he didn't fight me getting out of the car. I think he was interested in the mountain. He'd never been any place like that before.

"After I bought the lift tickets and he looked up the mountain and he saw the kids coming down the hill, his face lit up. He still didn't say anything, but I could see he was excited. When we got in the tube, he didn't even pretend to be upset anymore. He was absolutely thrilled. When we got to the bottom, he said, 'Let's do it again!'

"We spent the whole day on the mountain. And it changed everything. He saw me in a totally new light after that. He discovered that we could have fun together. So when we got home, we started doing rough and tumble play, throwing the ball around outside, wrestling inside, everything. We're good now. And it all started with that day on the mountain."

Spending fun time together with your child is not an optional elective to be squeezed in after the day's required work is done. It's essential. You have to plan for it. You have to insist on it. You must make time for it.

When I push parents on the importance of doing fun things with their kids, some parents say, "But what should we do?" My answer: choose something that you, the parent, love to do, and teach it to your kid. I learned to sail at summer camp as a teenager, and I love to sail every chance we get. We don't own a sailboat, but Marsh Creek State Park, near our home, rents catamarans and sailboats for a reasonable fee, and I'm teaching my daughter, Sarah, to sail. When we went sailing most recently, a gust of wind caught the sail and the catamaran capsized stern over bow, throwing both of us into the water. Sarah said it was the most fun she'd ever had.

If you like to hike, take your kid hiking with you. If you enjoy cooking, teach your kid to help prepare the meals you enjoy. If you love the beach, take your kid to the beach and play in the waves together. If you love to golf, teach your kid to golf, starting young. If you ski, take your kids to the slopes as soon as they are old enough to wear boots and get on skis or a snowboard. If you enjoy skeet shooting, get your kid a rifle and have her join you at the club. If you enjoy music, make music with your kid. Anything that gets you and your kid out of the routine, out of the house together to do something fun.

Instead of fathers teaching their sons to be men, I see men who are trying to be boys, asking their 11-year-old sons to teach them how to play video games. That's not what boys need. Don't try to be a child. Be the adult you want your child to become.

Kayden was 8 years old when his father was able to change his attitude with one day on the mountain. If Kayden had been 15, it might not have been so easy or so quick. The younger the child, the easier it is to change the child's attitude about fun and about you. Teenagers are often more of a challenge. But not always.

Bronson Bruneau* is an all-American teenage success story. As captain of his high school basketball team, he led his teammates to the Minnesota state championship. He was also an All-Conference football player (he played tight end). He graduated with the #2 grade point average in his class. The girl who graduated with the #1 GPA was his girlfriend. He was awarded eight different scholarships for college by local community groups. He earned extra cash by mowing his neighbors' lawns. Other community groups gave him their top awards for community service.[8] He went on to attend Duke University, where he played football for four years. He has been working since graduation and recently married a young woman. They hope to start a family in the next year or two.

As befits a successful student athlete in the United States, Bronson was popular in high school. He could have spent every night of his senior year in high school at a party or a friend's house. But when we spoke by telephone during his senior year, he told me that his favorite free time activity was just hanging out with his parents. On more than one occasion he declined invitations to parties in order to just stay home and play board games with his

---

*His real name.

parents, or to watch old movies with them. Now, years later, he's returned to Minnesota and lives near his parents. When we spoke again a few weeks ago, he told me that he still enjoys playing golf with his father and playing board games with his parents, now alongside his young bride.

Having spoken both with Bronson and with his older sister, Marlow,* I am confident that their parents are Just Right parents, that they are both strict and loving. Marlow told me how upset she often was with her parents when she was a teenager. She wasn't allowed to get her ears pierced until she turned 13. She was never allowed to see an R-rated movie until she was 17, and she had to give her parents advance notice of the movies she was going to see. She was never allowed to be home alone with a boy; at least one parent always had to be present. Her father insisted on interviewing every boy before the boy was allowed to date Marlow. She was never allowed to bring a boyfriend upstairs, even though her friends were engaging in all sorts of private trysts in *their* bedrooms.

"All through high school, I told my parents, 'I'm going to have to be in therapy for the rest of my life because of all the terrible things you're doing to me,'" Marlow told me. "I was always the odd girl out, the girl who wasn't allowed to do stuff that everybody else was doing. Then I went to the University of Virginia and after about two years there, seeing all the kids who were falling apart and who were doing all kinds of crazy things to wreck their own lives, I suddenly realized: *I'm NOT going to have to be in therapy now or later because of the way my parents raised me.*"

Despite—or perhaps because of—their parents' strictness, both Marlow and Bronson still enjoy spending time with their

---

*Her real name.

parents. They still watch old movies together. Dad and Bronson still like to shoot pool or play golf together.

Little things make the best happiness.[9]

Enjoy the time you have with your kids. That means no devices at mealtime—no TV on in the background, no looking at your phone at the dinner table. When you are sitting at the table with your child, the focus should be on the interaction between you and her. Listen to your child and talk with her.

We try to enforce this rule strictly in our home. No screens at the dinner table. No glancing at cell phones. No TV on during suppertime. No iPads. When my daughter was in first grade, she wrote down a list of topics to help her remember what she wanted to talk about at dinner that evening: food, books, animals, plants, numbers, letters, names, movies, toys, colors, and vehicles. My daughter's plan was to ask everyone at the table to name their favorite food, their favorite book, favorite animal, etc. It took us about an hour at the table to work through our favorite foods, favorite books, and favorite animals. Then it was time to clean up.

Likewise: no headphones, no earbuds allowed in the car. When my wife and I went to buy a car recently, my wife wanted heated rear seats. It turns out the only way to get heated rear seats was to purchase the Entertainment Package, which includes an entertainment system for the rear seats. I kept the promotional materials from the car dealer. One photo in the materials shows a mom in the front passenger seat, looking back and beaming at her two children in the rear seats. Both children are wearing headsets, looking at the screen while they play their video game. The mom seems to be saying, "Isn't this great! We can drive for hours, and I never have to talk with my kids at all!"

Everybody's in a rush. Take advantage of every moment you can. As I said earlier, time in the car should be time for kids and parents to talk. Don't permit your child to separate herself or himself from you by putting on a headset in the car, or anywhere that you are together.

Following this advice—no multitasking, devoting yourself 100 percent to your child when you are with her—requires time. A significant investment of time. Beyond time in the car together, how do you find the time to follow these guidelines?

It's about balance. Balance in your life and in the life of your child. You may have to cut back on your schedule and on your child's schedule. I have discussed this problem with many working parents, and I have become convinced that many of us are just trying to do too much and our kids are trying to do too much. One mom in our neighborhood mentioned that she is so busy every afternoon, chauffeuring her kids to their various activities, that they almost never have time for a meal at home. Instead, they order sandwiches on the run and eat in the car between ballet class and soccer practice. By the time they get home it's time for homework and then bed.

What message is being sent here? As I mentioned in the chapter on food, the unintended message is that relaxed time together as a family is the lowest priority of all, that being amazing and doing tons of amazing things is more important than having supper at home with family. Don't send that message.

Parents are overscheduled as well, trying to do too much in too little time, not getting enough sleep. But instead of cutting back on our own schedules, many of us parents act as though the answer is to book up our kids' schedules so that they are as stressed and overwhelmed as we are.

This sort of behavior is more common in the United States than elsewhere. Outside of North America, it's unusual to find adults who boast about how busy they are and how little sleep they get. Outside of North America, it's rare to find full-time parents who spend their days chauffeuring their children from one activity to another, even over the summer holiday.[10] As essayist and cartoonist Tim Kreider observes, "If you live in America in the 21st century you've probably had to listen to a lot of people tell you how busy they are.... It is, pretty obviously, a boast disguised as a complaint." He shares the experience of a friend who left New York City and moved to France. She "described herself as happy and relaxed for the first time in years. She still gets her work done, but it doesn't consume her entire day and brain.... What she had mistakenly assumed was her personality—driven, cranky, anxious and sad—turned out to be a deformative effect of her environment. It's not as if any of us wants to live like this.... It's something we collectively force one another to do."[11]

I spoke with a mother who has a daughter, Darby. Darby works hard at school. Her mother and father both support her academic ambitions, but they are cautious about giving her too much help with her homework. They don't want to be helicopter parents. She has soccer practice every Saturday plus every Tuesday afternoon, dance class two other days, and a computer coding class another day.

Darby is 8 years old.

When I asked Darby's mom why Darby is doing all those activities, she answered, "Because Darby really enjoys all those activities." That's great, I replied. But don't you think you need to teach her something about *balance*, about not being overscheduled?

Something about the joy of a quiet moment, maybe just lying on your back on the grass and looking at the sky?

Mom paused. She could see where I was going with this. "Computer coding is a really valuable skill," she said. "Especially for girls."

I didn't pursue the argument. I didn't have much hope of actually changing that mom's mind, and I don't see the point of arguing just to argue. Of course computer coding is a valuable skill. Especially for girls. But by cramming a child's life full of activities, at 8 years of age, with little time for reflection, with no quiet time for a relaxed parent-and-child supper, this mom is sending an unintended message: *what you **do** is more important than who you **are**.* And this parent is teaching her daughter that becoming more accomplished, honing her skills in this activity and that activity, matters more than free time, more than relaxation, more than good conversation and listening to others. More than family.

The focus on after-school activities for kids, like the culture of social media, is all about boosting the ego and inflating the self. *Look at my kid: she's an accomplished dancer, a skilled soccer player, and a whiz at computer coding.*

The same is true for parents: I have found many who are stretched thin with commitments at work, volunteering, and other chores which leave too little time for just having a relaxed meal at home with their child. Too many parents want to say, *Look at me*: I'm a successful professional, a great parent, and blah blah blah.

Like mother like daughter. Like father like son.

It's too much. We have everything backward. Forget about the accomplishments. Don't push your child to live her life as though she were continually preparing her college application. Teach her not to worry about being amazing in the eyes of other people. That means *doing less* and *becoming more*.

Making these changes may require some big adjustments in your personal life and in your professional job. You may have to move from one state to another in order to find a less demanding job or to live comfortably on a smaller income. That's OK. You have to be clear about what the priorities are.

You have to teach the meaning of life.

12

The Meaning of Life

When I visit schools, I often meet with students in groups both large and small. When I meet with middle or high school students, I engage them in back-and-forth questioning. I pose questions and I call on students who raise their hands.

What's the point of school? I sometimes ask. Why bother?

To get into a good college—that's the answer I hear most often.

So why do you have to go to college? I ask.

To get a good job, the students answer.

So why do you need a good job? I ask.

To earn lots of money, they answer.

So why do you need lots of money? I ask.

To have fun! they answer. *Obviously! Duh.* (At this point, I often hear some disgruntled muttering from the students—"Jeez! Who hired this guy?")

This dialogue is the basis for what I have come to call "the middle-class script." The script, as I have heard it preached at many schools, reads as follows:

1. *Work hard in school so you can get into a good college.*
2. *Get into a good college so you can get a good job.*
3. *Get a good job and you will make a good living and have a good life.*

There are several problems with this script. The first problem is that every line in it is false.

1. **Working hard in school is no guarantee of admission to a top college**. We all know stories of kids who worked hard, earned good grades, and didn't get into any of their top choices.

2. **Getting into a good college is no guarantee of a good job**. The media and the blogosphere are full of stories of young people who have earned bachelor's degrees from Princeton and Harvard and Stanford who are now pouring lattes at Starbucks or simply unemployed.[1]

3. **Getting a good job is no guarantee of having a good life**.

The implicit assumption of the middle-class script is that getting a good job—which at these schools always means a job that pays well—is the key to happiness. But the evidence doesn't provide strong support for that hypothesis. In a much-cited study, Nobel laureates Daniel Kahneman and Angus Deaton found that beyond a threshold income of about $75,000, more money doesn't buy more happiness.[2] That finding has been confirmed and replicated in a more recent study of more than 1.7 million individuals worldwide.[3]

If money doesn't guarantee happiness, what does? The answer is *the quality of your personal relationships*, beginning with your family. A good marriage, and a loving relationship with your children, is the best predictor of your long-term health and happiness, far better than your income.[4]

Apparently most American parents don't know that. In 2023, the Pew Research Center surveyed 3,757 parents nationwide. A large majority—88 percent—said that it was "very" or "extremely" important for their kids to be financially independent, which is a polite way of saying financially well-off. But only 21 percent of parents thought it was important for their kid to get married, and only 20 percent thought it was important for their kid to have a child of their own. Fully 46 percent of survey respondents said it was "not too important" or "not at all important" for their kid to get married or to have children of their own.[5]

This is weird. This was a survey not of the general population but of *parents* with children under 18 at home. Don't the majority of parents want to have grandchildren someday? Apparently not.

The middle-class script leads to a rise in the proportion of young people who are living alone, young people who prioritize their work over marriage, family, and friendships. The proportion of young Americans living alone is higher than it has ever been. In 1960, single-person households represented only 13 percent of American households. By 2021, that percentage had more than doubled to 28 percent.[6] And many young adults are simply "failing to launch." In one recent survey, fully half of young adults ages 18 to 29 were still living in their parents' home.[7] A 29-year-old man living in his parents' home doesn't count as a single-person household, but he is often a failure to launch, a failure to fulfill his potential to become independent and to start his own family. In another recent survey from the Pew Center, nearly six in 10 single adults said that they were not even *looking* for a relationship or even casual dates.[8] (For a deep dive into the factors driving the "failure to launch" phenomenon, please see the chapter titled "Failure to Launch" in the second edition of my book *Boys Adrift*.)

Some of these adults are thoroughly immersed in what podcaster and journalist Derek Thompson has christened "workism," in which one's job has morphed "into a kind of religion, promising identity, transcendence, and community"—the belief that work is, and should be, "the centerpiece of one's identity and life's purpose."[9] These people are so submerged in workism that they aren't even interested in having a relationship. "My job is my life" is a phrase I often hear from such people.

But here's the twist: I would estimate that more than 80 percent of the adults I see in the office don't like their jobs.[10] In a culture that preaches "get a good job, have a good life," they are restless and unhappy. They don't like their job, so they believe they don't have a good life. "Your job is *not* your life," I tell these people. "You are more than your job." Sometimes they hear what I'm saying. More often they don't. A 10-minute pep talk from a family doctor (me) can't undo the years of brainwashing from a culture which holds up achievement at work as the best guarantee of personal happiness and fulfillment.[11]

There is nothing new about people not enjoying their work. More than 150 years ago, Henry David Thoreau wrote that "most men lead lives of quiet desperation." What's different today is that young people are immersed in stories of billionaire entrepreneurs and YouTube influencers and TikTok celebrities who endlessly promote *themselves* and their brand. Your news feed now offers you a continual spew of amazing people bombarding you with their awesome amazingness. The rest of us feel inadequate. Less than. A failure.

So I ask: How does it happen that so many young people succumb to the toxic culture of workism? Which brings us back to the question, more seriously: What is school for?

I find that parents in the United States, more than in any other country where I have spoken to parents, have bought into the middle-class script. In Germany and in German-speaking Switzerland, for example, I have found that there is no shame if a 15-year-old chooses to train to become an auto mechanic rather than choosing the university track. And that's true even if both parents are professors at the university. Mechanics in Germany earn good money, just as they do in the United States, but I have found that mechanics in Germany are truly respected by their university-educated peers, which is less likely to be true in the USA. But those mechanics usually don't find their meaning of life in rebuilding engines. They find their meaning of life in their connections with other human beings.

Mechanics can earn good money in the United States as well, but there is a stigma, a lack of respect attached to being "blue-collar" in the United States today which I have found to be utterly lacking in Germany, Austria, and Switzerland. In the United States, it is hard to imagine the child of two professors choosing to go straight into "vocational training" to be a mechanic unless that child has been diagnosed with some sort of learning disability. Many Americans today regard "vocational training" as a low-prestige option for kids with below-average IQ or kids with learning disabilities.

At some level, sometimes subconsciously, many Americans—not only parents and students, but in many cases also teachers and school leaders—have accepted the idea that a primary purpose of K–12 schooling, maybe even *the* primary purpose, is to get accepted into a good college and to prepare for college. That's a mistake. The primary purpose of education should be to prepare for *life*, not for more school. And many of the skills needed to be successful in life are different from the skills needed to be admitted to a good college.

In order to be admitted to a selective university, it is usually necessary to have a good grade point average as well as good test scores (although test scores are becoming less important—in 2023, a majority of students applying to four-year colleges did not submit test scores).[12] The student will also need to have extracurricular activities which will impress the admissions staff. So a rational student will avoid classes that might interest her but in which she may be less certain of getting an A; instead, she enrolls in familiar classes which she knows she can ace. She may sign up for an after-school activity not primarily because it interests her but because she thinks it will look good on her college application. In short, she is not *living* so much as she is *performing*, putting on a show to impress the college admissions office. And what breaks my heart is that I see so many parents who are aiding and abetting this puppet show, parents who believe they are acting in their kid's best interest.

There are a few life trajectories—but only a few—in which this approach might almost make sense. If you are absolutely certain that you want to be a doctor, and you are sure that nothing else will bring you fulfillment and satisfaction, then the middle-class script might be a good fit for you. Work hard in school, get into a selective college. Work hard at college, get into med school. Work hard at med school, get into a good residency. Work hard in residency, get a good job at a good practice. Simple. The medical profession is a popular choice among college students, in part because the path to a good life seems clear at 17 years of age if you go that route.

As a practicing physician, I can tell you that many of my medical colleagues never did the hard work of figuring out, in childhood or adolescence, the answers to the really important questions. Those questions are *Who am I? What do I really want? What would make me happy?* Those are not trivial questions. The great American psychologist Dr. Abraham Maslow observed that many adults never answer those questions.[13] Maslow believed that those adults are often miserable because they are working hard at jobs they now hate in pursuit of goals that are no longer meaningful to them. I have seen some such adults among my own physician colleagues. I know a man who is a successful surgeon. He earns north of $800,000 a year, but he is wretched. "I'm a slave," he told me. "I'm working 80 hours a week at a job I just can't stand anymore. But I don't have a choice. I've got a big mortgage on a big house. I've got a wife who likes to fly first-class to Europe. I've got three kids in private school. I don't have any other options, no other way of earning this kind of money. And besides, I honestly don't know what else I'd really like to do. Mostly I just wish I could retire and live at the beach."

That man is right. He is a slave. Life is precious. Each minute is a priceless gift. No amount of money can reclaim lost time. If you are wasting your time on work you don't enjoy, in pursuit of goals which are no longer meaningful to you, you may come to be resentful about the time you are losing. If you are a physician, you may come to resent your patients. I have learned to recognize such physicians, and I try to steer my patients away from them.

But the straight-arrow path of the physician, from high school to college to med school to residency to high-paying job, is now a rare option. According to some labor force experts, in the 21st century most Americans will bounce from one job to another, even from one career to another, several times throughout their life.[14] And that's likely to become even more true as artificial intelligence makes inroads into fields such as computer coding which just a few years ago were marketed to high school kids as a sure thing. That sort of life, that bouncing-from-job-to-job life which many of our children will lead, demands a skill set very different from the skill set which works well in school. Your kids will have to be willing to try different things, to go in different directions, in order to find their niche, their calling, their vocation. And their niche/calling/vocation may change over time. If you and your kid are playing by the middle-class script, then school isn't preparing your kid for real life. Instead, school may be making your kid *less* prepared for real life by pushing your kid to be unduly cautious and risk averse.

The rules for success in life are different from the rules for getting admitted to a top college. *The willingness to fail* is one of the keys to success in real life, as I said earlier. To be a top student, you need to get As all the time, or at least most of the time. School— and the values inculcated at many schools today, both public and private—reinforces a reluctance to take risks, a reluctance to fail.

Your job as a parent is not to reinforce the middle-class script, but to challenge it. Empower your daughter or your son to take risks and congratulate them when they *fail*, because failure builds humility. And the humility born of failure can build growth and wisdom and an openness to new things in a way that success almost never can. Steve Jobs said something similar in his 2005 commencement speech at Stanford: "I didn't see it then, but it turned out that getting fired from Apple was the best thing that could have ever happened to me. The heaviness of being successful was replaced by the lightness of being a beginner again, less sure about everything. It freed me to enter one of the most creative periods of my life."[15]

Over the past 23 years, as I've visited more than 500 schools, I've been trying to understand what kids need and how schools help, or don't help. I have often been disappointed. Many schools I have visited, especially in the United States, embrace and broadcast the middle-class script. As a result, those schools often make kids more fragile rather than less. But there are some schools which have broken free of that script. One of those schools is Shore, the Australian school I mentioned earlier.

Robert Grant, sixth headmaster at Shore, was fond of making one particular remark to the parents of students newly enrolled at the school. He liked to say, "I hope your child will be *severely disappointed* during his time at this school." The parents were often confused. *Why would the headmaster wish for my child to be severely disappointed?* Mr. Grant would explain that if a student does not experience real disappointment at school, then he will be unprepared for disappointment when it comes in real life.

And disappointment will come. Dreams will be crushed. Loved ones will die. Relationships will end. The right education, alongside the right kind of upbringing, should prepare your son or your daughter to handle disappointment and failure, to slip loose of a dream when the dream is over, to move to another field of endeavor with no loss of enthusiasm. A few schools teach this, explicitly and well. But only a few. Some of the high schools which are regarded as "the best" because many of their graduates attend highly ranked colleges don't even attempt to teach these skills, the skills needed for success in *life*. Those schools are too busy preparing their students to get the best grades and the best test scores.

Robert Bly was a poet and philosopher. Dr. Marion Woodman was a psychoanalyst. Together they wrote a little-noticed book called *The Maiden King* about how girls become women and boys become men. They observed that many children and teens have the feeling that "something marvelous is going to happen."[16] Or as the protagonist of *Diary of a Wimpy Kid* puts it, "I'll be famous one day, but for now I'm stuck in middle school with a bunch of morons." Then sometime later, navigating through adolescence, the teenager "is hit with the awareness that something marvelous is *not* going to happen. That's the moment of The Great Disappointment."[17] In our culture, that moment is sometimes postponed until young adulthood, when the 20-something finally realizes that she isn't ever going to compete in the Olympics or have a million followers on TikTok or earn millions off her You-Tube channel.

Adolescence should be the time when kids learn about their own limits. In a world that contains nearly eight billion people, 99.99 percent of us are going to have to get used to the idea that we are not anybody special. Becoming a mature adult means reconciling yourself to the fact that you're not going to be a movie star. You're not going to be on the cover of *People* magazine. You're not going to be famous.

Our culture today does a terrible job of preparing kids for this moment and helping them make the transition to mature adulthood. On the contrary: kids are immersed in stories of ordinary kids just like them who rocketed to fame and fortune with minimal effort. At age 15, Charli D'Amelio started posting videos of herself dancing on TikTok. Two years later she was earning more than $17 million a year from TikTok,[18] where she now has over 150 million followers and has earned more than 11 *billion* likes.[19] But when you watch her TikTok videos, your first reaction is likely to be, *I don't get it. What's all the fuss about? She's not that special.* One girl I know watched some of Charli D'Amelio's TikTok videos and thought, *I can do that. I can do **better** than that. I'm a better dancer, everybody says so.* The girl I know went all in on making the perfect TikTok video. And it was the perfect TikTok video: funny, well-executed, catchy music. Two weeks after she posted it, she had seven likes and four shares. It fizzled. Nobody saw it.

When I speak on this topic to teens at a Jewish school or at a school with a Christian affiliation, I always quote Ecclesiastes 9:11: *The race is not to the swift, nor the battle to the strong...nor wealth to the brilliant...but time and chance happens to them all.* Why didn't your video go viral? Time and chance. There's nothing fair about it. Kids expect the world to be fair. But the world is not fair. The author of Ecclesiastes knew that. Wise people know it. We need to impart that wisdom to our kids.

In the chapter on education, I mentioned Suniya Luthar's finding that the children of affluent parents are now more likely to be depressed as adults compared to the children of lower-income parents. Luthar believes that the increased risk is attributable to the type of school those kids are attending, and I'm sure that's part of the story. But I wonder if there isn't more to the story. Speaking to high school students at a private school serving an affluent community, I asked the kids, "Where do you see yourself in 10 years? Raise your hand if you'd like to share with your peers where you see yourself in 10 years." A boy raised his hand. I called on him. The boy said, "I figure I'll have like, at least, 200 billion dollars. I mean, Mark Zuckerberg had *one* good idea, and he has like 120 billion dollars. I have like *eight* good ideas." I engaged the boy in conversation. He wasn't joking. He truly believes this.

What's going to happen to this boy five, 10 years down the road when he realizes he isn't going to have 200 billion dollars? He isn't going to have one billion dollars. He isn't going to be the next Mark Zuckerberg. He's going to be working at a job like the rest of us. He is likely to experience The Great Disappointment.

Maybe one reason that affluent children are at higher risk of The Great Disappointment compared with kids from lower-income families is that affluent kids have never learned humility. On the contrary, their self-esteem has been puffed up and their expectations of future greatness have been fanned. Well-meaning teachers and college counselors and school leaders tell these kids to "dream big." There's little or no recognition of how puffing up self-esteem and enlarging expectations to unrealistic proportions at age 15 can lead to disappointment and resentment at age 25.

Flashdance was a popular motion picture when it premiered, eventually becoming the third highest-grossing movie of 1983. Based on the true story of Maureen Marder, a construction worker by day who was an exotic dancer at night, it's about an 18-year-old girl who dreams of auditioning for a prestigious dance company. But she lacks the training and resources of many of the other girls. She is discouraged. At one point in the movie, she is ready to give up. Then her boyfriend Nick tells her, "When you give up your dream, you die." So she perseveres, and her dream comes true.

Many American parents and kids today are caught in the grip of what I sometimes call the *Flashdance* illusion. Movie as metaphor. Most of the kids I talk to nowadays have never seen *Flashdance*, they've never even heard of it, but they have seen dozens of other movies with the same theme. *Go for your dream. If you work hard enough, it will happen. If you build it, they will come.* And the parents often are stuck in the same script.

But it's a toxic script. It leads kids to focus on one trajectory, one story line: *initial failure must be met with the resolve to try harder in the same domain, leading to ultimate success.* The movie *Flashdance* might have been more interesting as a movie and more instructive for real life if halfway through, Jennifer Beals's character had said, "You know, maybe dancing just isn't my thing. Maybe I'll forget about dancing and instead go to Colorado and try my luck as a ski instructor. Or maybe I'll open a bed and breakfast in Nova Scotia."

The *Flashdance* metaphor is toxic for reasons similar to the reasons why the culture of Instagram and TikTok is toxic. It's all about *me*. It's all about what *I'm* doing, *my* success. For many middle-income and affluent parents, the deepest meaning of life they can offer their children is this notion of success. Conquering the world. Becoming top dog. That's become the new American dream: winning the jackpot of fame and fortune. Success equals fulfillment—or so many parents now seem to believe. As *New York Times* columnist David Brooks has observed, American culture today is based on the premise "that career and economic success can lead to fulfillment," an assumption which Brooks calls "the central illusion of our time."[20]

The flipside of the dream is what Mark Shiffman, professor of humanities at Villanova, calls "the game of fear": the concern so many young Americans now have that they will not find their place, that they will be less successful than their parents. "It has always been hard to answer life's deep and abiding questions," observes Shiffman. But he believes that contemporary American culture "makes it hard to ask them at all." He points out that young adults today have become accustomed to relying on institutionalized criteria to validate and affirm themselves. The result is a focus on what kids *do*, what they achieve, instead of on who they *are*, their character, their core, their soul.

It's part of your job as a parent to help your child develop character, self-control, Conscientiousness. To help your child learn what matters and what doesn't matter. Doing so, Professor Shiffman concludes, will give your child "clearer bearings amid life's uncertainties, a place to stand outside the game of fear. It also addresses what might be the deepest fear of all, which is that endless achievement might not add up to a meaningful life, that winning the races of academic and professional competition might not bring genuine happiness."[21]

The antidote to the culture of *Flashdance* and TikTok is to teach humility and gratitude. It's no longer all about *me*. It's about service to others. Integrity. Character. Even if my service and integrity and character are never noticed by anybody, and never result in any morsel of fame or fortune. It's finally about being and becoming the person you truly are meant to be, not the person you are pretending to be.

Real life does not conform to the conventions of the movies. We need to break free of this idea of life as being some sort of movie about personal success, triumphing over the odds, being victorious, climbing to the top of the pyramid. Let that go. Find another dream. The movie is not a good metaphor.

One of the most difficult obligations of responsible parenthood is to tell your son or your daughter that their dream isn't going to come true, that they need to find another dream. Parents who are unsure of their own authority, whose top priority is to please their child, will never speak these difficult truths. But if you don't, who will?

Which is more important, achievement or happiness? Wrong question.

Many parents have heard about "Tiger Moms" who are focused on their children's achievements, relentlessly pushing the child to do more. They may know some "Irish Setter Dads" who just want their kids to have a good time.[22] They wonder, should I push my kid harder to achieve? Or should I loosen up and let them relax?

But this question—achievement versus happiness—is based on false premises. There is no point in pushing your kid harder to achieve if he or she has no sense of a goal, or purpose, which gives some context to that achievement. Likewise, there isn't much point in letting your kids relax and do whatever they desire if you have not first *educated* their desire. If a parent hasn't educated their child's desire, and the kid has a device with Internet access, then it's likely that the girl is going to be on TikTok and the boy is going to be playing video games. You have to instill a desire for something better than social media and video games.

That's one of your tasks as a parent: to instill a sense of meaning, a longing for something higher and deeper than video games and social media. Without meaning, life comes to seem pointless and futile, and working hard to get good grades at school just becomes a "race to nowhere," to borrow the title of a documentary that makes that point. Without meaning, young people are more likely to become anxious and depressed.

Once children have a sense of meaning, they can pursue achievement with confidence because they know *why* that achievement is worth pursuing. Once desire has been educated, young people can enjoy free time more deeply and more fully, whether in reading a book, listening to music, or taking a walk through the woods. Or going on a fishing trip in Alaska.

In the previous chapter, I mentioned the importance of enjoying the time you spend with your child. Schedule a vacation with the objective of strengthening the parent-child bond. That's what Bill Phillips—remember the Breathalyzer?—was doing the morning of August 9, 2010, when he and his youngest son, Willy, 13 years old, climbed aboard a 12-seater amphibious floatplane in a remote corner of southwestern Alaska, on their way to some of the best salmon and trout fishing in the world, where the Nushagak River joins Lake Nerka. It would be a great adventure.

The plane—a single-engine De Havilland DHC built in 1957—never reached its destination. The pilot, Theron "Terry" Smith, 62 years old, had survived a stroke four years earlier and was grieving the recent death of his son-in-law, who had died in a plane crash.[23] The group boarded the floatplane around 11 a.m. Staff at their lodge called the fishing camp around 5 p.m. to ask when the party would be returning for dinner.[24] That's when the staff learned that the nine people who were on board the plane had never arrived at the fishing camp. Both civilian and Alaska Air National Guard aircraft were quickly dispatched to search the flight path.

One of the pilots spotted the wreckage of the plane. He thought, *no one could've survived such a crash*. The wreckage was lying on a 40-degree slope. There was a scar on the hillside where the plane had impacted and skidded up the steep hill. The scar was about 75 yards long. The front of the aircraft had been sheared completely off.[25]

Then the pilot heard another pilot on the radio: the other pilot had spotted someone waving for help. *Someone at the scene of the crash is waving for help.* That waving hand converted a recovery mission into a rescue mission. The pilots alerted the medical chain of command: *there is at least one person still alive down there.* But how to execute a rescue? There was no place for a helicopter to land. And time was short. Conditions on the hillside were cold and damp. A doctor, Dr. Dani Bowman, was helicoptered to the closest landing spot about 1,000 feet away. She forced a path to the crash site through dense brush "as fog and cold rain blanketed the area and nightfall set in," according to one news report.[26]

Willy Phillips had survived. His father, Bill Phillips, was dead. Willy had not been wearing a seat belt. When the plane hit the mountain, he was thrown forward into the open cockpit. His nose was completely smashed. The braces on his teeth were ripped off. His left foot and ankle were a mangled puddle of crushed bone. (Two other survivors who *had* been wearing a seat belt were unable to move because their pelvises had been fractured by the force of the impact against the seat belts.)[27] In the confusion and horror immediately following the impact—which the survivors agreed occurred with no warning—Willy realized, first, that his father was dead. Second, that he himself was injured. Third, that the plane was a tangle of debris. Later rescuers had to cut open the steel fuselage to extract the other survivors.

When we spoke recently, more than 13 years after the event, Willy told me that he didn't cry. "I knew I just had to figure out the solution to the situation." Willy managed to crawl out of the jumble of the broken aircraft, slippery with jet fuel and cold rain, and jump seven feet down to the ground to wave his sweatshirt at the first search aircraft flying low overhead, even though that jump further compounded his own injuries.

It's hard to imagine a stress much worse than witnessing the death of a beloved father and at the same time being in agonizing pain from broken bones. No one could have faulted Willy if he'd just crumpled into a ball next to his father's corpse. But instead, Willy heroically sought to summon help, and succeeded.

To this day, Willy credits his father with helping him to "keep my head level" after the crash. "For my entire life he had taught my brothers and me that getting overly frustrated or anxious in a moment doesn't help. My first instinct was to be the calmest person there. I didn't really see another option, it didn't feel right to talk about how bad a situation we were in, that didn't seem helpful."[28]

Most American parents do not prepare their child in any serious way for disappointment, for failure, for heartbreak. Bill and Janet did prepare their four sons, I believe. And that made all the difference.

I mentioned my visit to Shore, the school in Sydney, Australia. The headmaster, Dr. Timothy Wright, picked me up at the airport. We had agreed on the format for my two-day visit to the school. Half a day would be devoted to structured conversations with the students. I would ask the students questions, and they would answer. On the drive in from the airport, Dr. Wright said to me, "I want you to ask me some of the questions you're going to ask the students tomorrow."

"OK," I said. "Here's one: What's the purpose of school?"

He immediately answered, "Preparation for life." That's not a trivial answer. Dr. Wright constantly reminds his teachers, and his students, and their parents, that the main purpose of school is not to get into a top university but to prepare for life. The skills needed to get into a top university are not the same as the skills needed for success in life, as I mentioned a moment ago.

So I answered Dr. Wright as I would answer a student who said the same thing. I said, "OK, preparation for life. So what's the purpose of life?"

Dr. Wright again responded without hesitation. He said, "Human life is for three things: Meaningful work. A person to love. And a cause to embrace."

I paused. "OK," I said at last.

I'm not saying that Dr. Wright is the guru. I'm not saying that his formula is the answer we all must accept. But it is an answer. And I believe that *you must have an answer* when your child asks you, "Why should I work hard at school?" You must have some answer that's bigger than "getting admitted to Stanford" or "making a good living." You must offer a bigger picture. Some concept of what it's all about. Some understanding that experiences with people matter more than the acquisition of things.[29]

Willy Phillips told me that he believes his father's tough love helped him to survive and maybe even to thrive after the plane crash. "I am so grateful for it all," Willy told me. "I've met so many people who have this mentality that 'I am on this earth to make a ton of money, I've been in investment banking since I came out of the womb, and anything else is not worth my time.' And now I have a different perspective. My dad showed me how to be really grateful for the things that are in front of you, not expecting everything to be perfect, not expecting everything to go your way." More recently, Willy sent me an email in which he wrote, "that I do still in some shape or form interact with my dad—nearly every day. Sadly, I only knew the man for 13 years—much of which I can't remember due to head trauma from the crash. However, I've now had 13 years [since the crash] to build a relationship with him. Even to the point that my partner of the last 5 years will make comments—never having met my dad, mind you—like 'Oh, I feel like Bill would have LOVED this!' To me, this is proof of his colossal impact and enduring presence. I feel lucky to navigate the world having learned from him."[30]

You need to provide the big picture for your child, as Bill and Janet Phillips did for their sons. The most serious consequence of the shift from a parent-oriented culture to a peer-oriented culture is that **many parents are no longer able to provide that big picture to their children**. By the time an American child is 12 years old, she or he is more likely to look to peers than to parents for guidance about what really matters in life. But children are not competent to guide other children. That's what parents are for.

Without strong guidance from parents, children and teenagers turn to the marketplace for direction about what counts and what matters. But today, the American marketplace—the mainstream culture in which most American children and teenagers now take part—is focused narrowly and relentlessly on fame and wealth. In the culture of Drake and Bruno Mars and Charli D'Amelio and Cardi B and TikTok, fame and money are what matter most. But the pursuit of fame and wealth for their own sake impoverishes the soul. And because most of us will never be famous, and will never be billionaires, the end result of the pursuit of fame and wealth is frustration, envy, and resentment. Frustration: *I'm working as hard as I can but I'm not getting what I want, not even close.* Envy: *I wish I had what he/she has. Or even just a fraction.* Resentment: *Why him? Why her? Why not me? It's not fair.*

The past 10 years have witnessed a perfect storm of hammer blows to the fabric of society, coming at us from all different directions. The authority of parents has been undermined; social media and online video games have created virtual universes into which kids are lured and become unmoored; the culture of disrespect has eroded basic social norms. As NYU social psychologist Jonathan Haidt recently observed, the past 10 years have seen "the fragmentation of everything. It's about the shattering of all that had seemed solid, the scattering of people who had been a community...not only *between* red and blue, but within the left and within the right, as well as within universities, companies, professional associations, museums, and even families."[31]

If we are to have any shot at fixing this, at making this right, we have to begin by restoring the authority of parents, empowering parents to do the parents' job of creating and enforcing a meaningful system of values within the home. But as feminist social critic Mary Harrington recently observed, "Our biggest obstacle is an obsolete mindset that deprecates all duties beyond personal fulfillment, and views intimate relationships in instrumental terms, as means for self-development or ego gratification, rather than enabling conditions for solidarity.... The idea of mutual love coexisting with hierarchy is alien to a modern perspective, in which all such asymmetries are treated as exploitative by definition."[32] In other words, parents find it hard today to reconcile *I love you* with *because I'm your mother, that's why.* But finding that balance is at the core of authoritative, Just Right parenting.

As our society falls apart, kids need their parents more than ever to hold things together, to provide meaning and context and purpose. It's unreasonable to expect 10-year-olds or 12-year-olds or 14-year-olds or even 16-year-olds to do this on their own. No society has ever imposed that burden on children. But while the fragmentation of everything has made the role of parents more important than ever, the same fragmentation has undermined parents' ability to deliver.

I wrote this book to encourage you to step up, to be courageous, to do your job. I'm a parent myself. I know how difficult it is to assert parental authority in a society that undermines and disrespects parents. But if you don't do it, no one can do it for you, and your child will be adrift in a toxic culture.

You don't have to do this alone. Find allies. A good school, led by professionals who understand the challenges and who mindfully create a culture of respect within the school, can be immensely helpful. It has certainly been helpful to my wife and to me in raising our daughter. If you belong to a community of faith, then the church, the synagogue, or the mosque should be able to provide a community of men and women who share a tradition that teaches right and wrong, up and down, from a perspective profoundly at odds with the culture of TikTok and Instagram. That alternative perspective can be enormously helpful and grounding. Not all communities of faith offer this connection across generations, but some do. Find one that does. Good friends, extended family, and neighbors can help to provide the village that every child needs to become a fulfilled adult. But none of those people can take your place. They can support you, they can be your allies, but you must find the strength to be the first teacher of virtue for your child.

Being a good parent means—among other things—helping your daughter or son to find and to fulfill their true potential, their true identity. The answer given to me by Dr. Wright, headmaster at Shore, provides a road map for thinking about what that might mean, concretely. *Meaningful work. A person to love. And a cause to embrace.* What work might your child find most meaningful? How to prepare your child to give and receive love in a lasting relationship? How to help them find a cause, something larger than themselves, that they can champion with enthusiasm?

The Conscientious child or teen is more likely to develop into a Conscientious adult: a woman or man mature enough to set meaningful goals and to work toward them with integrity. To serve others. To be the best person they can be.

To find their meaning of life.

Conclusion

You and I are not the only ones trying to raise kids right in a culture which is likely to steer them wrong. I have met like-minded parents across the United States and around the world. Together, you and I and other parents like us can create a community of parents who understand the challenges, parents who are trying to build a culture of respect that works in the 21st century.

We need to reevaluate our values.[1] As recently as 40 years ago, our popular culture celebrated the lives of ordinary people in television shows like *The Cosby Show* and *Family Ties*. The characters depicted in those shows were not famous or wealthy. But they were good role models for children because the characters depicted in those shows were good people. Today, popular American culture—especially the culture of children and teenagers—revolves around famous influencers on TikTok and Instagram and celebrity entertainers like Drake, Taylor Swift, and Cardi B. As journalist Alina Tugend has observed, we parents "end up convinced that being average will doom our children to a life that will fall far short of what we want for them." The very word "ordinary" has become a derogatory term. Author, professor, and podcaster Brené Brown suggests that in 21st-century America, "an ordinary life has become synonymous with a meaningless life."[2]

We Americans have gone far astray in the past three decades with regard to understanding what kids need to become fulfilled and independent adults. We have undermined the authority of teachers and of parents. We have allowed kids to be guided by same-age peers rather than insisting on the primacy of guidance from adults. As a result, American kids now are growing up to be less adaptive and less resilient than they could be.

But you can change that, in your own home, starting today.

If you live in the United States and you want your child to grow up to be happy, productive, and fulfilled, then you will have to parent your child in ways which will differ from those of many of your neighbors. Your neighbors may not understand. They may whisper to one another about how strict you are. You don't allow your 11-year-old son to play violent video games like *Grand Theft Auto* or *Call of Duty*. He must feel so Isolated! Your 13-year-old daughter is one of only two girls in her class who doesn't have her own page on Instagram. How Awful!

You will be *so* uncool.

Don't be intimidated. Lend your neighbor your copy of this book. Meanwhile, you will have to be courageous, for the sake of your child. So that he or she can grow up to be brave.

And humble.

Like you.

Throughout the world, parents in developed countries are increasingly confused about their role. Should they be their child's best friend or their child's authoritative guide? Many parents are twisting themselves in knots trying to be the cool peer of their child one moment and the authoritative parent the next. My advice: Don't do that. Your job is to be the authoritative parent, not the cool kid. The parent-child relationship differs from the relationship between same-age peers. Understand the differences. I have found that advice to be every bit as necessary in Edinburgh and Auckland and Brisbane as it is in Dallas and New York and Seattle.

But there are other challenges which are uniquely American. In this book I have highlighted three:

1. **Culture:** The culture of disrespect is mingled with the culture of "Live for Now." When one sees the Pepsi "Live for Now" billboard in England or in New Zealand, it's easy to recognize the message of "Live for Now" as an American import which anyone can freely accept or reject. But here in the United States, the culture of "Live for Now" / "Whatever Floats Your Boat" / "You Do You" is our native culture. It is the default culture which American kids encounter if we set them loose to navigate on their own, as some notables would have us do.[3] Without authoritative guidance, it is the culture which they will adopt as their own.

2. **Medication:** In the United States, it has become common to medicate children with powerful psychiatric drugs as a first resort rather than a last resort. As I explained in Chapter 3, that's a big reason why American kids are now much more likely to be on medication compared with kids outside North America. We are experimenting on children in a way

that has no precedent, with medications whose long-term risks are largely unknown.

3. **Overscheduling:** As I mentioned in Chapter 11, we Americans like to boast about how busy we are. The nonstop grind of school and activities and homework begins early in the morning and continues late into the night. In America, parents routinely brag about how busy and overscheduled they are. That's not healthy. Find a different perspective. Boast about how you and your child spent an afternoon lying on the grass, looking up at the sky, trying to find shapes in the clouds.

To be a wise parent in the United States today, you must understand these challenges. Be the authoritative guide: introduce your child to a worldview more meaningful than "Live for Now." Resist the pressures to medicate your child except as a last resort rather than as the first intervention. Don't give in to the temptation to overschedule. Teach your child that relaxed time with family is more important than cramming two or three more extracurricular activities into the week.

Every human relationship is characterized by responsibilities, but the responsibilities differ depending on the relationship.

A physician has responsibilities to a patient: to evaluate the patient's signs and symptoms, to make a diagnosis, to determine the best treatment, and to explain the treatment, all to be done objectively and without being influenced by third parties such as drugmakers or employers or insurance companies.

A friend has responsibilities to a friend: to be kind, to be trustworthy, to be available to the best of their ability in times of need.

A husband has responsibilities to his wife, and a wife to her husband. Each has made a commitment to cherish the other, forsaking all others, for as long as they both shall live.

Each of these relationships—between physician and patient, between friends, and between husband and wife—begins with a choice. You choose your doctor. You choose your friend. You choose your spouse. But your child didn't choose you. The parent-child relationship is unchosen. And while you and your partner may have chosen to have *a* child, you didn't choose to have *this* child. So the unchosenness applies in both directions, though somewhat differently for parents than for children.

Earlier I mentioned the author Ayn Rand. Her name at birth was Alisa Rosenbaum. She didn't choose that name; it was given to her by her parents. She rejected the name her parents gave her and took another name of her own choosing. In one of her most famous books, *The Virtue of Selfishness*, she wrote, "No man can have a right to impose an unchosen obligation on another man" (this was back in 1964, when "man" meant "human being"). But the whole premise of this book is that parents do have the right to impose obligations and expectations on their children. More than once, parents have told me of their child complaining, "I didn't ask to be born into this family." The child feels that because he or she didn't choose to be in this family, he or she shouldn't be bound by the family rules.[4] As I mentioned earlier, Ayn Rand never had a child and never wrote seriously about parenting or the parent-child relationship.

But there is no greater responsibility between human beings than the responsibility of a parent to a child. It is the parent's responsibility not only to feed and to clothe and to shelter the child, but also to transmit the parent's culture to the child, to instill a longing for virtue, and to teach the meaning of life—*why are we here?*—according to the parent's best understanding. Each of us, as parents, must clearly explain to our child that Ayn Rand's commandment—that nobody can impose an unchosen obligation on another—might be reasonable among adults, but it doesn't apply within the family. Our daughter didn't choose to be born into our family, but she is bound by our family rules. I didn't choose my daughter, but I am bound by the obligations of a father to a daughter.

An old-fashioned word for "unchosen obligation" is *duty*. Contemporary mainstream culture scorns the idea of duty—"whatever floats your boat / if it feels good, do it"—and in so do-ing, the culture has undermined the authority of parents to do their job. The result has been a collapse of parenting worldwide, perhaps more so in North America than elsewhere. The collapse of parenting has led, not surprisingly, to an explosion in the prev-alence of anxiety and depression among children and teenagers, and to an extraordinary rise in the proportion of kids who are fragile in ways unknown in previous generations.

For the sake of your child, you have to create an alternative culture in your home. A culture of respect. An affirmation of duty: of parents to their children, and of children to their parents.

You have to assert without apology the primacy of the parent-child relationship over relationships between same-age peers.

You have to teach that family comes first, despite living in a culture where family ties are seldom respected.

You must teach your child that every choice he or she makes has immediate, far-reaching, and unforeseen consequences.[5]

You must help your child to find meaning in their life that is not about their latest accomplishment, or how they look, or how many friends they have, but about who they *are*, their truest self.

You must judge your success as a parent not by how many friends your child has, not by grade point average or test scores or athletic prowess, not by an acceptance letter from a famous college or university, but by whether your child is on the road to fulfilling his or her potential, capable of governing his or her needs and desires instead of being governed by them.

Do not allow yourself to be paralyzed by your own inadequacies. You may not be a perfect model of honesty and integrity. Neither am I. There may be dark places in your own soul, things that you are ashamed of. I have them too. You may feel silly trying to preach to your child about virtue and character because you know how far astray you have gone in the past, including the recent past. I have often felt the same way.

But too bad. To borrow an analogy from the classroom: Raising your child to know and care about virtue and character is not a special extra-credit assignment reserved for the superior parent. It is mandatory for all parents. And when you are given a mandatory assignment, you must do your best, regardless of your own shortcomings.[6] Regardless of whether your peers—other parents—are paying attention to the assignment or not.

There is no greater responsibility.

I wish you all the best. For you and for your child. And I hope we will be in touch.

Acknowledgments

My first debt is to the parents and children who have come to see me in the office, from 1989 to the present, in Maryland and in Pennsylvania. Conducting more than 120,000 office visits with children and parents from diverse backgrounds has provided me with a firsthand education which cannot be found in any book, on any website, or on any social media.

My next debt is to the more than 500 schools, across the United States and worldwide, where I have visited over the past 23 years. Observing classrooms, talking with students and teachers, meeting with school administrators, and listening to parents have all been invaluable in working through the issues in this book. Lists of my school visits from 2005 to the present may be found at www.leonardsax.com/schedule/.

I am grateful to the families and individuals who have agreed to be quoted by name in this book: to Janet Phillips and her four sons, Andrew, Colter, Paul, and especially Willy; to Beth Fayard, her husband, Jeff Jones, and their children, Grace, Claire, and Roland, a.k.a. Bubby; to Dr. Meg Meeker and her son, Walter; and to Bronson Bruneau and his sister Marlow Phillips (wife of Andrew).

Throughout this book, I contrast the United States with other countries. I am most indebted to those hosts outside of North America who have invited me to visit their school or their community and who have taught me something about the lived experiences of children and teenagers in other countries. I am especially grateful to Josep Maria Barnils of Barcelona, Spain; Jan Butler of Hobart, Tasmania, former head of the Australasian Girls' Schools Alliance; Rebecca Cody, former principal of Woodford House in New Zealand and of MLC in Western Australia and now principal of Geelong Grammar in Victoria; Melanie L'Eef of Christchurch, New Zealand; Anne Everest in Edinburgh, Scotland; Andrew Hunter, who as headmaster at Merchiston Castle School in Edinburgh, Scotland, graciously put me up at his home on two occasions and taught me so much about how Scotland differs from England, as well as connected me with boys who are passionate about distinguishing genuine Scottish textiles from imported imitations; Christine Jenkins in Melbourne, Victoria; Robyn Kronenberg of Hobart, Tasmania, with special thanks for a crash course in Australian football at the Melbourne Cricket Ground; Dr. Jane Muncke of Zurich, Switzerland; Judith Poole, former headmistress of Abbotsleigh in Wahroonga, New South Wales, who as an American has a special gift for explaining Australian culture to Americans like me; Belinda Provis, formerly principal of Seymour College in Adelaide, Australia, and now principal of All Saints' College in Perth; Karen Spiller, former principal of St Aidan's Anglican Girls School near Brisbane, Australia; Dr. Ralph Townsend, former headmaster of Winchester College in Winchester, England; Dr. Timothy Wright, former headmaster of Sydney Church of England Grammar School, a.k.a. "Shore," and his colleagues David Anderson and Cameron Paterson; and Garth Wynne, former headmaster of Christ Church Grammar School in Perth, Australia. Each of these individuals has taught me something about how their culture differs from American culture. However, mention of these individuals here does not imply that they endorse anything I have written in the book. I just wanted to say thank you.

Also a thank you to those schools in the United States and Canada which have opened their doors to me, making it possible for me to meet with students, listen to teachers, and share strategies with parents. I am especially grateful to those schools which have hosted me on repeat visits to follow the effects of various interventions over time. Among these, I am most grateful to JSerra Catholic High School in San Juan Capistrano, California, where I have visited on nine separate occasions over the past seven years, and especially Pat Reidy, vice president of Mission and Faith at JSerra. I also appreciate the opportunity to have visited the Barack Obama Male Leadership Academy, a public school in Dallas, Texas, where I spent eight days on four separate visits. I have visited nine schools in the Hillsdale College network of public charter schools, sharing with them and learning from them different strategies to inspire boys and girls to become men and women of character.

Dr. Gordon Neufeld is a key authority cited in this book. I am grateful that he agreed to meet with me face-to-face during the writing of the book, and I especially appreciated his insights on how Canadian culture is growing more similar to, but is still distinct from, mainstream American culture. I am also grateful to NYU professor Jonathan Haidt for generously sharing with me the manuscript of his book *The Anxious Generation* four months in advance of publication so that I could draw on his insights in writing the revised edition of this book.

Felicia Eth has been my literary agent for more than 20 years. This is our fourth book together. I am grateful for her patience, her guidance, and her advocacy.

I thank the whole team at Basic Books, but most especially Lara Heimert, publisher, for believing in the book; for her editorial insights and suggestions, which have greatly improved the book; and for encouraging me to write this second edition. I also thank Roger Labrie for a meticulous edit of the manuscript for the first edition; and Duncan McHenry, for his many thoughtful and constructive suggestions in his line-by-line edit of the second edition. Any errors which remain are solely my responsibility.

The director of my family medicine residency program, Dr. Nikitas Zervanos, often remarked that the most important measure of any person's life is neither income, nor professional achievement, nor even happiness, but the quality of that person's closest personal relationships. He urged us to make our spouse and our children our highest priority. Family should come before work, Dr. Zervanos taught us.

I think he's right. And I have tried to live according to that rule. How well I have succeeded is not for me to judge; you will have to ask my wife, Katie, and my daughter, Sarah. I am indebted to Katie for any common sense which might be found in this book. I am indebted to Sarah for giving me a reason to write this book. I researched and wrote this book in hopes of becoming a better father.

I am also thankful for my wife's parents, Bill and Joan, who have lived with us for the past 16 years. My daughter is fortunate to have not one, not two, but four adults in the home who love her. My background growing up Jewish in a suburb of Cleveland,

Ohio, is very different from Katie's, who grew up Protestant on a farm in Lancaster County, Pennsylvania. We teach our daughter our different cultures, celebrating both. Or at least we try.

That's my family. Everything I do, I do for them.

Finally, I want to remember my late mother, Dr. Janet Sax, who as a pediatrician devoted her professional life to teaching parents how to guide their children. In the years before her death, she and I had countless conversations about the topics I address here. She had a vast depth and breadth of firsthand experience with children and adolescents acquired in more than 30 years of clinical practice. Throughout the book, I have often thought, *What would Mom have said?*

Wherever you are, Mom, I hope you like the book.

Notes

Introduction: Parents Adrift

1. Lists of my events from 2005 through the present are available at https://www.leonardsax.com/schedule/.

Chapter 1: The Culture of Disrespect

1. Kathy Kiely, "Obama accepts Wilson's outburst apology," *USA Today*, September 10, 2009, https://abcnews.go.com/Politics/obama -accepts-wilsons-outburst-apology/story?id=8538361.

2. Carl Hulse, "House rebukes Wilson for shouting 'you lie,'" *New York Times*, September 15, 2009, https://www.nytimes.com /2009/09/16/us/politics/16wilson.html.

3. Katie Rogers, "After shouts of 'liar' and worse, Biden takes on his detractors in real time," *New York Times*, February 8, 2023, https:// www.nytimes.com/2023/02/08/us/politics/biden-state-of-the-union .html.

4. Matt Young, "MTG was 'honored' to call Biden a liar, refuses to apologize," *The Daily Beast*, February 9, 2023, https://www.thedailybeast .com/mtg-was-honored-to-call-biden-a-liar-refuses-to-apologize.

5. Libby Cathey, "GOP leaders defend members calling Biden a 'liar' during State of the Union," ABC News, February 8, 2023, https://abcnews .go.com/Politics/gop-leaders-defend-members-calling-biden-liar-state /story?id=96980039.

6. Jeff Darcy, "Rep. Bowman fire alarm pull: Darcy cartoon," *Cleveland Plain Dealer*, October 5, 2023, https://www.cleveland.com /darcy/2023/10/rep-jamaal-bowman-bogus-fire-alarm-pull-darcy -cartoon.html.

7. Bowman claims that he pulled the alarm by mistake, thinking it would open a locked door. However, surveillance video shows him making no effort to use the door in question after pulling the alarm. See Kayla Guo, "Jamaal Bowman charged with setting off false fire alarm," *New York Times*, October 25, 2023, https://www.nytimes .com/2023/10/25/us/politics/jamaal-bowman-fire-alarm.html. You can watch the surveillance video of Bowman pulling the fire alarm, and then walking away without trying to open the door, at https:// www.cnn.com/2023/09/30/politics/jamaal-bowman-pulls-fire-alarm /index.html.

8. Three Democrats—Chris Pappas of New Hampshire, Jahana Hayes of Connecticut, and Marie Gluesenkamp Perez of Washington— joined with Republicans to censure Bowman. Five Democrats voted "present." See Summer Concepcion, "House censures Rep. Jamaal Bowman for pulling fire alarm," NBC News, December 7, 2023, https://www.nbcnews.com/politics/congress/house-vote-censuring -rep-jamaal-bowman-pulling-fire-alarm-rcna128492. The vote to censure Joe Wilson in 2009 was slightly less partisan: that resolution passed 240 to 179, with 233 Democrats and seven Republicans voting for the measure, 167 Republicans and 12 Democrats voting against the measure, and five Democrats voting "present." Associated Press, "House votes to rebuke Rep. Wilson," September 15, 2009, https:// www.nbcnews.com/id/wbna32858805.

9. Matthew Lynch, "The story of American education and the Mc- Guffey Readers," *The Edvocate*, September 2, 2018, https://www.thee dadvocate.org/story-american-education-mcguffey-readers/.

10. The quotes from John Dewey and the National Education As- sociation both come from David Brooks's article, "How America got mean: devoid of moral education, generations are growing up in a

morally inarticulate, self-referential world," *The Atlantic*, August 14, 2023.

11. Katherine Schaeffer, "Among many U.S. children, reading for fun has become less common, federal data shows," Pew Research Center, November 12, 2021, https://www.pewresearch.org/fact-tank /2021/11/12/among-many-u-s-children-reading-for-fun-has -become-less-common-federal-data-shows/.

12. Yasaman Madanikia and Kim Bartholomew, "Themes of lust and love in popular music lyrics from 1971 to 2011," *Sage Open*, volume 4, 2014, online at https://journals.sagepub.com/doi/full /10.1177/2158244014547179.

13. See my essay for *Public Discourse*, "Why WAP matters," August 30, 2020, online at https://www.thepublicdiscourse.com /2020/08/70643/.

14. See my essay for *Psychology Today*, "You and your [expletive] invited: mixed messages at the Grammys," February 2, 2018, https://www.psychologytoday.com/us/blog/sax-sex/201802/you -and-your-expletive-invited.

15. Jon Caramanica, "Drake rebuilt hip-hop in his image," *New York Times*, June 19, 2022, https://www.nytimes.com/2022/06/19 /arts/music/drake-honestly-nevermind-review.html.

16. Forty-nine of Drake's Top Ten hits on the Billboard Hot 100 have explicit profanity. See Daniel Parris, "The rise of explicit music: a statistical analysis," June 29, 2023, https://www.statsignificant .com/p/the-rise-of-explicit-music-a-statistical.

17. According to Billboard, Drake owns many all-time records on the Billboard Hot 100: he has had the most Top Ten hits of any artist ever (78), and the most songs in the Top 100 (332); see Xander Zellner, "Here are the Hot 100 records that Drake has (and hasn't) broken," *Billboard*, October 16, 2023, https://www.billboard.com /lists/drake-hot-100-records/; for the updated numbers shown here as of June 14, 2024, see https://www.billboard.com/artist/drake /chart-history/hsi/. By comparison, Taylor Swift has had 59 songs

make the Top Ten on the Billboard Hot 100 and 263 songs in the Billboard Hot 100 as of June 14, 2024, https://www.billboard.com /artist/taylor-swift/chart-history/hsi/. The Beatles had 34, https:// www.billboard.com/lists/the-beatles-top-songs-billboard-hot-100/. Michael Jackson had 30, https://www.billboard.com/artist/michael -jackson/, including two that reached the Top Ten after his death.

18. My source for this statement is Michael Schneider's article "100 most-watched TV series of 2022–23," *Variety*, May 29, 2023, https://variety.com/2023/tv/news/most-popular-tv-shows-highest -rated-2022-2023-season-yellowstone-football-1235623612/. Among the top 20 shows, I found just one—*Blue Bloods*—which at least occasionally depicts a parent as knowledgeable, competent, and responsible.

19. Spencer Kornhaber, "What gives SZA her edge," *The Atlantic*, December 14, 2022, https://www.theatlantic.com/culture/archive /2022/12/sza-sos-2022-album-review/672462/.

20. "Music business," *Hype Bot*, April 16, 2019, https://www .hypebot.com/hypebot/2019/04/the-weeks-youtube-music-charts -bts-blackpink-muse-soundgarden-lil-nas-x-and-more.html.

21. Bill Maher, *What This Comedian Said Will Shock You* (New York: Simon & Schuster, 2024), p. 76.

22. Biologists and anthropologists are still arguing whether any animals other than humans truly exhibit culture. For more on this point, please see Melvin Konner's discussion of this issue in his book *The Evolution of Childhood: Relationships, Emotion, Mind* (Cambridge: Harvard University Press, 2010), especially the section titled "Does Nonhuman Culture Exist?" pp. 579–592. There is now fairly good evidence that chimpanzees in the wild do have a rudimentary "culture": consistent variations which distinguish one community from the next, which are sustained across generations, and which do not appear to be genetically programmed. Chimpanzees in the Kibale rainforest of Uganda often use sticks to get food, while chimpanzees in the Budongo rainforest rarely use sticks, although sticks are just as readily available in the Budongo as in the Kibale. The Budongo chimps prefer

to use their fingers. These differences between the two neighboring groups of wild chimpanzees occupying similar habitats appear to be socially learned, not innate. See Thibaud Gruber, Richard Wrangham, and colleagues, "Wild chimpanzees rely on cultural knowledge to solve an experimental honey acquisition task," *Current Biology*, volume 19, pp. 1806–1810, 2009. The two groups have different table manners, if you like. Josep Call and Claudio Tennie, reviewing the findings of Gruber, Wrangham, and colleagues, liken the differences between the two communities of wild chimpanzees to human differences in table manners. See their article "Animal culture: chimpanzee table manners?" *Current Biology*, volume 19, pp. R981–R983, 2009.

23. See Konner (previous note) for a lengthy defense of this statement. If you like, you can jump directly to Part IV, "Enculturation," pp. 595–727.

24. For a 500+ page intensive primer on neuroplasticity, see *Neuroplasticity: From Bench to Bedside*, edited by Angelo Quartarone and colleagues, *Handbook of Clinical Neurology*, volume 184, pp. 2–512, 2022. When I refer to the buzz about neuroplasticity, I am thinking of articles such as Shufei Yin and colleagues, "Intervention-induced enhancement in intrinsic brain activity in healthy older adults," *Scientific Reports*, 2014, volume 4, online at https://www.sciencedirect.com/handbook/handbook-of-clinical-neurology/vol/184/suppl/C.

25. See for example Jacqueline Johnson and Elissa Newport, "Critical period effects in second language learning: the influence of maturational state on the acquisition of English as a second language," *Cognitive Psychology*, volume 21, pp. 60–99, 1989. For a reevaluation of the critical period hypothesis, see Jan Vanhove's "The critical period hypothesis in second language acquisition: a statistical critique and a reanalysis," *PLOS One*, July 25, 2013, online at http://journals.plos.org/plosone/article?id=10.1371/journal.pone.0069172#pone-0069172-g009.

26. Robert Fulghum, *All I Really Need to Know I Learned in Kindergarten: Uncommon Thoughts on Common Things* (New York: Ivy, 1988).

27. All quotations are from Yamamoto Tsunetomo, *Hagakure: The Book of the Samurai*, translated by William Scott Wilson (Boston: Shambhala, 2012). For more of the same, see Thomas Cleary's book *Code of the Samurai: A Modern Translation of the Bushido Shoshin-shu of Taira Shigesuke* (Tokyo: Tuttle, 1999). For a more scholarly overview of Japanese life in the era from the establishment of the Tokugawa Shogunate in 1603 to the Meiji Restoration of 1868, see Charles Dunn's book *Everyday Life in Traditional Japan* (Tokyo: Tuttle, 1969).

28. American anxiety about the perceived decline in the achievement of American students relative to Japanese and German students in particular was expressed in the Reagan-era federal report published in 1983 titled *A Nation at Risk*. For a perceptive critique of this report and of the early-1980s anxiety about American education, see Richard Rothstein's essay "*A Nation at Risk* twenty-five years later," April 7, 2008, http://www.cato-unbound.org/2008/04/07/richard-rothstein/nation-risk-twenty-five-years-later.

29. For more about why American schools switched from an emphasis on socialization to an emphasis on early literacy and numeracy, please see Chapter 2 of my book *Boys Adrift*, second edition (New York: Basic Books, 2016).

30. Superintendent Jerry D. Weast was not hesitant to blow his own horn and to boast about the wisdom of phasing out art, music, and games in order to make more time for phonics. See his article titled "Why we need rigorous, full-day kindergarten" in the May 2001 issue of *Principal* magazine. For some of the positive buzz, see Marian Wright Edelman, "Getting it right, right from the start," October 18, 2013, https://www.huffpost.com/entry/getting-it-right-right-fr_b_4124791. But Dr. Weast's reforms were not universally welcomed. For a taste of the pushback, see Allen Flanigan's letter, "Let the kids play," *Washington Post*, February 20, 2000.

31. David Brooks, "How America got mean: devoid of moral education, generations are growing up in a morally inarticulate, self-referential world," *The Atlantic*, August 14, 2023.

32. The literal translation of *Statusunsicherheit* would be "status insecurity" or "status uncertainty," but "role confusion" is a more idiomatic translation considering the context.

33. This paragraph is my summary of the relevant aspects of Norbert Elias's essay "Changes in European standards of behaviour in the twentieth century," pp. 23–43 in his book *The Germans: Power Struggles and the Development of Habitus in the Nineteenth and Twentieth Centuries*, edited by Michael Schröter, translated by Eric Dunning (New York: Columbia University Press, 1998).

34. James S. Coleman, *The Adolescent Society: The Social Life of the Teenager and Its Impact on Education* (New York: Free Press, 1961), pp. 5–6.

35. The study was Ellen Galinsky's interviews with 1,000 American adolescents, which she documented in her book *Ask the Children: The Breakthrough Study That Reveals How to Succeed at Work and Parenting* (New York: HarperCollins, 2000). In Jennifer Senior's analysis of Galinsky's study in Senior's book *All Joy and No Fun: The Paradox of Modern Parenthood* (New York: HarperCollins, 2014), p. 194, Senior summarizes Galinsky's findings as "During adolescence, that ingratitude is additionally seasoned with contempt."

36. Alana Newhouse, "Everything is broken," *Tablet*, January 14, 2021, https://www.tabletmag.com/sections/news/articles /everything-is-broken.

37. See for example Jennifer Szalai, "The problem of misinformation in an era without trust," scroll down to "the 'crisis of authority,'" *New York Times*, December 31, 2023, https://www.nytimes.com/2023/12/31 /books/review/elon-musk-trust-misinformation-disinformation.html.

38. Pew Research Center, "Public trust in government: 1958–2023," September 19, 2023, https://www.pewresearch.org/politics /2023/09/19/public-trust-in-government-1958-2023/.

39. This passage, in which I share my encounter with a high school student who prefers *Superbad* to *Hamlet*, is drawn from my essay for *Public Discourse*, "Why WAP matters," August 30, 2020, online at https://www.thepublicdiscourse.com/2020/08/70643/.

40. This is a central theme of Dr. Neufeld's book, written with Gabor Maté, *Hold On to Your Kids: Why Parents Need to Matter More Than Peers*, second edition (Toronto: Vintage Canada, 2013).

41. For this analysis of Megan's behavior, I am indebted to *Hold On to Your Kids*, previous reference. I explore Dr. Neufeld's perspective at greater length in Chapter 7.

42. Neufeld and Maté, *Hold On to Your Kids*, p. 7.

43. Neufeld and Maté, pp. 15–16. Emphasis in original.

44. My discussion here of the politics of parenting is adapted from my article on this topic for the Institute for Family Studies, "Do your political beliefs affect your parenting?" April 4, 2023, https://ifstudies.org/blog/do-your-political-beliefs-affect-your-parenting-.

45. Kimberly Zapata, "What is gentle parenting?" *Parents* magazine, August 17, 2023, https://www.parents.com/parenting/better-parenting/style/what-is-gentle-parenting/.

46. Janet Lansbury, "3 reasons kids don't need toilet training (and what to do instead)," August 2014, https://www.janetlansbury.com/2014/08/3-reasons-kids-dont-need-toilet-training-and-what-to-do-instead/, accessed December 20, 2023.

47. Jessica Winter, "The harsh realm of 'gentle parenting,'" *The New Yorker*, March 23, 2022, https://www.newyorker.com/books/under-review/the-harsh-realm-of-gentle-parenting.

48. Winter, previous note.

49. Catherine Gimbrone and colleagues, "The politics of depression: diverging trends in internalizing symptoms among US adolescents by political beliefs," *SSM—Mental Health*, volume 2, 2022, https://www.sciencedirect.com/science/article/pii/S2666560321000438.

50. Michelle Goldberg, "Don't let politics cloud your view of what's going on with teens and depression," *New York Times*, February 24, 2023, https://www.nytimes.com/2023/02/24/opinion/social-media-and-teen-depression.html.

51. Jon Haidt, "Why the mental health of liberal girls sank first and fastest," March 9, 2023, https://www.afterbabel.com/p/mental-health-liberal-girls.

52. Alison Barton and Jameson Hirsch, "Permissive parenting and mental health in college students: mediating effects of academic entitlement," *Journal of American College Health*, volume 64, pp. 1–8, 2016.

53. Grace Wischerth and colleagues, "The adverse influence of permissive parenting on personal growth and the mediating role of emotional intelligence," *Journal of Genetic Psychology*, volume 177, pp. 185–189, 2016.

54. Holly Shakya, Nicholas Christakis, and James Fowler, "Parental influence on substance use in adolescent social networks," *Archives of Pediatrics and Adolescent Medicine*, volume 166, pp. 1132–1139, 2012.

55. Ming Cui and colleagues, "Parental indulgence: profile and relations to college students' emotional and behavioral problems," *Journal of Child and Family Studies*, 2018, full text at https://fincham .info/papers/2018%20JCFS%20Cui%20online.pdf.

56. W. Bradford Wilcox, "Focused on their families: religion, parenting, and child wellbeing," Center for Research on Child Wellbeing, 2002, online at https://core.ac.uk/download/pdf/6885426.pdf.

Chapter 2: Food

1. The figures for the early 1970s come from Cheryl Fryar and colleagues, "Prevalence of obesity among children and adolescents: United States, trends 1963–1965 through 2009–2010," published by the Centers for Disease Control and Prevention, full text online at www.cdc.gov/nchs/data/hestat/obesity_child_09_10/obesity _child_09_10.htm. The figures for 2020 come from the National Health and Nutrition Examination Survey (NHANES) Data Files, June 14, 2021, online at https://stacks.cdc.gov/view/cdc/106273, accessed July 8, 2023.

2. Some parents are confused about when to use the term "obese" versus "overweight." Several parents have chided me for using the word "obese" because they think it is derogatory. "You should say

'overweight' instead," these parents tell me. But the two terms have precise definitions, which differ. In the United States, the term "overweight," for children, has been defined by the NIH as having a body mass index (BMI) between the 85th and 95th percentiles of the age- and sex-specific reference values established by the CDC growth chart published in the year 2000. "Obese," for children, means having a body mass index (BMI) above the 95th percentile on the CDC growth chart published in the year 2000. See Cynthia Ogden and Katherine Flegal, "Changes in terminology for childhood overweight and obesity," Centers for Disease Control and Prevention, June 25, 2010, online at www.cdc.gov/nchs/data/nhsr/nhsr025.pdf. You can download the year 2000 CDC growth charts at www.cdc.gov/growth charts/2000growthchart-us.pdf. BMI calculators are widely available on the Web, for example at www.nhlbi.nih.gov/guidelines/obesity /BMI/bmicalc.htm.

Some examples may help make this more concrete. A 15-year-old boy who is 5'8" tall would be obese if he were over 180 pounds. If he were 155 pounds, he would be overweight but not obese. A 15-year-old girl who is 5'4" tall would be obese if she were 168 pounds or more. If she were 142 pounds, she would be overweight but not obese. Remember that these rules apply to children and adolescents, not adults.

3. Jaime Gahche and colleagues, "Cardiorespiratory fitness levels among U.S. youth aged 12–15 years: United States, 1999–2004 and 2012," NCHS Data Brief 153, May 2014, https://www.cdc.gov/nchs /data/databriefs/db153.pdf. This was the most recent study of fitness trends available for American kids as of 2024.

4. The quotes from Dr. Fulton and Dr. Blackburn are from Gretchen Reynolds's article "This is our youth," *Well* (blog), *New York Times*, July 9, 2014, http://well.blogs.nytimes.com/2014/07/09 /young-and-unfit/.

5. I would add that this boy's public school district has cut back on PE as a cost-saving measure, and also in order to devote more time to teaching reading, writing, and math. When he does have "physical

education" in his schedule, what passes for PE is often a health class on puberty, the importance of gaining explicit verbal consent before kissing anybody, etc. All conducted with the children sitting in chairs.

Note for healthcare providers: this child was also taking Adderall 30 mg every morning. Adderall, like all amphetamines, tends to accelerate the resting heart rate. This boy's resting heart rate at the time of my evaluation was 108 beats per minute. As a result, he has diminished cardiac reserve: when his heart rate climbs above 150, his cardiac output will decrease. In addition, stimulant medications such as Adderall, Ritalin, Concerta, etc. also decrease the threshold for anxiety. Kids who are taking these medications become anxious more easily than kids who are not taking these medications.

In this case, it was clear that this child was simply out of shape: his lungs were clear and his peak flow was normal. In other similar cases, I have seen similar children diagnosed as having "exercise-induced asthma." Many parents, and even some physicians, seem to believe that exercise-induced *shortness of breath* equals exercise-induced *asthma* even in the absence of wheezing on auscultation. But that's not accurate. Many kids who have exercise-induced shortness of breath are simply out of shape. Yet I know several physicians who seem to find it easier to say, *your child has exercise-induced asthma* and prescribe an inhaler, rather than say, *your child is out of shape because he doesn't get enough exercise.*

I am not the only physician to express concern that American kids are being diagnosed with "exercise-induced asthma" when the correct diagnosis is "exercise-induced breathlessness" due to being out of shape. See for example Yun Shim, Autumn Burnette, and colleagues, "Physical deconditioning as a cause of breathlessness among obese adolescents with a diagnosis of asthma," *PLOS One*, April 23, 2013, https://journals.plos.org/plosone/article?id=10.1371/journal .pone.0061022.

6. For more evidence regarding the role of endocrine disruptors in promoting overweight—as well as suggestions for how to protect your child from these substances in foods, beverages, creams, lotions,

and shampoos—please take a look at Chapter 5 of my book *Boys Adrift* (second edition) and Chapter 4 of my book *Girls on the Edge* (second edition).

7. Megumi Hatori and colleagues, "Time-restricted feeding without reducing caloric intake prevents metabolic diseases in mice fed a high-fat diet," *Cell Metabolism*, volume 15, pp. 848–860, 2012. See also Amandine Chaix, Satchidananda Panda, and colleagues, "Time-restricted feeding is a preventative and therapeutic intervention against diverse nutritional challenges," *Cell Metabolism*, volume 20, pp. 991–1005, 2014.

Those studies concerned mice. For evidence that the same phenomenon holds true in humans, see M. Garaulet and colleagues, "Timing of food intake predicts weight loss effectiveness," *International Journal of Obesity*, volume 37, pp. 604–611, 2013. For a useful overview of the practical implications of this research, see Gretchen Reynolds's article "A 12-hour window for a healthy weight," *Well* (blog), *New York Times*, January 15, 2015, http://well.blogs.nytimes .com/2015/01/15/a-12-hour-window-for-a-healthy-weight/. The quote from Dr. Panda is taken from Reynolds's article.

8. Frank Elgar, Wendy Craig, and Stephen Trites, "Family dinners, communication, and mental health in Canadian adolescents," *Journal of Adolescent Health*, volume 52, pp. 433–438, 2013.

9. Jerica Berge and colleagues, "The protective role of family meals for youth obesity: 10-year longitudinal associations," *The Journal of Pediatrics*, volume 166, pp. 296–301, 2015.

10. See for example:

- Amber Hammons and Barbara Fiese, "Is frequency of shared family meals related to the nutritional health of children and adolescents?" *Pediatrics*, volume 127, pp. 1565–1574, 2011.
- Jayne Fulkerson and colleagues, "A review of associations between family or shared meal frequency and dietary and weight status outcomes across the lifespan,"

Journal of Nutrition, Education, and Behavior, volume 46, pp. 2–19, 2014.

- Dianne Neumark-Sztainer and colleagues, "Family meals and adolescents: what have we learned from Project EAT (Eating Among Teens)?" *Public Health Nutrition*, volume 13, pp. 1113–1121, 2010.

11. Rebecca Davidson and Anne Gauthier, "A cross-national multi-level study of family meals," *International Journal of Comparative Sociology*, volume 51, pp. 349–365, 2010.

12. Quoted in Julie Jargon and Andrea Petersen, "Family dinners are key to children's health. So why don't we eat together more?" *Wall Street Journal*, October 8, 2022.

13. Daniel Miller, Jane Waldfogel, and Wen-Jui Han, "Family meals and child academic and behavioral outcomes," *Child Development*, volume 83, pp. 2104–2120, 2012.

14. Incidentally, the lead investigator on that Boston University study which purported to show the unimportance of family dinners per se gave a different message in his interview with the *Wall Street Journal*. Professor Daniel Miller told columnist Carl Bialik, "I have a family, I have kids. We still try to eat meals together and I would encourage other families to do so." See Bialik's column titled "What family dinners can and can't do for teens," *Wall Street Journal*, November 29, 2013, online at https://www.wsj.com/articles /BL-NB-1302.

15. Amanda Trofholz and colleagues, "Associations between TV viewing at family meals and the emotional atmosphere of the meal, meal healthfulness, child dietary intake, and child weight status," *Appetite*, volume 108, pp. 361–366, 2017.

16. Sources for this figure include the Nielsen *Report on Television: The First 50 Years*, published in 2000, which documents that American kids in 1965 only watched TV for 10 hours a week. Other sources include John P. Robinson's article "Television and leisure time: yesterday, today, and (maybe) tomorrow," *Public Opinion Quarterly*,

volume 33, pp. 210–222, 1969, and also Robinson's article "Changes in American life: 1965–2005," *Social Indicators Research*, volume 93, pp. 47–56, 2009.

17. The survey I am referring to here was published by Common Sense Media on March 9, 2022, and is titled "The Common Sense census: media use by tweens and teens, 2021," online at https://www.commonsensemedia.org/research/the-common-sense-census-media-use-by-tweens-and-teens-2021. They found that average entertainment screen time for tweens was 5 hours and 33 minutes per day, which works out to 38.85 hours per week. For teens, average entertainment screen time per day was 8 hours 39 minutes per day, which works out to just over 60 hours per week.

18. See for example, "Dodgeball banned after bullying complaint," *Headline News*, March 28, 2013, online at https://www.wcvb.com/article/dodgeball-banned-after-bullying-complaint/8179338.

19. Noreen McDonald, "Active transportation to school: trends among US schoolchildren, 1969–2001," *American Journal of Preventive Medicine*, volume 32, pp. 509–516, 2007. For evidence of further decline since 2001, and comparison of the United States with Canada, see Linda Rothman, Alison Macpherson, and colleagues, "The decline in active school transportation (AST): a systematic review of the factors related to AST and changes in school transport over time in North America," *Preventive Medicine*, volume 111, pp. 314–322, 2018.

20. In a meta-analysis of studies involving 30,002 children 2 to 18 years of age, and 604,509 adults over 18 years of age, Francesco Cappuccio and his colleagues found that decreased sleep was more strongly associated with obesity for children than for adults. Specifically, the odds ratio—the likelihood of being obese if you are sleep-deprived—was 1.89 for children and 1.55 for adults. In other words, the sleep-deprived child is 89 percent more likely to be obese compared with the child who is not sleep-deprived. See Cappuccio and colleagues, "Meta-analysis of short sleep duration and obesity in children and adults," *Sleep*, volume 31, pp. 619–626, 2008. For an

especially persuasive longitudinal study, see the study by Julie Lu-meng and colleagues, "Shorter sleep duration is associated with increased risk for being overweight at ages 9 to 12 years," *Pediatrics*, volume 120, pp. 1020–1029, 2007, full text online at http://pediatrics.aappublications.org/content/120/5/1020.full.

21. See for example Shahrad Taheri and colleagues, "Short sleep duration is associated with reduced leptin, elevated ghrelin, and increased body mass index," *PLOS Medicine*, 2004, full text online at http://www.plosmedicine.org/article/info%3Adoi%2F10.1371%2Fjournal.pmed.0010062. See also Chantelle Hart and colleagues, "Changes in children's sleep duration on food intake, weight, and leptin," *Pediatrics*, volume 132, pp. e1473–e1480, 2013.

22. Centers for Disease Control and Prevention, "How much sleep do I need?" September 14, 2022, accessed July 9, 2023, https://www.cdc.gov/sleep/about/.

23. Centers for Disease Control and Prevention, "High school students sleep data," https://www.cdc.gov/sleep/data-research/facts-stats/high-school-students-sleep-facts-and-stats.html, accessed June 14, 2024.

24. Katherine Keyes and colleagues, "The great sleep recession: changes in sleep duration among US adolescents, 1991–2012," *Pediatrics*, volume 135, pp. 460–468, 2015. For the trend lines for high school students 2009–2021, see Centers for Disease Control and Prevention, "High school students sleep data," https://www.cdc.gov/sleep/data-research/facts-stats/high-school-students-sleep-facts-and-stats.html, accessed June 14, 2024.

25. See for example Jean Twenge, Garrett Hisler, and Zlatan Krizan, "Associations between screen time and sleep duration are primarily driven by portable electronic devices: evidence from a population-based study of U.S. children ages 0–17," *Sleep Medicine*, volume 56, pp. 211–218, 2019.

26. See for example Jennifer Falbe and colleagues, "Sleep duration, restfulness, and screens in the sleep environment," *Pediatrics*, volume 135, pp. e367–e375, 2015. See also Jean Twenge and colleagues,

"Decreases in self-reported sleep duration among U.S. adolescents 2009–2015 and association with new media screen time," *Sleep Medicine*, volume 39, pp. 47–53, 2017. See also Lauren Hale and colleagues, "Youth screen media habits and sleep: sleep-friendly screen behavior recommendations for clinicians, educators, and parents," *Child and Adolescent Psychiatric Clinics of North America*, volume 27, pp. 229–245, 2018.

27. Meg Pillion, Michael Gradisar, and colleagues, "What's 'app'-ning to adolescent sleep? Links between device, app use, and sleep outcomes," *Sleep Medicine*, volume 100, pp. 174–182, 2022.

28. Garrett Hisler, Jean Twenge, and Zlatan Krizan, "Associations between screen time and short sleep duration among adolescents varies by media type: evidence from a cohort study," *Sleep Medicine*, volume 66, pp. 92–102, 2020.

29. Yingyi Lin, Mark Tremblay, and colleagues, "Temporal and bi-directional associations between sleep duration and physical activity/sedentary time in children: an international comparison," *Preventive Medicine*, volume 111, pp. 436–441, 2018.

30. Michelle Short, Sarah Blunden, and colleagues, "Cognition and objectively measured sleep duration in children: a systematic review and meta-analysis," *Sleep Health*, volume 4, pp. 292–300, 2018.

31. Amanda Chue, Kathleen Gunthert, and colleagues, "The role of sleep in adolescents' daily stress recovery: negative affect spillover and positive affect bounce-back effects," *Journal of Adolescence*, volume 66, pp. 101–111, 2018.

32. Robert Roberts and Hao Duong, "The prospective association between sleep deprivation and depression among adolescents," *Sleep*, volume 37, pp. 239–244, 2014.

33. Robert Roberts and Hao Duong, "Is there an association between short sleep duration and adolescent anxiety disorders?" *Sleep Medicine*, volume 30, pp. 82–87, 2017.

34. For an overview of this topic, see the article by Daphne Korczak and colleagues, "Are children and adolescents with psychiatric illness at risk for increased future body weight? A systematic review," *Developmental Medicine and Child Neurology*, volume 55, pp. 980–987,

2013. Some of the articles which demonstrate this phenomenon—of the defiant child being more likely to become overweight or obese—include (in alphabetical order):

- Sarah Anderson and colleagues, "Externalizing behavior in early childhood and body mass index from age 2 to 12 years: longitudinal analyses of a prospective cohort study," *BMC Pediatrics*, volume 10, 2010, full text online at www.biomedcentral.com/1471-2431/10/49/.

- Roxanna Camfferman and colleagues, "The association between overweight and internalizing and externalizing behavior in early childhood," *Social Science and Medicine*, volume 168, pp. 35–42, 2016. These researchers found that "externalizing and internalizing behavior were both associated with later overweight [but] no significant associations in the other direction were found." In other words, defiant behavior is associated with later overweight, but overweight is not associated with later defiant behavior.

- Ivonne P. M. Derks and colleagues, "Testing bidirectional associations between child aggression and BMI: results from three cohorts," *Pediatric Obesity*, volume 27, pp. 822–829, 2019.

- Cristiane Duarte and colleagues, "Child mental health problems and obesity in early adulthood," *The Journal of Pediatrics*, volume 156, pp. 93–97, 2010.

- Daphne Korczak and colleagues, "Child and adolescent psychopathology predicts increased adult body mass index: results from a prospective community sample," *Journal of Developmental and Behavioral Pediatrics*, volume 35, pp. 108–117, 2014.

- Julie Lumeng and colleagues, "Association between clinically meaningful behavior problems and overweight in children," *Pediatrics*, volume 112, pp. 1138–1145, 2003.

- A. Mamun and colleagues, "Childhood behavioral problems predict young adults' BMI and obesity: evidence from a birth cohort study," *Obesity*, volume 17, pp. 761–766, 2009.
- Sarah Mustillo and colleagues, "Obesity and psychiatric disorder: developmental trajectories," *Pediatrics*, volume 111, pp. 851–859, 2003.
- Daniel Pine and colleagues, "Psychiatric symptoms in adolescence as predictors of obesity in early adulthood: a longitudinal study," *American Journal of Public Health*, volume 87, pp. 1303–1310, 1997, full text online at www.ncbi.nlm.nih.gov/pmc/articles/PMC1381090/.
- B. White and colleagues, "Childhood psychological function and obesity risk across the lifecourse," *International Journal of Obesity*, volume 36, pp. 511–516, 2012.

35. The study I am citing here was published by Julie Lumeng and her colleagues, "Association between clinically meaningful behavior problems and overweight in children," *Pediatrics*, volume 112, pp. 1138–1145, 2003. Although these authors use the term "overweight," their definition of "overweight" is actually the 2010 definition for "obese."

36. Anna Bardone and colleagues, "Adult physical health outcomes of adolescent girls with conduct disorder, depression, and anxiety," *Journal of the American Academy of Child and Adolescent Psychiatry*, volume 37, pp 594–601, 1998.

Chapter 3: School

1. Brittany Wallman and Megan O'Matz, "Violent kids take over Florida's classrooms, and they have the law on their side," *South Florida Sun-Sentinel*, December 10, 2019, online at https://projects .sun-sentinel.com/teenage-time-bombs/how-schools-manage -violent-kids/. This particular student had a psychiatric diagnosis,

which these reporters believe prevented him from being charged or subjected to more serious discipline than a three-day suspension. See also Nicole Linsalata, "3 transported after Northeast High School student attacks staff members," 7 News Miami, August 23, 2019, https://wsvn.com/news/local/rescue-crews-respond-to-fight-at-northeast-high-school-in-oakland-park/.

2. Susan McMahon and colleagues, "Violence directed against teachers: results from a national survey," *Psychology in the Schools*, volume 51, pp. 753–766, 2014, https://onlinelibrary.wiley.com/doi/full/10.1002/pits.21777. The quote is from page 761.

3. Susan McMahon and colleagues, "Rates and types of student aggression against teachers: a comparative analysis of U.S. elementary, middle, and high schools," *Social Psychology of Education*, volume 25, August 1, 2022.

4. Email from the teacher in question, April 22, 2023.

5. See my article "The unspeakable pleasure," for *First Things*, April 10, 2018, https://www.firstthings.com/web-exclusives/2018/04/the-unspeakable-pleasure.

6. To be precise: the PISA examination is administered to students who are between age 15 years 3 months and age 16 years 2 months at the time of the test, https://www.oecd.org/pisa/aboutpisa/pisa-based-test-for-schools-faq.htm.

7. In 2000, American students outranked Poland and Germany on the math portion of the PISA. In 2012, Polish and German students outranked American students on the math portion. The numbers I present from the 2000 administration of the PISA are taken from Figure 10, "Mathematics and science literacy average scores of 15-year-olds, by country," in *Outcomes of Learning: Results from the 2000 Program for International Student Assessment of 15-Year-Olds in Reading, Mathematics, and Science Literacy* (Washington, DC: National Center for Education Statistics, December 2001).

8. These data are taken from OECD (2014), PISA 2012 Results: *What Students Know and Can Do: Student Performance in Mathematics,*

Reading, and Science, http://dx.doi.org/10.1787/9789264208780-en,
Figure 1.2.13, "Comparing countries' and economies' performance
in mathematics."

9. OECD, *PISA 2022 Results: The State of Learning and Equity in
Education,* volume 1 (Paris: OECD Publishing, 2023), Table I.1, online at https://www.oecd-ilibrary.org/education/pisa-2022-results
-volume-i_53f23881-en.

10. In defense of the United States: the United States did much better on the reading assessment than on the math assessment. Here is
how the United States did in reading on the latest PISA assessment
(see previous note for citation):

1. South Korea 515
2. **United States** 504
3. New Zealand 501
4. Australia 498
5. United Kingdom 494
6. Finland 490
7. Poland 489
8. Denmark 489
9. Sweden 487
10. Switzerland 483
11. Italy 482
12. Germany 480
13. Austria 480
14. Belgium 479
15. Portugal 477
16. Norway 477
17. Latvia 475
18. France 474
19. Spain 474
20. Hungary 473

There are a number of theories as to why the United States scores
above average on the reading assessment and (now) far below average

on the math assessment. One explanation I find persuasive is that young Americans with high achievement in math have many professional options available to them which will pay much better than teaching in K–12 education. Young Americans with high achievement in reading may not have as many high-paying options available. So a talented reader may choose to become a teacher, whereas a talented young mathematician is unlikely to choose a career in K–12 education. However, my focus here is on the drop in math achievement among American students between 2000 and 2022.

11. Amanda Ripley, *The Smartest Kids in the World: And How They Got That Way* (New York: Simon and Schuster, 2013), p. 136. Ripley is analyzing PISA data. She concludes that as of 2007, Poland was spending about $39,964 to educate one student from age 6 to 15, the age at which students take the PISA examination. The United States spent about $105,752 to educate one student from age 6 to 15. Figures are in US dollars, "converted using purchasing power parity." See the note in Ripley, *The Smartest Kids in the World*, p. 281.

12. The "utilitarian and spare" quote is from Ripley, *The Smartest Kids in the World*, p. 52.

13. Ripley, *The Smartest Kids in the World*, p. 214. Ripley quotes Andreas Schleicher, the key person behind the PISA exam from its inception through the present day, who observes that "In most of the highest-performing systems, technology is remarkably absent from classrooms. . . . It does seem that those systems place their efforts primarily on pedagogical practice rather than digital gadgets."

14. Jessica Grose, "Every tech tool in the classroom should be ruthlessly evaluated," *New York Times*, April 24, 2024, https://www.nytimes.com/2024/04/24/opinion/ed-tech-classroom.html.

15. Ripley makes the case against American sports throughout her book. This quote actually comes from her October 2013 article for *The Atlantic*, "The case against high school sports," online at http://www.theatlantic.com/magazine/archive/2013/10/the-case-against-high-school-sports/309447/.

16. Ripley, *The Smartest Kids in the World*, p. 85.

17. Ripley, *The Smartest Kids in the World*, p. 93. She is citing a National Council on Teacher Quality report titled "It's easier to get into an education school than to become a college football player," available online at http://issuu.com/nctq/docs/teachers_and_football _players. The report is a modified PowerPoint.

18. Ripley, *The Smartest Kids in the World*, p. 59.

19. Ou Lydia Liu, Katrina Crotts Roohr, and colleagues, "Are fourth-year college students better critical thinkers than their first-year peers?" *Educational Measurement: Issues and Practice*, 2021/2022, volume 41, pp. 64–79, online at https://onlinelibrary .wiley.com/doi/abs/10.1111/emip.12430.

20. See pages 29–32 under the heading "The Necessity of the Social" in the book *Aspiring Adults Adrift: Tentative Transitions of College Graduates* by Richard Arum and Josipa Roksa (Chicago: University of Chicago Press, 2014).

21. Here I am following Arum and Roksa's summary on page 35 of their book *Aspiring Adults Adrift* (see previous citation) of the work of Philip Babcock and Mindy Marks.

22. Arum and Roksa, *Aspiring Adults Adrift*, p. 35.

23. Kevin Carey, "Americans think we have the world's best colleges. We don't," *New York Times*, June 28, 2014, http://www.nytimes .com/2014/06/29/upshot/americans-think-we-have-the-worlds-best -colleges-we-dont.html.

24. This comment was posted by a reader of Carey's article. To read the full comment, go to Carey's article (the link is in the preceding note), click on comments, then click on "Reader Picks," then scroll down to the second comment by "OSS Architect."

25. My discussion of "the best school" is adapted from my essay on this topic for the Institute for Family Studies, "When is the 'best' school not the best school?" August 9, 2021, https://ifstudies.org/blog /when-is-the-best-school-not-the-best.

26. Suniya Luthar and Karen D'Avanzo, "Contextual factors in substance use: a study of suburban and inner-city adolescents," *Developmental Psychopathology*, volume 11, pp. 845–867, 1999.

27. See for example Suniya Luthar and Shawn Latendresse, "Children of the affluent: challenges to well-being," *Current Directions in Psychological Science*, volume 14, pp. 49–53, 2005.

28. Harold Koplewicz, Anita Gurian, and Kimberly Williams, "The era of affluence and its discontents," *Journal of the American Academy of Child and Adolescent Psychiatry*, volume 48, pp. 1053–1055, 2009.

29. Suniya Luthar and Nina Kumar, "Youth in high-achieving schools: challenges to mental health and directions for evidence-based interventions," in *Handbook of School-Based Mental Health Promotion*, Springer, pp. 441–458, 2018.

30. Suniya Luthar, Nina Kumar, and Nicole Zillmer, "High-achieving schools connote risks for adolescents: problems documented, processes implicated, and directions for interventions," *American Psychologist*, volume 75, pp. 983–995, 2020.

31. Richard Göllner, Rodica Ioana Damian, and colleagues, "It's not only who you are but who you are with: high school composition and individuals' attainment over the life course," *Psychological Science*, volume 29, pp. 1785–1796, 2018.

32. Francis Vergunst, Richard Tremblay, and colleagues, "Association between childhood behaviors and adult employment earnings in Canada," *JAMA Psychiatry*, volume 76, pp. 1044–1051, 2019.

33. Terrie Moffitt and colleagues, "A gradient of childhood self-control predicts health, wealth, and public safety," *Proceedings of the National Academy of Sciences*, volume 108, pp. 2693–2698, 2011.

34. Brent Roberts and colleagues, "The power of personality: the comparative validity of personality traits, socioeconomic status, and cognitive ability for predicting important life outcomes," *Perspectives in Psychological Science*, volume 2, pp. 313–345, 2007.

35. Suniya Luthar and I spoke via Zoom on September 22, 2021.

36. We could have afforded a small home on a tiny lot in Bryn Mawr, but my wife and I wanted our daughter to have a big backyard to run around in, and big backyards are crazy expensive in Bryn Mawr.

Chapter 4: Medication

1. See for example Joseph Biederman and colleagues, "Pediatric mania: a developmental subtype of bipolar disorder?" *Biological Psychiatry*, volume 48, pp. 458–466, 2000.

2. Rob Waters, "Children in crisis? concerns about the growing popularity of the bipolar diagnosis," *Psychotherapy Networker*, September 24, 2009.

3. Rob Waters, *Psychotherapy Networker* (see previous note).

4. The *Newsweek* cover story, written by Mary Carmichael, was titled "Growing up bipolar," published May 17, 2008, online at www .newsweek.com/growing-bipolar-maxs-world-90351.

5. See for example Gardiner Harris and Benedict Carey, "Researchers fail to reveal full drug pay," *New York Times*, June 8, 2008, www .nytimes.com/2008/06/08/us/08conflict.html.

6. When the news broke about the millions of dollars paid to Biederman and his two friends, the only penalty which Harvard Medical School imposed was a one-year embargo on receiving more money from drug companies. Biederman never had to pay the money back. At the time of his death in January 2023, he still retained his position as a director of psychiatric research at Harvard Medical School. As of June 2024, his Harvard web page—https://researchers.mgh.harvard .edu/profile/3048456/Joseph-Biederman—still made no mention of his death, still listed him as the current Chief of Clinical and Research Programs in Pediatric Psychopharmacology, still prominently mentioned his various honors, and still made no mention of the fact that he accepted millions from the drug companies and failed to disclose that fact until Senator Grassley forced him to.

7. Elizabeth Root, *Kids Caught in the Psychiatric Maelstrom: How Pathological Labels and "Therapeutic" Drugs Hurt Children and Families* (Santa Barbara: ABC-CLIO, 2009), p. 40.

8. Elizabeth Roberts, "A rush to medicate young minds," *Washington Post*, October 8, 2006, online at http://www.washingtonpost .com/wp-dyn/content/article/2006/10/06/AR2006100601391.html.

9. Martin Holtmann and colleagues, "Bipolar disorder in children and adolescents in Germany: national trends in the rates of inpatients, 2000–2007," *Bipolar Disorders,* volume 12, pp. 155–163, 2010, full text available online at http://onlinelibrary.wiley.com /doi/10.1111/j.1399-5618.2010.00794.x/full. The German researchers found a significant increase in diagnosis for adolescents 15 to 19 years of age, and a small "nonsignificant" decline in diagnosis of bipolar disorder for children under 15 years of age. It may have been a "nonsignificant" decline from the German perspective, but nevertheless it was a *decline,* not a huge increase as was observed in the United States. Even among adolescents, Holtmann and colleagues note that an adolescent in the United States is still much more likely (about 40 times more likely) to be diagnosed with bipolar disorder than an adolescent in Germany (204 / 5.22 = 39.1). For more, see Holtmann, p. 159.

10. Juan Carballo and colleagues, "Longitudinal trends in diagnosis at child and adolescent mental health centres in Madrid, Spain," *European Child and Adolescent Psychiatry,* volume 22, pp. 47–49, 2013.

11. Kirsten van Kessel and colleagues, "Trends in child and adolescent discharges at a New Zealand psychiatric inpatient unit between 1998 and 2007," *The New Zealand Medical Journal,* volume 125, pp. 55–61.

12. Holtmann and colleagues, "Bipolar disorder in children and adolescents in Germany," pp. 156, 159.

13. Anthony James and colleagues, "A comparison of American and English hospital discharge rates for pediatric bipolar disorder, 2000 to 2010," *Journal of the American Academy of Child and Adolescent Psychiatry,* volume 53, pp. 614–624, 2014.

14. These guidelines are based on the research of professors Craig Anderson and Doug Gentile. I present their research, and explain the guidelines at greater length, in Chapter 3 of my book *Boys Adrift: The Five Factors Driving the Growing Epidemic of Unmotivated Boys and Underachieving Young Men,* second edition (New York: Basic Books, 2016).

15. Gabrielle Weiss and Lily Hechtman, "The hyperactive child syndrome," *Science*, volume 205, pp. 1348–1354, 1979.

16. Sarah Sparks, "Attention deficit rates skyrocket in high school," *Education Week*, August 23, 2021, https://www.edweek.org/teaching-learning/attention-deficit-rates-skyrocket-in-high-school-mentoring-could-prevent-an-academic-freefall/2021/08.

17. I first used the phrase "the medicalization of misbehavior" in the first edition of my book *Why Gender Matters* (New York: Doubleday, 2005), p. 199.

18. For a review of the relation between these antipsychotic medications and **weight gain**, see the article by Dr. James Roerig and colleagues, "Atypical antipsychotic-induced weight gain," *CNS Drugs*, volume 25, pp. 1035–1059, 2011. See also José María Martínez-Ortega and colleagues, "Weight gain and increase of body mass index among children and adolescents treated with antipsychotics: a critical review," *European Child and Adolescent Psychiatry*, volume 22, pp. 457–479, 2013. For a review of the relation between these medications and **diabetes**, specifically in children, see the article by William Bobo and colleagues titled "Antipsychotics and the risk of Type 2 diabetes mellitus in children and youth," *JAMA Psychiatry*, volume 70, pp. 1067–1075, 2013.

19. José María Martínez-Ortega and colleagues, "Weight gain and increase of body mass index among children and adolescents treated with antipsychotics: a critical review," *European Journal of Child and Adolescent Psychiatry*, volume 22, pp. 457–479, 2013.

20. In the review by William Bobo and colleagues (cited above), the risk remained elevated for one year following discontinuation of the antipsychotic. At one year after discontinuation, there was no statistically significant difference in risk of diabetes between those who had discontinued the antipsychotic medication and those children who remained on the medication.

21. Centers for Disease Control and Prevention, "U.S. teen girls experiencing increased sadness and violence," February 13, 2023, updated March 9, 2023, https://www.cdc.gov/media/releases/2023/p0213-yrbs.html.

Chapter 5: Screens

1. Jenny Radesky, Niko Kaciroti, Heidi Weeks, and others, "Longitudinal associations between use of mobile devices for calming and emotional reactivity and executive functioning in children aged 3 to 5 years," *JAMA Pediatrics*, volume 177, pp. 62–70, 2023.

2. Ippei Takahashi, Taku Obara, and Mami Ishikuro, "Screen time at age 1 year and communication and problem-solving developmental delay at 2 and 4 years," *JAMA Pediatrics*, published online August 21, 2023, https://jamanetwork.com/journals/jamapediatrics/fullarticle/2808593.

3. Dr. Beth Long's comments are drawn from our email correspondence, January 21, 23, 24, 25, and 26, 2023.

4. Jonathan Haidt, *The Anxious Generation: How the Great Rewiring of Childhood Is Causing an Epidemic of Mental Illness* (New York: Penguin, 2024).

5. Centers for Disease Control and Prevention, "Youth risk behavior survey: data summary and trends report," April 27, 2023, full text online at https://www.cdc.gov/healthyyouth/data/yrbs/pdf/YRBS_Data-Summary-Trends_Report2023_508.pdf.

6. Quoted in Michelle Goldberg, "Don't let politics cloud your view of what's going on with teens and depression," *New York Times*, February 24, 2023.

7. This statement is drawn from Jonathan Haidt's slide "% US Teens (12–17) who had a major depression in the last year," based on data from the United States National Survey on Drug Use and Health, in Jonathan Haidt and Jean Twenge (ongoing), "Adolescent mood disorders since 2010: A collaborative review," unpublished manuscript, New York University, online at https://tinyurl.com/Teen MentalHealthReview. Note that the slide title is entered as a graphic, not as text, so you won't find it if you do a word search. Instead, scroll down to the end of section 1.1.1.

8. See Haidt and Twenge, previous citation, which as of January 7, 2024, lists 23 different studies showing a rise in anxiety and/or depression among American teens in recent years.

9. Jean Twenge, *Generations: The Real Differences Between Gen Z, Millennials, Gen X, Boomers, and Silents—and What They Mean for America's Future* (New York: Atria, 2023), p. 392.

10. *Social Media and Youth Mental Health: The U.S. Surgeon General's Advisory*, May 23, 2023, online at https://www.hhs.gov/sites/default/files/sg-youth-mental-health-social-media-advisory.pdf.

11. The figures from 2012 and 2018 come from Felix Richter, "Teens' social media usage is drastically increasing," *Statista*, October 9, 2018, https://www.statista.com/chart/15720/frequency-of-teenagers-social-media-use/.

12. Jonathan Rothwell, "Teens spend average of 4.8 hours on social media per day," Gallup, October 13, 2023, https://news.gallup.com/poll/512576/teens-spend-average-hours-social-media-per-day.aspx.

13. Jonathan Haidt and Jean Twenge (ongoing), "Social media and mental health: A collaborative review," unpublished manuscript, New York University. Accessed at tinyurl.com/SocialMediaMentalHealthReview (not to be confused with the other Haidt/Twenge collaboration, cited above, which focuses on changes in mental health but not on social media).

14. Jean Twenge, *Generations* (cited above), p. 410.

15. Haidt and Twenge, "Social media and mental health" (cited above), click on 1.4.1, "Studies on social comparison."

16. Rea Alonzo, Junayd Hussain, and colleagues, "Interplay between social media use, sleep quality, and mental health in youth: a systematic review," *Sleep Medicine Reviews*, volume 56, 2021, https://doi.org/10.1016/j.smrv.2020.101414.

17. Haidt and Twenge, "Social media and mental health" (cited above), click on Question Three, "Do experiments show a causal effect of social media use on mental health outcomes?"

18. Ayala Arad, Ohad Barzilay, and Maayan Perchick, "The impact of Facebook on social comparison and happiness: evidence from a natural experiment," SSRN Electronic Journal, January 2017, http://dx.doi.org/10.2139/ssrn.2916158.

19. Luca Braghieri, Ro'ee Levy, and Alexey Makarin, "Social media and mental health," *American Economic Review*, volume 112, pp. 3660–3993, November 2022, https://www.aeaweb.org/articles?id=10.1257/aer.20211218.

20. Interview with Nikki Waller, "Why AI will make our children more lonely," *Wall Street Journal*, May 29, 2023.

21. Kaitlyn Tiffany, "No one knows exactly what social media is doing to teens," *The Atlantic*, June 13, 2023.

22. Matti Vuorre and colleagues, "There is no evidence that associations between adolescents' digital technology engagement and mental health problems have increased," *Clinical Psychological Science*, volume 9, pp. 823–835, 2021.

23. Candice L. Odgers, "The great rewiring, unplugged," *Nature*, volume 628, pp. 29–30, April 4, 2024, https://www.nature.com/articles/d41586-024-00902-2.epdf.

24. Amy Orben is quoted in Madeleine Aggeler's article "Are smartphones bad for us?" *The Guardian*, January 10, 2024, https://www.theguardian.com/lifeandstyle/2024/jan/10/smartphone-screentime-good-bad-expert-advice.

25. Mary Harrington, "Normophobia," *First Things*, April 2024, https://www.firstthings.com/article/2024/04/normophobia.

26. Matthew Crawford, "The flight from normal," May 6, 2024, https://substack.com/home/post/p-144134037.

27. C. S. Lewis, *The Magician's Nephew* (London: HarperCollins, 1955/2010), p. 117.

28. *Pathways: How Digital Design Puts Children at Risk*, 5Rights Foundation, July 2021, pp. 66–86.

29. Center for Countering Digital Hate, "Deadly by design," December 9, 2022, online at https://counterhate.com/wp-content/uploads/2022/12/CCDH-Deadly-by-Design_120922.pdf.

30. Erin Ryan and Stephanie Hovis, "Collaborative starvation and the invisible podium: using Twitter as a 'how to' guide to spread eating disorders," *Journal of Entertainment and Media Studies*, volume 1, pp. 26–58, 2015.

31. Julie Jargon, "TikTok feeds teens a diet of darkness: self-harm, sad-posting and disordered videos abound on the popular app," *Wall Street Journal*, May 13, 2023.

32. Jargon, previous citation.

33. "TikTok users and growth statistics (2024)," SignHouse, June 14, 2023, https://www.usesignhouse.com/blog/tiktok-stats.

34. L. Ceci, "Average TikTok video length from August 2022 to January 2023," *Statista*, March 17, 2023, https://www.statista.com /statistics/1372569/tiktok-video-duration-by-number-of-views/.

35. Jeff Temple, Jonathan Paul, and Patricia van den Berg, "Teen sexting and its association with sexual behaviors," *JAMA Pediatrics*, volume 166, pp. 828–833, 2012.

36. Emily Van de Riet, "3 Nigerian men charged in 'sextortion' suicide death of 17-year-old football star," Gray News / KKTV, May 5, 2023, https://www.kktv.com/2023/05/05/3-nigerian-men-charged -sextortion-suicide-death-17-year-old-football-star/.

37. Julie Jargon, "Teen boys are falling for a Snapchat nude-photo scam," *Wall Street Journal*, November 18, 2023.

38. Yalda Uhls and Patricia Greenfield, "The rise of fame: an historical content analysis," *Cyberpsychology*, volume 5, 2011, https:// cyberpsychology.eu/article/view/4243/3289.

39. Haidt, *The Anxious Generation*, 2024.

40. Meghan Bobrowsky, "A shot at social-media fame lures 50 million contenders—and Lorenzo Mitchell," *Wall Street Journal*, October 22, 2021.

41. This statistic comes from Bobrowsky's article, previous citation.

42. This statistic, and the quote from Sarah Peretz, also come from Bobrowsky's article cited above.

43. Yuanling Yuan, "SignalFire's creator economy market map," SignalFire, November 29, 2020, accessed July 3, 2023, https://signal fire.com/creator-economy/.

44. Sarah Min, "86% of young Americans want to become a social media influencer," CBS News, November 8, 2019, https://www

.cbsnews.com/news/social-media-influencers-86-of-young-americans
-want-to-become-one/.

45. Verity Johnson, "I was Insta-famous and it was one of the worst
things to happen in my 20s," *The Guardian*, July 18, 2019.

46. Christian Smith and colleagues, *Lost in Transition: The Dark
Side of Emerging Adulthood* (New York: Oxford University Press,
2011), p. 36, emphasis in original.

47. Justin McCarthy, "U.S. approval of interracial marriage at new
high of 94%," Gallup, September 10, 2021, https://news.gallup.com
/poll/354638/approval-interracial-marriage-new-high.aspx.

48. Simone Kühn and Jürgen Gallinat, "Brain structure and func-
tional connectivity associated with pornography consumption: the
brain on porn," *JAMA Psychiatry*, volume 71, pp. 827–834, 2014.

49. Paul Wright, Robert Tokunaga, and Debby Herbenick, "Pornography, masturbation, and relational satisfaction," *The Journal
of Sex Research*, 2022, https://doi.org/10.1080/00224499.2022.213
1705.

50. H. A. Hazony, "Conservatives don't get the porn crisis," *First
Things*, June 26, 2023, https://www.firstthings.com/web-exclusives
/2023/06/conservatives-dont-get-the-porn-crisis.

51. Kimberly Nelson and Emily Rothman, "Should public health
professionals consider pornography a public health crisis?" *American
Journal of Public Health*, volume 110, pp. 151–153, 2020.

52. Erik Hedegaard, "The dirty mind and lonely heart of John
Mayer," *Rolling Stone*, June 6, 2012.

53. No byline, "John Mayer's dating history: Jessica Simpson, Jennifer Aniston, Katy Perry and more," *US Weekly*, July 7,
2023, https://www.usmagazine.com/celebrity-news/pictures/john
-mayers-famous-girlfriends-20121110/.

54. Rob Tannenbaum, "The Playboy interview with John Mayer,"
Playboy, February 4, 2010.

55. Michael B. Robb and Supreet Mann, *Teens and Pornography*
(San Francisco: Common Sense Media, 2023).

56. Quoted by Laura Garnett in her article "3 reasons more sex will bring you more success," *Inc.*, February 12, 2016, https://www.inc.com/laura-garnett/3-reasons-more-sex-will-bring-you-more-success.html.

57. Andrew Court, "AI is transforming porn industry," *New York Post*, February 23, 2023, https://nypost.com/2023/02/23/how-ai-is-changing-sex-industry-it-will-never-be-as-interesting/.

58. Josh Taylor, "Uncharted territory: do AI girlfriend apps promote unhealthy expectations for human relationships?" *The Guardian*, July 21, 2023.

59. Pranshu Verma, "AI fake nudes are booming. It's ruining real teens' lives," *Washington Post*, November 5, 2023, https://www.washingtonpost.com/technology/2023/11/05/ai-deepfake-porn-teens-women-impact/.

60. See for example Christian Laier, Jaro Pekal, and Matthias Brand, "Cybersex addiction in heterosexual female users of internet pornography can be explained by gratification hypothesis," *Cyberpsychology, Behavior, and Social Networking*, volume 17, pp. 505–511, 2014.

61. Pascal-Emmanuel Gobry, "A science-based case for ending the porn epidemic," *Ethics and Public Policy Center*, December 15, 2019, https://eppc.org/publication/a-science-based-case-for-ending-the-porn-epidemic/.

62. Marlow Stern, "Why porn has gotten so rough," *The Daily Beast*, August 4, 2019, https://www.thedailybeast.com/why-porn-has-gotten-so-rough.

63. Chanel Contos, "Sexual choking is now so common that many young people don't think it even requires consent. In a sexual landscape shaped by pornography, far too many incorrectly believe that choking is routine and risk-free," *The Guardian*, December 7, 2022, https://www.theguardian.com/commentisfree/2022/dec/08/sexual-choking-is-now-so-common-that-many-young-people-dont-think-it-even-requires-consent-thats-a-problem.

64. David Kushner, "A brief history of porn on the internet," *Wired*, April 9, 2019, https://www.wired.com/story/brief-history-porn-internet/.

65. Gobry, cited above.

66. Kassondra Cloos and Julie Turkewitz, "Hundreds of nude photos jolt Colorado school," *New York Times*, November 6, 2015.

67. Clare Morell, Patrick Brown, and colleagues, *Raising a Family in the Digital Age: A Technology Guide for Parents*, Ethics and Public Policy Center, August 2022, https://eppc.org/wp-content /uploads/2022/08/EPPC-Parents-Guide-to-Technology.pdf, scroll down to page 8, "Parental Control Software, Hardware, and Apps."

68. Netsanity, "Beating the secrets: what parents should know about 'vault apps,'" *Medium*, April 17, 2017, https://medium.com /netsanity-posts/beating-the-secrets-what-parents-should-know -about-vault-apps-645f86964953.

69. Kyle Gratton, "Red Dead Redemption 2 cost about $540 million to make," *Screen Rant*, August 21, 2021, https://screenrant.com /red-dead-redemption-2-cost-rockstar-development/.

70. The numbers for *Avatar* (2009), $77 million opening weekend and $237 million budget, come from the movie's entry on IMDB, https://www.imdb.com/title/tt0499549/?ref_=nv_sr_srsg_3_tt _8_nm_0_q_avatar.

71. The full text of the relevant guidance from the American Academy of Pediatrics reads, "Recommend that children not sleep with devices in their bedrooms, including TVs, computers, and smartphones. Avoid exposure to devices or screens for 1 hour before bedtime." See American Academy of Pediatrics, Council on Communications and Media, "Media use in school-age children and adolescents," *Pediatrics*, November 1, 2016, volume 138, pp. 1–6. This policy was officially reaffirmed by the AAP in July 2022; see https:// publications.aap.org/pediatrics/article/150/4/e2022059284/189561 /AAP-Publications-Reaffirmed.

72. My daughter, Sarah, accompanied me on a visit to JSerra Catholic High School in San Juan Capistrano on August 15, 2022. Patrick Reidy, vice president for Mission and Faith, interviewed Sarah and me. Mr. Reidy's conversation with Sarah is heard in the first eight minutes of the 32-minute interview, online at https://www.jserra

.org/lion-life/podcast/detail/~board/plugged-in-with-pat-reidy
-podcast/post/teen-culture-with-dr-sax, accessed December 1, 2023.

73. This prohibition is a matter of United States federal law. See
United States Department of Justice, "Obscenity," March 29, 2021,
https://www.justice.gov/criminal-ceos/obscenity, scroll down to
"Obscenity Law and Minors."

74. The state of Louisiana has taken the lead in making it harder for
minors under 18 to access pornography. See for example Kevin Mc-
Gill, "Judge tosses challenge to Louisiana's age verification law aimed
at porn websites," Associated Press, October 4, 2023. For more on the
Louisiana story, see Nancy Rommelmann, "The woman who stood
up to the porn industry—and won," *The Free Press*, September 21,
2023, https://www.thefp.com/p/laurie-schlegel-stood-up-to-porn.

75. See for example "AG Henry joins lawsuit against Meta for
endangering kids' mental health with addictive, harmful content,"
October 24, 2023, https://www.attorneygeneral.gov/taking-action
/ag-henry-joins-lawsuit-against-meta-for-endangering-kids-mental
-health-with-addictive-harmful-content/.

Chapter 6: Theybies

1. For more about Zyler and Kadyn, see Julie Compton, "Boy
or girl? Parents raising 'theybies' let kids decide," NBC News, July
19, 2018, https://www.nbcnews.com/feature/nbc-out/boy-or-girl
-parents-raising-theybies-let-kids-decide-n891836.

2. This sentence is a fair summary of the current guidelines of the
American Academy of Pediatrics, published in 2018 and reaffirmed
by the Academy in 2023, as I show in my essay "Politicizing pediatrics: how the AAP's transgender guidelines undermine trust in
medical authority," *Public Discourse*, March 13, 2019, https://www
.thepublicdiscourse.com/2019/03/50118/. The citation for the AAP
guidelines is Jason Rafferty and colleagues, American Academy of Pediatrics Policy Statement, October 1, 2018, "Ensuring comprehensive

care and support for transgender and gender-diverse children and adolescents," published in *Pediatrics*, volume 142, October 2018.

3. Nicholas Malfitano, "Parents of first-graders in Mount Lebanon get go-ahead to sue over transgender lessons," *Pennsylvania Record*, June 8, 2023, https://pennrecord.com/stories/643631678 -parents-of-first-graders-in-mount-lebanon-get-go-ahead-to-sue -over-transgender-lessons.

4. Eugene Volokh, "First-grade teacher's 'pursu[ing] her own transgender agenda outside the curriculum' may violate constitutional parental rights," *Reason*, June 1, 2023.

5. Malfitano, 2023, cited above.

6. No byline given, "Lebo Pride steps up to support transgender students in Mt. Lebanon legal battle," *QBurgh*, February 17, 2024, https://qburgh.com/lebo-pride-steps-up-to-support-transgender -students-in-mt-lebanon-legal-battle/.

7. My discussion here of the AAP guidelines for transgender and gender-diverse children is adapted from my essay for *Public Discourse* titled "Politicizing pediatrics: how the AAP's transgender guidelines undermine trust in medical authority," March 13, 2019, https://www.thepublicdiscourse.com/2019/03/50118/.

8. Jason Rafferty and colleagues, American Academy of Pediatrics Policy Statement, October 1, 2018, "Ensuring comprehensive care and support for transgender and gender-diverse children and adolescents," published in *Pediatrics*, volume 142, October 2018.

9. Kenneth Zucker and colleagues, "A developmental, biopsychosocial model for the treatment of children with gender identity disorder," *Journal of Homosexuality*, volume 59, pp. 369–397.

10. Devita Singh and colleagues, "A follow-up study of boys with gender identity disorder," *Frontiers in Psychiatry*, 2021, full text online at https://www.ncbi.nlm.nih.gov/pmc/articles/PMC8039393/.

11. See for example Kenneth Zucker, "On the 'natural history' of gender identity disorder in children," *Journal of the American Academy of Child and Adolescent Psychiatry*, volume 47, pp. 1361–1363, 2008.

12. The report cited by the AAP was written by D. C. Haldeman, "The practice and ethics of sexual orientation conversion therapy," *Journal of Consulting and Clinical Psychology*, volume 62, pp. 221–227, 1994.

13. Girls and women were not only prohibited from performing tea ceremony in samurai Japan (1603–1868), they were not allowed even to *attend*. See for example Adam Acar, "Tea ceremony in Japan," no date given, https://mai-ko.com/travel/culture-in-japan/tea-ceremony/japanese-tea-ceremony/.

14. That was the first book which popped up on Amazon Kids+ when I looked for recommendations for an 8-year-old on May 20, 2023.

15. Theresa Thorn (author) and Noah Grigni (illustrator), *It Feels Good to Be Yourself: A Book About Gender Identity* (New York: Henry Holt, 2019).

16. See my paper "How common is intersex? A response to Anne Fausto-Sterling," *Journal of Sex Research*, volume 39, pp. 174–178, 2002.

17. Zachary Mettler, "School district refuses to rescind controversial sex ed curriculum for kindergartners," *Daily Citizen*, September 29, 2022, https://dailycitizen.focusonthefamily.com/school-district-refuses-to-rescind-controversial-sex-ed-curriculum-for-kindergartners/.

18. Nina Power, "The trans war on tomboys," *Compact*, January 24, 2023, online at https://compactmag.com/article/the-trans-war-on-tomboys, emphasis added.

19. Katie J. M. Baker, "When students change gender identity, and parents don't know," *New York Times*, January 22, 2023.

20. The lawsuit—including the flyer, on page 11—is posted online at https://www.documentcloud.org/documents/23200909-will-eau-claire-complaint.

21. Baker, *New York Times*, cited above.

22. The statement about California, New Jersey, and Maryland, as well as the quote from Jon Davidson, are taken from Baker's article for the *New York Times*, cited above.

23. See for example GoFundMe's page "Gender-Affirming Care Fundraising," https://www.gofundme.com/c/gender-confirmation -surgery-fundraising, accessed June 1, 2023.

24. Sue Reid, "How children as young as 13 are asking strangers online to crowdfund their sex change drugs," January 28, 2022, https://www.dailymail.co.uk/news/article-10453837/How-children -young-13-asking-strangers-online-crowdfund-sex-change-drugs .html.

Chapter 7: Fragile

1. Ellen Beate Hansen Sandseter and Leif Edward Ottesen Kennair, "Children's risky play from an evolutionary perspective: the anti-phobic effects of thrilling experiences," *Evolutionary Psychology*, volume 9, April 2011, online at https://journals.sagepub.com/doi/full /10.1177/147470491100900212.

2. Friedrich Nietzsche, *Götzen-Dämmerung*, "Sprüche und Pfeile" §8, *Aus der Kriegsschule des Lebens*, 1888.

3. My discussion of the *Waldkindergarten* in Oberammergau and the cult of safetyism is drawn from an essay I wrote for *Psychology Today*, "Lessons from Germany: children climbing trees," October 2019, https://www.psychologytoday.com/us/blog/sax-sex/201910 /lessons-germany-children-climbing-trees.

4. This story took place before 2015, when the College Board transitioned AP Physics into two years and two separate AP courses, one for mechanics and one for electricity and magnetism.

5. Jean Twenge, "Generational differences in mental health: are children and adolescents suffering more, or less?" *American Journal of Orthopsychiatry*, volume 81, pp. 469–472, 2011.

6. This distinction is not assessed by the census. The American census asks where you live and who else lives with you. If you are an adult living alone, then you are a head of household. The fact that you are supported by your parents is not readily apparent in the data published by the census.

7. For the raw data on which these tables are based, go to http://stats.oecd.org/Index.aspx?DatasetCode=ALFS_SUMTAB. Click on "LFS [Labour Force Statistics] by sex and age," then click on "LFS by sex and age—indicators," then click on table B1: "Employment/population ratios by selected age groups." Customize your table for ages 25 to 34 by clicking on "Age." Accessed December 1, 2023. The data in my table are for the year 2022.

8. David Leonhardt, "The idled young Americans," *New York Times*, May 5, 2013, http://www.nytimes.com/2013/05/05/sunday-review/the-idled-young-americans.html.

9. See Helu Jiang and Faisal Sohail, "Skill-biased entrepreneurial decline," *Review of Economic Dynamics*, volume 48, pp. 18–44, 2023, Figure 1.

10. See Jiang and Sohail (previous reference), Figure 11.

11. For the study itself, see the Hathaway and Litan citation in the next note. This quote comes from Thomas Edsall's column commenting on the Hathaway and Litan report. Edsall's column is titled "America out of whack," *New York Times*, September 23, 2014.

12. Ian Hathaway and Robert Litan, "Declining business dynamism in the United States: a look at states and metros," May 5, 2014, online at https://www.brookings.edu/wp-content/uploads/2016/06/declining_business_dynamism_hathaway_litan.pdf.

13. The rise in the prevalence of anxiety and depression among American teenagers has been more pronounced for girls than for boys. For a consideration of the several factors underlying that girl/boy difference, please see Chapters 1 through 4 of the second edition of my book *Girls on the Edge: The Four Factors Driving the New Crisis for Girls* (New York: Basic Books, 2020).

14. I am not the first to suggest the cheerleader/coach analogy to different parenting styles. See for example "Motivating teenagers: how do you do it?" by psychologist Dan Griffin, February 14, 2014, http://www.slate.com/articles/life/family/2014/02/motivating_teenagers_how_do_you_do_it.html.

15. Annebet van Mameren, "The education system in the Netherlands," October 12, 2023, https://www.expatica.com/nl/education /children-education/dutch-education-system-100816/.

16. Stefanie Busse, "Local Swiss school and the working parent," *Swiss Education Consulting*, June 26, 2016, https://swisseducation consulting.ch/local-school-and-the-working-parent/.

17. Personal communication January 2014 from Dr. Eva Shimaoka, my medical school classmate then living in Switzerland.

18. I attended Lomond Elementary School in Shaker Heights, Ohio, for kindergarten through sixth grade. Lunch was at home every day, with rare exceptions such as a school picnic. My junior high school, Byron Junior High School, where I attended seventh grade, was the first school I attended which had a cafeteria.

19. Neufeld and Maté, *Hold On to Your Kids*, p. 140.

20. Here I am paraphrasing the aphorism, "Success means moving from one failure to the next with no loss of enthusiasm." There is no consensus regarding the source of this aphorism. Although it is often attributed to Winston Churchill, scholars of Churchill's life insist that he never said it. It may have originated with Abraham Lincoln.

Chapter 8: What Matters?

1. Angela Duckworth and colleagues, "Who does well in life? Conscientious adults excel in both objective and subjective success," *Frontiers in Psychology*, volume 3, article 356, September 2012, online at http://journal.frontiersin.org/Journal/10.3389/fpsyg.2012.00356 /full.

2. See for example Margaret Kern and Howard Friedman, "Do conscientious individuals live longer? A quantitative review," *Health Psychology*, volume 27, pp. 505–512, 2008. See also Tim Bogg and Brent Roberts, "The case for conscientiousness: evidence and implications for a personality trait marker of health and longevity," *Annals of Behavioral Medicine*, volume 45, pp. 278–288, 2013. Specifically

regarding the finding that childhood conscientiousness as measured at age 10 predicts a lower risk of obesity at age 51, see Sarah Hampson and colleagues, "Childhood conscientiousness relates to objectively measured adult physical health four decades later," *Health Psychology*, volume 32, pp. 925–928, 2013.

3. See Helen Cheng and Adrian Furnham, "Personality traits, education, physical exercise, and childhood neurological function as independent predictors of adult obesity," *PLOS One*, November 8, 2013. The abstract of this paper is confusing: it says that Conscientiousness was "significantly associated with adult obesity." That's true, but the correlation was *negative*: the more Conscientious the child was, the less likely that child was to become obese as an adult. See also Sarah Hampson and colleagues, "Childhood conscientiousness relates to objectively measured adult physical health four decades later," *Health Psychology*, volume 32, pp. 925–928, 2013.

4. See Robert Wilson and colleagues, "Conscientiousness and the incidence of Alzheimer disease and mild cognitive impairment," *Archives of General Psychiatry*, volume 64, pp. 1204–1212, 2007. See also Paul Duberstein, "Personality and risk for Alzheimer's disease in adults 72 years of age and older," *Psychology and Aging*, volume 26, pp. 351–362, 2011.

5. Tim Bogg and Brent Roberts, "The case for conscientiousness: evidence and implications for a personality trait marker of health and longevity," *Annals of Behavioral Medicine*, volume 45, pp. 278–288, 2013. See also Terrie Moffitt, Richie Poulton, and Avshalom Caspi, "Lifelong impact of early self-control: childhood self-discipline predicts adult quality of life," *American Scientist*, volume 101, pp. 352–359, 2013. See also José Causadias, Jessica Salvatore, and Alan Sroufe, "Early patterns of self-regulation as risk and promotive factors in development: a longitudinal study from childhood to adulthood in a high-risk sample," *International Journal of Behavioral Development*, volume 36, pp. 293–302, 2012, full text online at http://www.ncbi .nlm.nih.gov/pmc/articles/PMC3496279/.

In a careful study of data from seven different cohort studies—from the United Kingdom, from Germany, from Australia, and from the United States—researchers found that after adjusting for health behavior, marital status, age, sex, and ethnicity, only Conscientiousness, and no other Big Five personality trait, predicted longer life. See Markus Jokela and colleagues, "Personality and all-cause mortality: individual-participant meta-analysis of 3,947 deaths in 76,150 adults," *American Journal of Epidemiology*, volume 178, pp. 667–675, 2013.

6. Angela Duckworth and colleagues, "Who does well in life? Conscientious adults excel in both objective and subjective success," *Frontiers in Psychology*, volume 3, article 356, September 2012, online at http://journal.frontiersin.org/Journal/10.3389/fpsyg.2012.00356 /full. Duckworth and colleagues found that although Conscientiousness is positively associated with life satisfaction, Emotional Stability and Extraversion are more strongly positively associated with life satisfaction. However, Emotional Stability has no association, positive or negative, with wealth, whereas Conscientiousness is positively associated with wealth. Extraversion demonstrates a small-to-medium association with wealth, but no association with income and no positive association with health. Conscientiousness is positively associated with wealth, with income, and with health, as well as with life satisfaction.

7. Silvia Mendolia and Ian Walker, "The effect of non-cognitive traits on health behaviours in adolescence," *Health Economics*, volume 23, pp. 1146–1158, 2014.

8. Brent Roberts and colleagues, "The power of personality: the comparative validity of personality traits, socioeconomic status, and cognitive ability for predicting important life outcomes," *Perspectives on Psychological Science*, volume 2, pp. 313–345, 2007.

9. These findings are drawn from Figure 2 in Terrie Moffitt and colleagues, "A gradient of childhood self-control predicts health, wealth, and public safety," *Proceedings of the National Academy of Sciences*, volume 108, pp. 2693–2698, 2011.

10. Unfortunately we do not yet have a scholarly and comprehensive biography of Jim Morrison. The closest is the biography by James Riordan and Jerry Prochnicky, *Break on Through: The Life and Death of Jim Morrison* (New York: William Morrow, 2006).

11. These figures are from Terrie Moffitt, Richie Poulton, and Avshalom Caspi, "Lifelong impact of early self-control: childhood self-discipline predicts adult quality of life," *American Scientist*, volume 101, pp. 352–359, 2013. These figures are from page 355.

12. For a survey of interventions to boost self-control in young children, see the review by Alex Piquero and colleagues, "Self-control interventions for children under age 10 for improving self-control and delinquency and problem behaviors," *Campbell Systematic Reviews*, 2010, #2 (117 pages). Piquero and colleagues accept Michael Gottfredson and Travis Hirschi's assertion that interventions to boost self-control are not effective for children over 10 to 12 years of age. I don't accept that assertion. Gottfredson and Hirschi are basing their assessment on their experience (pre-1990) with teenage juvenile delinquents. I concede that there is evidence that the criminal justice system is not effective in boosting self-control in incarcerated teenagers: see for example Ojmarrh Mitchell and Doris MacKenzie, "The stability and resiliency of self-control in a sample of incarcerated offenders," *Crime and Delinquency*, volume 52, pp. 432–449, 2006. But data based on incarcerated juvenile offenders may not be valid for parents like you and me, assuming that your child has not been convicted of a felony. More to the point: I have personally seen numerous cases in my own practice where kids over age 10 have reformed and become more Conscientious because parents implemented some of the strategies described in this book. Even very simple interventions, such as repeatedly telling a child to "Stop and think!" before they act can have profound and lasting beneficial consequences, even in kids who have been diagnosed with ADHD: see for example Molly Reid and John Borkowski, "Causal attributions of hyperactive children: implications for teaching strategies and self-control," *Journal of Educational Psychology*, volume 79, pp. 296–307, 1987.

The more general premises here are that *personality can change at any age* and that *increased Conscientiousness is beneficial.* For evidence supporting these premises, see the study by Christopher Boyce and colleagues, "Is personality fixed? Personality changes as much as 'variable' economic factors and more strongly predicts changes to life satisfaction," *Social Indicators Research*, volume 111, pp. 287–305, 2013; and also see Christopher Magee and colleagues, "Personality trait change and life satisfaction in adults: the roles of age and hedonic balance," *Personality and Individual Differences*, volume 55, pp. 694–698, 2013. Magee and colleagues find, not surprisingly, that the older you are, the less likely your personality is to change. I am not asserting that it is easy for a 65-year-old to become more Conscientious. But I have seen 15-year-olds who have become more Conscientious.

13. This is the British cohort study. For an overview, see Tyas Prevoo and Bas ter Weel, "The importance of early conscientiousness for socio-economic outcomes: evidence from the British Cohort Study," IZA Discussion Paper 7537, July 2013, available online at http://ftp.iza.org/dp7537.pdf.

14. James J. Heckman and Yona Rubinstein, "The importance of noncognitive skills: lessons from the GED testing program," *AEA Papers and Proceedings*, May 2001, p. 145, full text available at https://www.aeaweb.org/articles?id=10.1257/aer.91.2.145.

15. These quotes come from Dr. Heckman's essay, "Lacking character, American education fails the test," online at https://heckmanequation.org/resource/lacking-character-american-education -fails-the-test/, accessed November 26, 2023.

16. Carol Dweck, "The secret to raising smart kids," *Scientific American Mind*, volume 18, pp. 36–43, 2008.

17. You can read Dr. Dweck's description of her classic study and many more studies like it in her book *Mindset: The New Psychology of Success* (New York: Ballantine, 2007).

18. Christopher Bryan, Gabrielle Adams, and Benoit Monin, "When cheating would make you a cheater: implicating the self

prevents unethical behavior," *Journal of Experimental Psychology*, volume 142, pp. 1001–1005, 2013.

19. Many of the points made in this section were made by Adam Grant in his essay "Raising a moral child," published on the front page of the Sunday Review in the *New York Times*, April 13, 2014, and online at http://www.nytimes.com/2014/04/12/opinion/sunday /raising-a-moral-child.html.

20. Christopher Bryan, unpublished study of 3- to 6-year-olds, cited by Adam Grant in his essay "Raising a moral child," see previous note.

21. I first encountered this statistic in the article by Richard Pérez-Peña, "Studies find more students cheating, with high achievers no exception," *New York Times*, September 7, 2012. Mr. Pérez-Peña is citing a survey of 40,000 American youth conducted by the Josephson Institute, "The Ethics of American Youth," available online at https://charactercounts.org/2012-report-card/, accessed August 14, 2023.

22. Richard Pérez-Peña, "Studies find more students cheating, with high achievers no exception," *New York Times*, September 7, 2012, online at http://www.nytimes.com/2012/09/08/education/studies -show-more-students-cheat-even-high-achievers.html.

23. Quoted in Richard Pérez-Peña, "Studies find more students cheating, with high achievers no exception," see previous note.

24. Raquel Coronell Uribe and Kelsey J. Griffin, "The graduating class of 2023 by the numbers," *The Harvard Crimson*, May 3, 2023, https://features.thecrimson.com/2023/senior-survey/academics/.

25. Allysia Finley, "Claudine Gay and the cheating crisis on campus," *Wall Street Journal*, January 7, 2024.

26. William James, *Principles of Psychology* (Notre Dame, IN: University of Notre Dame Press, originally published in 1892, republished in 1985), volume 2, pp. 449–450.

27. Proverbs 22:6, New King James Version. For an introduction to the scholarship regarding the provenance of the book of Proverbs,

I recommend Robert Alter's *The Wisdom Books: Job, Proverbs, and Ecclesiastes* (New York: W. W. Norton, 2011), pp. 183–192.

28. See the results of the survey by Common Sense Media, "Teens and pornography," January 2023, online at https://www.common sensemedia.org/research/teens-and-pornography.

29. Will Durant, *The Story of Philosophy: The Lives and Opinions of the World's Greatest Philosophers from Plato to John Dewey* (New York: Pocket Books, 1927/1991).

30. See for example Dov Peretz Elkins, *The Bible's Top 50 Ideas: The Essential Concepts Everyone Should Know* (New York: SPI Books, 2006), p. 229. See also Robert Alter's discussion of Deuteronomy 6:7 on p. 641 of his *The Hebrew Bible, Volume 1: The Five Books of Moses* (New York: W. W. Norton, 2019).

31. Adam Grant, "Raising a moral child," published on the front page of the Sunday Review in the *New York Times*, April 13, 2014, and online at http://www.nytimes.com/2014/04/12/opinion/sunday /raising-a-moral-child.html.

32. C. S. Lewis, *Mere Christianity*, Book IV, chapter 7, "Let's Pretend" (San Francisco: Harper San Francisco, 2009 [1952]), p. 188.

33. William Deresiewicz, *Excellent Sheep: The Miseducation of the American Elite and the Way to a Meaningful Life* (New York: Free Press, 2014), p. 26.

34. Jennifer Finney Boylan, "A Common Core for all of us," *New York Times*, March 23, 2014, Sunday Review, p. 4.

35. Talbot Brewer, "The great malformation," *Hedgehog Review*, summer 2023, https://hedgehogreview.com/issues/theological -variations/articles/the-great-malformation.

Chapter 9: Misconceptions

1. Among researchers, this study—the National Longitudinal Study of Adolescent Health—is known as the "Add Health" study. "Add" is spelled with a capital A and two lower-case d's. I find this

jargon confusing. Many of us might assume that "Add" in this context has something to do with ADHD, Attention Deficit Hyperactivity Disorder, formerly known as ADD. But the Add Health study has nothing directly to do with ADHD and was not developed with ADHD in mind.

2. Two separate analyses of the same database have come to the same conclusion in this regard. See Matthew Johnson, "Parent-child relationship quality directly and indirectly influences hooking up behavior reported in young adulthood through alcohol use in adolescence," *Archives of Sexual Behavior*, volume 42, pp. 1463–1472, 2013; and also see Kathleen Roche and colleagues, "Enduring consequences of parenting for risk behaviors from adolescence into early adulthood," *Social Science and Medicine*, volume 66, pp. 2023–2034, 2008.

3. Matthew Johnson and Nancy Galambos, "Paths to intimate relationship quality from parent-adolescent relations and mental health," *Journal of Marriage and Family*, volume 76, pp. 145–160, 2014.

4. Emily Harville and colleagues, "Parent-child relationships, parental attitudes toward sex, and birth outcomes among adolescents," *Journal of Pediatric and Adolescent Gynecology*, volume 27, pp. 287–293, 2014.

5. The use of the terms "Too Hard," "Too Soft," and "Just Right" in place of "authoritarian," "permissive," and "authoritative" is not original. I am borrowing that usage from Judith Rich Harris, *The Nurture Assumption: Why Children Turn Out the Way They Do*, revised and updated (New York: Free Press, 2009), p. 44. I disagree with Ms. Harris on almost every point of substance, but I do like her simpler formulation of Baumrind's categories.

6. For example, in his 2001 presidential address to the Society for Research on Adolescence, Laurence Steinberg said, "Studies of American samples show that as a general rule, adolescents fare better when their parents are authoritative, regardless of their racial or social background or their parents' marital status. This finding has been confirmed in samples from countries around the world that

have extreme diversity in their value systems, such as China, Pakistan, Hong Kong, Scotland, Australia, and Argentina."

Quoted in Diana Baumrind, "Authoritative Parenting Revisited: History and Current Status," in Robert Larzelere, Amanda Sheffield Morris, and Amanda Harrist (editors), *Authoritative Parenting: Synthesizing Nurturance and Discipline for Optimal Child Development*, American Psychological Association, 2013, p. 11.

7. Baumrind, "Authoritative Parenting Revisited," 2013, p. 12.

8. See for example Baumrind's article, "The impact of parenting style on adolescent competence and substance abuse," *The Journal of Early Adolescence*, volume 11, pp. 56–95, 1991. Although these findings are not well-known to many American parents, this article has been influential among scholars in the field of parenting; as of December 2023, it had been cited in more than 7,700 other articles, according to Google Scholar.

9. Baumrind, "Authoritative Parenting Revisited," 2013, p. 13.

10. Baumrind, "Authoritative Parenting Revisited," 2013, p. 13. The researcher Baumrind is criticizing here is Alfie Kohn and his book *Unconditional Parenting: Moving from Rewards and Punishments to Love and Reason* (New York: Atria, 2005).

11. Baumrind, "Authoritative Parenting Revisited," 2013, p. 13.

12. My appearance on the *TODAY* show with Dr. Meeker was broadcast on April 26, 2014. NBC has taken the episode down, I don't know why, but it's still archived at https://archive.org/details /KNTV_20140426_090700_Today/start/2160/end/2220, accessed December 23, 2023. Our segment begins at 02:42 (scroll to the right until you get to 02:42). For me, as I said, the highlight of the day was not being on TV but having the chance to talk with Dr. Meeker in the green room.

13. A useful review of the mechanisms by which brain development in adolescence influences socialization, delay of gratification, etc. is provided by Sarah-Jayne Blakemore and Kathryn Mills in their paper "Is adolescence a sensitive period for sociocultural processing?" *Annual Review of Psychology*, volume 65, pp. 187–207, 2014.

14. See Douglas Gentile, Craig Anderson, and colleagues, "Mediators and moderators of long-term effects of violent video games on aggressive behavior," *JAMA Pediatrics*, volume 168, pp. 450–457, 2014. See also Craig Anderson, Douglas Gentile, and Katherine Buckley, *Violent Video Game Effects on Children and Adolescents: Theory, Research, and Public Policy* (New York: Oxford University Press, 2007).

15. See Jan Hoffman's article "Cool at 13, adrift at 23," *New York Times*, June 23, 2014. In this article, Hoffman is reporting on a study by Joseph Allen and colleagues which was subsequently published under the title, "What ever happened to the 'cool' kids? Long-term sequelae of early adolescent pseudomature behavior," *Child Development*, volume 85, pp. 1866–1880, 2014. It may also be relevant to note that popular adolescents were less likely to comply with COVID-19 restrictions during the pandemic compared with their less-popular peers: see Wendy Ellis and colleagues, "Staying safe or staying popular? Popularity and reputation concerns predict adherence and adjustment during the COVID-19 pandemic," *Youth and Society*, volume 55, pp. 1287–1306, 2023. See also Sunmi Seo and Kristina McDonald, "What happens to the popular kids?" chapter 14 in Martin Jones (editor), *Peer Relationships in Classroom Management* (New York: Routledge, 2022).

16. Mansoor Iqbal, "Twitch revenue and usage statistics 2024," January 8, 2024, https://www.businessofapps.com/data/twitch-statistics/.

17. In the scholarly literature, the confusion between *happiness* and *pleasure* is often couched in terms of "eudaimonic well-being"—that's real happiness—and "hedonic well-being"—that's mere pleasure. Incidentally, some scholars believe that *gratitude* is key to becoming truly happy; and they observe that this premise is fundamental to Judaism, Christianity, and Islam. See Robert Emmons and Cheryl Crumpler, "Gratitude as a human strength: appraising the evidence," *Journal of Social and Clinical Psychology*, volume 19, pp. 56–69, 2000.

18. David Brooks, "Baseball or soccer?" *New York Times*, July 10, 2014, http://www.nytimes.com/2014/07/11/opinion/david-brooks-baseball-or-soccer.html.

19. Arthur C. Brooks, "Love people, not pleasure," *New York Times*, July 18, 2014, http://www.nytimes.com/2014/07/20/opinion/sunday/arthur-c-brooks-love-people-not-pleasure.html?src=xps.

20. This teacher spoke during a presentation I gave to parents at Hillview Middle School in Menlo Park, California, on October 22, 2013. The school to which the teacher was referring was NOT Hillview Middle School.

Chapter 10: *Humility*

1. The now-defunct Center on Wealth and Philanthropy at Boston College surveyed 120 very wealthy families—average net worth $78 million—and found that they are "a generally dissatisfied lot, [with] deep anxieties involving love, work, and family." The study was never published in a scholarly journal, but anecdotes from the study were reported in Graeme Wood's article "Secret fears of the super-rich," *The Atlantic*, April 2011, https://www.theatlantic.com/magazine/archive/2011/04/secret-fears-of-the-super-rich/308419/.

2. Diana Boer and Ronald Fischer, "How and when do personal values guide our attitudes and sociality? Explaining cross-cultural variability in attitude-value linkages," *Psychological Bulletin*, volume 5, pp. 1113–1147, September 2013.

3. Gian Vittorio Caprara, Guido Alessandri, and Nancy Eisenberg, "Prosociality: the contribution of traits, values, and self-efficacy beliefs," *Journal of Personality and Social Psychology*, volume 102, pp. 1289–1303, 2012.

4. Paul K. Piff, Pia Dietze, Matthew Feinberg, and colleagues, "Awe, the small self, and prosocial behavior," *Journal of Personality and Social Psychology*, volume 108, pp. 883–899, 2015, https://www.apa.org/pubs/journals/releases/psp-pspi0000018.pdf.

5. See for example Kirsten Weir, "Nurtured by nature: psychological research is advancing our understanding of how time in nature can improve our mental health and sharpen our cognition," *Monitor on Psychology*, volume 51, April/May 2020, https://www.apa.org /monitor/2020/04/nurtured-nature.

6. "Life is what happens while you are making other plans" is a paraphrase of John Lennon's 1980 song "Beautiful Boy," which contains this line: *"Life is what happens to you while you're busy making other plans."* In the song, Lennon is speaking to his son Sean Taro Ono Lennon, who was 4 years old at the time. Lennon was shot and killed on December 8, 1980, just three weeks after the record was released on November 17, 1980.

7. My discussion here is adapted from my essay for the Institute for Family Studies, "An Elon Musk school or a Mother Teresa school?" February 28, 2023, https://ifstudies.org/blog/parents -choice-an-elon-musk-school-or-a-mother-teresa-school.

8. "Everybody can be great, because anybody can serve" is of course a quote from Dr. Martin Luther King Jr. See for example "'Everybody can be great, because anybody can serve,'" Wayne Meisel, *Huffington Post*, https://www.huffpost.com/entry/everybody -can-be-great-because-anybody-can-serve_b_2476044.

9. I am paraphrasing Alina Tugend's paraphrase of David Mc-Cullough Jr.'s notorious 2012 commencement speech: "that just because they've been told they're amazing doesn't mean that they are." Tugend's article is titled "Redefining success and celebrating the ordinary," *New York Times*, June 29, 2012, www.nytimes .com/2012/06/30/your-money/redefining-success-and-celebrating -the-unremarkable.html.

10. See the paper by Alex Wood and colleagues, "Gratitude predicts psychological well-being above the Big Five facets," *Personality and Individual Differences*, volume 46, pp. 443–447, 2009. Robert Emmons and Michael McCullough found that simply telling people to "count their blessings" had significant and sustained benefits: see their paper "Counting blessings versus burdens: An experimental

investigation of gratitude and subjective well-being in daily life," *Journal of Personality and Social Psychology*, volume 84, pp. 377–389, 2003; see also their follow-up paper "Gratitude in intermediate affective terrain: Links of grateful moods to individual differences and daily emotional experience," *Journal of Personality and Social Psychology*, volume 86, pp. 295–309, 2004.

11. See Alex Wood and colleagues, 2009 (previous note), for a discussion of gratitude as a *cause* of well-being rather than a *result* of well-being.

12. This insight is borrowed from C. S. Lewis, *The Screwtape Letters* (New York: HarperCollins 1942/1996), p. 138, where a senior devil advises a junior tempter: "We direct the fashionable outcry of each generation against those vices of which it is least in danger.... The game is to have them all running about with fire extinguishers whenever there is a flood, and all crowding to that side of the boat which is already nearly gunwale under. Thus we make it fashionable to expose the dangers of enthusiasm at the very moment when they are all really becoming worldly and lukewarm; a century later, when we are really making them all Byronic and drunk with emotion, the fashionable outcry is directed against the dangers of the mere 'understanding.'"

13. For Professor Lancy's own presentation of this work, see his 2012 paper "The Chore Curriculum," online at https://www.research gate.net/publication/303126722_The_chore_curriculum/link/5767e c0508aedbc345f78044/download. For some context on how and why American parents don't know about this, see Joe Pinsker's article "The way American parents think about chores is bizarre," *The Atlantic*, December 26, 2018, https://www.theatlantic.com/family /archive/2018/12/allowance-kids-chores-help/578848/.

14. This comment is taken from an interview which Mr. Washington did on Oprah's talk show on October 31, 2006.

15. Kat Eschner, "John D. Rockefeller was the richest person to ever live. Period," *Smithsonian*, January 10, 2017, https://www .smithsonianmag.com/smart-news/john-d-rockefeller-richest-person

-ever-live-period-180961705/; and also Tom Nicholas and Vasiliki Fouka, "John D. Rockefeller: the richest man in the world," Harvard Business School, December 2014, https://www.hbs.edu/faculty /Pages/item.aspx?num=47167.

Chapter 11: *Joy*

1. Daniel Kahneman, Alan Krueger, David Schkade, and colleagues, "Toward national well-being accounts," *AEA Papers and Proceedings*, pp. 429–434, May 2004, downloaded from http://www2 .hawaii.edu/~noy/300texts/nationalwellbeing.pdf, accessed September 12, 2023.

2. Daniel Kahneman, David Schkade, Claude Fischler, Alan Krueger, and Amy Krilla, "The structure of well-being in two cities: life satisfaction and experienced happiness in Columbus, Ohio; and Rennes, France," chapter 2 in Ed Diener, Daniel Kahneman, and John Helliwell, *International Differences in Well-Being* (New York: Oxford University Press, 2010), p. 26.

3. All three quotes in this section come from Kahneman, Schkade, and colleagues, p. 29 (see previous note).

4. Jennifer Senior, *All Joy and No Fun: The Paradox of Modern Parenthood* (New York: Ecco [HarperCollins], 2014), pp. 55–59.

5. The figure for 1975 comes from Suzanne Bianchi and colleagues, "Housework: who did, does or will do it, and how much does it matter?" *Social Forces*, volume 91, pp. 55–63, 2012. The figure for 2022 comes from the US Bureau of Labor Statistics, "Average hours per day parents spent caring for and helping household children as their main activity," https://www.bls.gov/charts/american-time-use /activity-by-parent.htm#, accessed December 29, 2023, according to which fathers spent an average of 0.94 hours per day caring for or helping children in their household. Multiplying 0.94 hours per day times seven days in a week yields 6.58 hours per week, which I have rounded to 6.6 hours per week. Mothers spent an average of

1.69 hours per day caring for or helping children in their household, which works out to 11.8 hours per week.

6. Jennifer Senior, *All Joy and No Fun: The Paradox of Modern Parenthood* (New York: Ecco [HarperCollins], 2014), p. 57.

7. Senior, *All Joy and No Fun*, p. 59.

8. At my request, Mr. Bruneau provided me with a list of his awards. Some of the awards reflect academic and/or athletic achievement; others reflect community services; and still others, such as being elected to the Homecoming Court, are simply a measure of popularity. Mr. Bruneau demonstrates that it is still possible to be popular in the United States without being disrespectful to parents. It helps to be a champion athlete.

9. This is my paraphrase of Nietzsche's aphorism in *Also Sprach Zarathustra*, "Wenig macht die Art des besten Glücks" (a little makes for the best kind of happiness).

10. For more than two decades now, we have had good evidence that Americans work more hours per week, on average, than workers in Europe. See for example Jerry Jacobs and Kathleen Green, "Who are the overworked Americans?" *Review of Social Economy*, volume 56, pp. 442–459, 1998. For a more anecdotal account of the cultural contrast on this parameter between the USA and Europe, see John de Graaf's cover story for *The Progressive*, "Wake up Americans: it's time to get off the work treadmill: we need to come up with a different approach to work," *The Progressive*, pp. 22–24, September 2010. Pete Grieve recently observed that the average American now works 400 hours a year more than the average German. That's the equivalent of 10 extra weeks of full-time work per year. See his article "Americans work hundreds of hours more a year than Europeans," *Money*, January 6, 2023, https://money.com/americans-work-hours-vs-europe-china/.

Although Americans work more hours than workers in any European country, they do not work more hours than workers in China, India, or South Korea. The average worker in China and in India puts in more than 2,100 hours per year, significantly more than the average American (see Grieve's article).

While it's fairly easy to find documentations that Americans work longer hours per week, on average, than workers in other developed countries, it's harder to find any documentation that Americans *boast* of being busy more so than in other countries. That's my personal observation. It's also an observation shared by Tim Kreider in his essay for the *New York Times* (next note).

11. Tim Kreider, "The 'busy' trap," *New York Times*, July 1, 2012.

Chapter 12: *The Meaning of Life*

1. See for example Jennifer Lee's story for the *New York Times*, "Generation limbo," August 31, 2011, profiling graduates of Harvard, Dartmouth, and Yale who are now working odd jobs to make ends meet; and also Noam Scheiber, "The revolt of the college-educated working class," *New York Times*, June 22, 2023; also see Lisa Miller's article "Adrift, broke, and disillusioned: how a struggling bartender became the face of a resurgent left," *Intelligencer*, February 11, 2022, documenting how Alexandria Ocasio-Cortez was a college graduate barely making ends meet as a bartender and waitress when she decided to run for Congress.

The fixation on getting into a "top" college or university is not only unjustified by the data on long-term outcomes; it is also harmful to adolescents, narrowing their focus and limiting their horizons. For a poignant account of the damage done by this obsession, see Frank Bruni's book *Where You Go Is Not Who You'll Be: An Antidote to the College Admissions Mania* (New York: Hachette, 2015).

2. Daniel Kahneman and Angus Deaton, "High income improves evaluation of life but not emotional well-being," *Proceedings of the National Academy of Science*, volume 107, pp. 16489–16493, September 7, 2010, https://www.pnas.org/doi/10.1073/pnas.1011492107.

3. Andrew Jebb, Louis Tay, and colleagues, "Happiness, income satiation and turning points around the world," *Nature Human*

Behaviour, volume 2, pp. 33–38, 2018, https://www.nature.com /articles/s41562-017-0277-0. For data contradicting this conclusion, see Matthew Killingsworth, "Experienced well-being rises with income, even above $75,000 a year," *Proceedings of the National Academy of Sciences*, volume 118, January 18, 2021, https://www.pnas.org /doi/10.1073/pnas.2016976118.

4. Liz Mineo, "Good genes are nice, but joy is better: Harvard study, almost 80 years old, has proved that embracing community helps us live longer, and be happier," *Harvard Gazette*, April 11, 2017, https://news .harvard.edu/gazette/story/2017/04/over-nearly-80-years-harvard -study-has-been-showing-how-to-live-a-healthy-and-happy-life/.

5. Rachel Minkin and Juliana Menasce Horowitz, "Parenting in America today: mental health concerns top the list of worries for parents; most say being a parent is harder than they expected," Pew Research Center, January 24, 2023, https://www.pewresearch.org /social-trends/2023/01/24/parenting-in-america-today/.

6. United States Census Bureau, "Census Bureau releases new estimates on America's families and living arrangements," November 29, 2021, https://www.census.gov/newsroom/press-releases/2021 /families-and-living-arrangements.html.

7. Dipo Fadeyi and Juliana Menasce Horowitz, "Americans more likely to say it's a bad thing than a good thing that more young adults live with their parents," Pew Research Center, August 24, 2022, https://www.pewresearch.org/short-reads/2022/08/24/americans -more-likely-to-say-its-a-bad-thing-than-a-good-thing-that-more -young-adults-live-with-their-parents/.

8. Risa Gelles-Watnick, "For Valentine's Day, 5 facts about single Americans," Pew Research Center, February 8, 2023, https://www .pewresearch.org/short-reads/2023/02/08/for-valentines-day-5-facts -about-single-americans/.

9. Derek Thompson, "Workism is making Americans miserable," *The Atlantic*, February 24, 2019, https://www.theatlantic.com /ideas/archive/2019/02/religion-workism-making-americans-miser able/583441/.

10. I am aware that the majority of American workers say they are satisfied with their jobs. In one recent survey, for example, 51 percent of workers said that they were "extremely" or "very" satisfied with their job (see Juliana Menasce Horowitz and Kim Parker, "How Americans view their jobs," Pew Research Center, March 30, 2023, https://www.pewresearch.org/social-trends/2023/03/30/how-americans-view-their-jobs/). But I think that question isn't quite right. A worker might answer Yes to the question "Are you very satisfied with your job?"—because that worker knows you have to work some kind of job—but still might answer NO to the question "If you didn't have to work to survive, would you still work the job you have now?" When I offer to write a patient a note excusing them from work for a few days due to illness, the great majority of patients will accept my offer, even though they don't really, medically, need the time off.

11. David Brooks, "Five lies our culture tells us: the cultural roots of our political problems," *New York Times*, April 25, 2019, https://www.nytimes.com/2019/04/15/opinion/cultural-revolution-meritocracy.html.

12. Jeremy Bauer-Wolf, "College applicants still aren't submitting SAT, ACT scores at pre-pandemic levels," *Higher Ed Dive*, March 30, 2023. As of March 30, 2023, only 43 percent of applicants had submitted SAT or ACT scores, and only 4 percent of colleges still require them—a huge decline from 2019, when 55 percent of colleges still required SAT or ACT scores.

13. One of Maslow's core ideas was the idea of a hierarchy of needs. Everyone needs to fulfill basic human needs, such as the need for food, clothing, and shelter. Most human beings also have a need for love and for belonging. Once those needs are fulfilled, Maslow believed that people would want respect and esteem from their peers. At the top of Maslow's hierarchy was the need for self-actualization, to fulfill one's deepest purpose. Maslow believed that a narrow focus on achieving wealth would not satisfy, because ultimately human beings want more than the satisfaction of appetites. In Maslow's perspective,

each person must discover on their own what they need to become "self-actualized." See for example his book *The Farther Reaches of Human Nature*, reprint edition (New York: Penguin, 1993).

I am aware of the criticisms of Maslow's theories: see for example Mahmoud Wahba and Lawrence Bridwell, "Maslow reconsidered: a review of research on the need hierarchy theory," *Organizational Behavior and Human Performance*, volume 15, pp. 212–240, 1976. I am not asking you to swallow Maslow's theories whole. I am merely pointing out that figuring out what you want out of life, what will truly make you happy, is not a trivial task. On the contrary, it is a substantial task because the answer differs for each person.

My other point here is that the contemporary American answer is lacking. The unspoken assumption in contemporary American culture is that material success—earning lots of money—will provide a satisfying life. Arthur C. Brooks recently observed that this basic assumption of 21st-century American life is not compatible with research findings on this issue. If you have read Chapter 8 of this book, that will not come as a surprising finding. As you will recall from that chapter, Conscientiousness predicts life satisfaction more strongly than income. And a life devoted to the pursuit of money *for its own sake* may not be a life characterized by high levels of Conscientiousness. See Arthur Brooks's article "Love people, not pleasure," *New York Times*, July 18, 2014.

14. The government reports that younger Baby Boomers—born between 1957 and 1964—held more than 12 different jobs, on average, between the ages of 18 and 54. See US Bureau of Labor Statistics, "Number of jobs, labor market experience, marital status for those born 1957–1964," August 22, 2023, https://www.bls.gov/news.release/pdf/nlsoy.pdf. *Forbes* magazine reported that 60 percent of younger American workers now switch jobs every three years or less: Kate Taylor, "Why Millennials are ending the 9 to 5," August 23, 2013. In one recent survey, 22 percent of workers planned to change jobs within the next six months: Rakesh Kochhar and colleagues, "Majority of U.S. workers

changing jobs are seeing real wage gains," Pew Research Center, July 28, 2022, https://www.pewresearch.org/social-trends/2022/07/28/majority-of-u-s-workers-changing-jobs-are-seeing-real-wage-gains/.

A job change is different from a career change. The US Bureau of Labor Statistics does not seek to track career changes because "no consensus has emerged as to what constitutes a career change.... What about the case of a web site designer who was laid off from a job, worked for six months for a lawn-care service, and then found a new job as a web site designer? Might that example constitute two career changes? If not, why not? Is spending six months at the lawn-care service long enough to consider that a career? How long must one stay in a particular line of work before it can be called a career? Until a consensus emerges among economists, sociologists, career-guidance professionals, and other labor market observers about the appropriate criteria that should be used for defining careers and career changes, BLS [Bureau of Labor Statistics] and other statistical organizations will not be able to produce estimates on the number of times people change careers in their lives." US Bureau of Labor Statistics, "NLS FAQs," https://www.bls.gov/nls/questions-and-answers.htm#anch43, accessed December 17, 2023.

Such disclaimers aside, Lori Amato estimates that the average American worker will now change careers between three and seven times in a lifetime. See her article, "What is the average number of career changes in a person's lifetime?" Unmudl, November 1, 2023, https://unmudl.com/blog/average-career-changes.

15. The full text of Steve Jobs's 2005 commencement address is online at http://news.stanford.edu/news/2005/june15/jobs-061505.html.

16. Robert Bly and Marion Woodman, *The Maiden King: The Reunion of Masculine and Feminine* (New York: Holt, 1998), p. 20.

17. Bly and Woodman, *The Maiden King*, p. 20. Bly and Woodman cite Joseph Chilton Pearce, *Evolution's End: Claiming the Potential of Our Intelligence* (New York: HarperCollins, 1992), as the source of

the idea of "The Great Disappointment": see chapter 22 in Pearce's book, especially p. 190.

18. Todd Spangler, "TikTok's highest-earning stars: Charli and Dixie D'Amelio raked in $27.5 million in 2021," *Variety*, January 7, 2022, https://variety.com/2022/digital/news/tiktok-highest -paid-charli-dixie-damelio-1235149027/.

19. https://www.tiktok.com/@charlidamelio?lang=en, accessed December 14, 2023.

20. David Brooks, "The ambition explosion," *New York Times*, November 27, 2014, online at http://www.nytimes.com/2014/11/28 /opinion/david-brooks-the-ambition-explosion.html.

21. Mark Shiffman, "Majoring in fear," *First Things*, November 2014, pp. 19–20.

22. "Tiger Mom" is a reference to Amy Chua's book *Battle Hymn of the Tiger Mother* (New York: Penguin, 2011). "Irish Setter dad" is a reference to P. J. O'Rourke's article "Irish Setter Dad," *Washington Examiner*, April 4, 2011, https://www.washingtonexaminer.com /weekly-standard/irish-setter-dad.

23. These details about Theron "Terry" Smith come from the Associated Press, "Ted Stevens plane crash: NTSB issues report on cause of crash that killed Alaska senator," May 25, 2011, www.huffington post.com/2011/05/24/ted-stevens-plane-crash-n_n_866585.html.

24. According to the published reports which appeared within hours of the plane crash—before any of the four survivors had been interviewed—the plane had taken off around 3 p.m. that afternoon. However, Willy and his mother, Janet, have told me that the plane took off around 11 a.m. that morning. More than six hours passed before anyone knew that they were missing.

25. The pilot who thought "no one could've survived such a crash" is Eric Shade, owner of Shannon's Air Taxi, as reported by Mark Thiessen and Becky Bohrer for the Associated Press, August 12, 2010, "Waving hand first clue of AK crash survivors," https:// www.sandiegouniontribune.com/2010/08/11/pilot-waving-hand -1st-clue-of-ak-crash-survivors/. The description of the crash scene is

taken from the remarks of Jonathan Davis, an officer with the Alaska Air National Guard, as reported by Jim Kavanagh in his article, "Rescuers battled weather, terrain at Alaska crash site," CNN, August 11, 2010, http://www.cnn.com/2010/US/08/11/alaska.crash.conditions/.

26. This description is taken from the Associated Press account, previous note. Dr. Dani Bowman was helicoptered to a nearby site and forced her way through the brush: no byline, "Anchorage doctor among first to aid crash victims," Liberty Broadband, August 12, 2010, https://www.libertybroadband.com/news/detail/212 /anchorage-doctor-among-first-to-aid-crash-victims.

27. The details of Willy's injuries, and of the injuries to the survivors, come from Willy's interview with me via Zoom on May 22, 2023.

28. Darren McKenzie and Patrick Kiteley, "The boy who survived a plane crash in Alaska," BBC Radio 5, May 3, 2019, https://www.bbc .com/news/world-47537221.

29. This sentence is a paraphrase of Arthur Brooks's op-ed "Love people, not pleasure," *New York Times*, July 18, 2014.

30. Email from Willy Phillips, December 13, 2023.

31. Jonathan Haidt, "Why the past 10 years of American life have been uniquely stupid," *The Atlantic*, May 2020, https://www.the atlantic.com/magazine/archive/2022/05/social-media-democracy -trust-babel/629369/.

32. Mary Harrington, *Feminism Against Progress* (Washington, DC: Regnery, 2023), pp. 21, 32.

Conclusion

1. My call to "reevaluate our values" is an allusion to Nietzsche's call for *Umwertung aller Werte*, a reevaluation of all values. Nietzsche's point is that in the traditional European world before the Enlightenment, most people looked to religion as the foundation of their values. In the contemporary world, many people no longer accept religious doctrine or the Bible as the foundation of their moral

perspective. Nietzsche was arguably the first to recognize that in such a world, *nothing* about morality can be taken for granted. He made this point emphatically in one of his last books, *Twilight of the Idols*, where he wrote,

"Christianity is a system, a whole view of things thought out together. By breaking out of it a fundamental concept [*einen Hauptbegriff*], the faith in God, one destroys [*zerbricht*] the whole: nothing necessary remains between your fingers.... Christian morality is a command; its origin is transcendent; it is beyond all criticism, all right to criticism; it has truth only if God is the truth, it stands and falls with faith in God. When the English actually believe that they know 'intuitively' what is good and evil, when they subsequently suppose that it is no longer necessary to have Christianity as the guarantee of morality, that is merely the effects of the dominion of the Christian value judgment and an expression of the strength and depth of this dominion: such that the origin of English morality has been forgotten, such that the very-conditionality [*das Sehr-Bedingte*] of its right to existence is not perceived. For the English, morality is not yet a problem."

The translation is my own. Where my translation departs from the usual English translations, I have shown the German original in brackets. Nietzsche is using the word "English" to mean "those who speak English." He had no interest in the distinctions between English and Scottish and Irish and American. For more of my writing on Nietzsche, please see my article in the *Journal of Medical Biography*, volume 11, pp. 47–54, 2003.

Nietzsche's *conclusions* about values are very different from mine. But he and I start from the same *premise*: namely, that in a post-Christian era, nothing can be taken for granted. All values must be reevaluated. We now live in the world which Nietzsche prophesied in 1888: a world in which all moralities are in question. All values must therefore be reevaluated. The point I am making here is that if you do not undertake this task explicitly and seriously, and you happen to live in the United States today, then it is likely that your children will adopt the values of American popular culture, a culture in which what matters most is the pursuit of fame, wealth, or "whatever floats your boat."

2. Quoted in Alina Tugend's op-ed for the *New York Times*, "Redefining success and celebrating the ordinary," June 29, 2012.

3. Here I am referring to Jennifer Finney Boylan. See her article "A Common Core for all of us," *New York Times*, March 23, 2014, Sunday Review, p. 4.

4. The ideas in this paragraph about "unchosen obligation" are adapted from Giles Fraser's essay, "Harry and Meghan's moral exile," *UnHerd*, December 15, 2022, https://unherd.com/2022/12/harry-and-meghans-moral-exile/.

5. In Chapter 10, I described Beth Fayard and Jeff Jones as "Just Right" parents. In my conversations with Beth, more than once she has told me that she strives to teach her children that "every choice you make has immediate, far-reaching, and unforeseen consequences."

6. Here I am paraphrasing C. S. Lewis's comment about duties which are "not a sort of special exercise for the top class" but which are mandatory. Lewis observes that when one is faced "with an optional question in an examination paper, one considers whether or not one can do it or not; faced with a compulsory question, one must do the best one can." *Mere Christianity* (San Francisco: HarperCollins, 2009), pp. 195, 100–101.

Index

AAP. *See* American Academy of
    Pediatrics
Aaron (pseudonym), 149–151,
    155–156, 159–161, 163, 226
Abigail (pseudonym), 213–214
academic achievement
    and cheating, 181–182, 209–212
    vs. chores, time spent on, 229
    in college, 72–74
    and fragility, 151–156
    at high-achieving schools, 75–79
    outcomes associated with, 77–78,
        174, 179
    in US vs. other countries, 66–74
acceptance, unconditional, 160–161,
    164, 168, 196
achievement
    drive to achieve, 125–126
    vs. happiness, 265–266
    See also academic achievement;
        success
ACLU, 143
activities
    in absence of social media, 129
    in college admission, 256
    in culture of busyness, 247–250, 278
    cutting back on, 52–53, 79, 166,
        247–250, 278

in enjoyment of parent-child time,
    241–244
importance of diversifying, 90–91,
    201
meals scheduled around, 52–53,
    166, 247
outdoor, 53–54, 220–221
Adderall, 87, 89, 92, 93
addiction
    age at start of, 201
    to drugs and alcohol, 175
    to porn, 117, 120, 127
    to video games, 126, 201, 207
ADHD, 87–93
    medication for, 85, 87–90
    rise in diagnosis of, 9, 91–93
    and sleep deprivation, 88–90, 92–93
adolescence, length of, 20–21, 31–32,
    102
affluent children
    depression in, 75–76, 261–262
    at high-achieving schools, 75–79
affluenza, 75–76
alcohol use, 7–9, 175
allies, 272
All I Really Need to Know (Fulghum),
    22–23
All Joy and No Fun (Senior), 239–240

primary attachment in, 34–36,
166–167
responsibilities in, 278–281
timing of transfer of allegiance in,
167–168
unconditional love in, 160–161, 164
ways of establishing primacy in,
162–168
parenting styles
politics linked to, 37–41
types of, 195–198
See also specific styles
Paterson, Cameron, 62–63
peers
culture of, 31–32, 42–43, 98
importance of parents vs., 4, 25–27,
31–36
instability of relationships with, 33,
98, 160
opinions of, 25–26, 159–160, 165,
167–168
as primary attachment, 34–36,
166–167
See also parent-child vs. peer
relationships
Peretz, Sarah, 113
perfectionism, 107
permissive (Too Soft) parents,
195–199
definition of, 195
negative outcomes with, 40, 194, 195
politics of, 37–41
strictness vs. love in, 196–197
perseverance, 223
personality traits, associated with
positive outcomes, 78, 171–176
persuasion, in virtuous behavior,
184–185
pessimism, 39
Pew Research Center, 253, 254
Phillips, Andrew, 183–184, 230
Phillips, Bill, 7–9, 183–184, 229–231,
266–270

Phillips, Janet, 7–9, 229–232,
268, 270
Phillips, Willy, 266–270
phones. *See* smartphones
PISA. *See* Program for International
Student Assessment
Playboy (magazine), 120, 121
play time, 53–54
pleasure, misconceptions about,
206–209
Poland, 69–70, 72
politics
culture of disrespect in, 13–15
parenting styles linked to, 37–41
popular culture
culture of disrespect in, 15–19, 29,
64
humility as antidote to, 217–218
self-control as sin in, 182–183
popularity, effects of restricting
technology on, 200–204
pornography, 116–123
child, 122
frequency of viewing, 116, 118
gender differences in use of,
119–120, 127
government regulation of, 130
negative effects of, 117–120
parental monitoring of, 117,
120–123
recommended rules for, 129
unsolicited links to, 109
Power, Nina, 141
power differentials, decline of, 25–27
praise
for bad behavior, 5–6
for identity vs. behavior,
179–181
Program for International Student
Assessment (PISA), 66–71
pronouns, 141, 143, 145
Proverbs, Book of, 185–186
Przybylski, Andrew, 107

vocational training, 255–256
Vyvanse, 87, 89, 92

walking, 54
Washington, Denzel, 233
wealth
  affluenza and, 75–76
  in happiness, 252–253
  high-achieving schools and, 77–79
  personality traits associated with, 78, 171–176
  See also affluent children
weight
  fitness and, 45–47
  as topic on social media, 109–110
  See also obesity
"whatever floats your boat," 29, 164, 182–183, 189, 208, 277, 280
Wilcox, Brad, 40
Williams, Megan, 134–135
willingness to fail, 168, 258–259
Wilson, Joe, 13–14
Winter, Jessica, 38
women

changes in roles of, 139–140
  enjoyment of parenting among, 237–240
  time spent parenting, 239–240
  See also girls
Woodman, Marion, 260
work. *See* jobs
workism, 254–255
World of Warcraft (video game), 124
Wright, Timothy, 11–12, 268–269, 273

Yamamoto Tsunetomo, 22–23
yardwork, 229–231
young adults
  with authoritative parents, 194
  economic role of, 158–159
  failure to launch, 156, 167, 253–254
  living with parents, 156, 253–254
  with permissive parents, 40
  unemployed, 156–158

Zuckerberg, Mark, 158, 262
Zyprexa, 95

About the Author

CREDIT: COURTESY OF THE AUTHOR

Leonard Sax, MD, PhD, is a board-certified family physician, psychologist, and author of *Why Gender Matters, Boys Adrift,* and *Girls on the Edge.* Dr. Sax has visited more than 500 schools worldwide and has appeared on major radio and television programs including the *TODAY* show, CBS, CNN, Fox, and NPR's *Weekend Edition.* Sax lives with his family in Chester County, Pennsylvania.